ADVANCE PRAISE FOR

How to Be Single and Happy

"Jenny Taitz offers a skillful guide to uncovering your strength and contentment as an individual, allowing you to live more fully. Using engaging case studies and solid research, *How to Be Single and Happy* invites new insights into the stories we tell ourselves about relationships. This book is a gift for anyone who longs for real happiness."   —SHARON SALZBERG,
bestselling author of *Lovingkindness* and *Real Love*

"You don't need to wait to find your partner to find happiness. Drawing on a wealth of evidence and experience as a therapist, Jenny Taitz has written a book that's as uplifting as it is practical."
—ADAM GRANT,
New York Times bestselling author of *Give and Take*,
Originals, and *Option B* (with Sheryl Sandberg)

"What if, instead of treating the unprecedented rise of single people as a crisis, we all searched for ways to make going solo easier, more social, even happy? In her clinical work, and now, in this excellent book, Jenny Taitz has done pioneering work to help people achieve more fulfilling relationships regardless of their marital status. I recommend strongly."   —ERIC KLINENBERG,
professor of sociology, New York University; *New York Times* bestselling author of *Going Solo* and
Modern Romance (with Aziz Ansari)

"At the heart of this honest and engaging book is a key insight—namely that our emotions are sometimes but not always helpful. And when emotions are not helpful—such as when we're in the grip of anxiety about being alone forever—Dr. Taitz shows us how

we can use scientifically documented methods for freeing ourselves from their painful grip. If you're suffering in your quest for the Right One (or miserable from being with the Wrong One), this book is a must-read!" —JAMES GROSS, PH.D.,
professor of psychology, Stanford University

"*How to Be Single and Happy* is an excellent guide to living your life now rather than waiting for the perfect partner. Dr. Taitz has written a powerful and practical guide based on the best scientific research and self-help tools to free you from the myth that only married people can be happy. With a personal and engaging style, Dr. Taitz gives you the tools to living a full life as a single person. I will recommend this wonderful book to anyone who thinks that being single is something to escape from."

—ROBERT L. LEAHY, PH.D.,
author of *The Jealousy Cure*

"We all yearn for connection and belonging, but our minds get in the way, pulling us into rumination, worry, judgment, and other soul killers. This wise and compassionate volume helps us reconnect with our values and bring them into our hearts and our relationships with others. This book is for you if you think it is time to set aside loneliness and 'not good enough,' and to let go of 'what if . . .' and 'if only.' This book is for you if you think it is time to live."

—STEVEN C. HAYES,
co-developer of Acceptance and Commitment Therapy (ACT);
author of *Get Out of Your Mind and Into Your Life*

HOW TO
BE SINGLE
and Happy

HOW TO ♥ BE SINGLE

and Happy

Science-Based Strategies *for* Keeping Your Sanity While Looking *for a* Soul Mate

JENNIFER L. TAITZ,
Psy.D., A.B.P.P.

A TarcherPerigee Book

An imprint of Penguin Random House LLC
375 Hudson Street
New York, New York 10014

TarcherPerigee with tp colophon is a registered trademark of
Penguin Random House LLC.

Most TarcherPerigee books are available at special quantity discounts for bulk purchase for
sales promotions, premiums, fund-raising, and educational needs. Special books or book
excerpts also can be created to fit specific needs. For details, write: SpecialMarkets@
penguinrandomhouse.com.

Library of Congress Cataloging-in-Publication Data

Names: Taitz, Jennifer L., author.
Title: How to be single and happy : science-based strategies for keeping your
sanity while looking for a soul mate / Jenny Taitz.
Description: First Edition. | New York : TarcherPerigee, 2018. | Includes
bibliographical references.
Identifiers: LCCN 2017037238| ISBN 9780143130994 (paperback) | ISBN
9781524704810 (E-book)
Subjects: LCSH: Self-actualization (Psychology) | Single people—Psychology.
| Happiness. | BISAC: SELF-HELP / Personal Growth / Happiness. |
PSYCHOLOGY / Interpersonal Relations.
Classification: LCC BF637.S4 T395 2018 | DDC 155.6/42—dc23
LC record available at https://lccn.loc.gov/2017037238

Printed in the United States of America
9th Printing

For my mother,

Dr. Jo Seletz, the strongest and

most independent woman I know

CONTENTS

INTRODUCTION

Lonely, Loony, and Me

I wish I could show you when you are lonely or in darkness
the astonishing light of your own being. —HAFIZ

D ON'T YOU KNOW about the 'singles crisis'? There literally aren't enough eligible men for women," Rachel* explained, reaching for a tissue as she sat on my therapy couch, in a trendy hat. Ironically, given her single status, and her articulated negative feelings about it, she worked in the wedding planning industry. "I'm thirty-four and the only person in my group of friends who is still single," she continued, tears welling up. "And now my hair is falling out because of a hormone thing." (Her hair looked lovely to me, falling nicely around her face from under her beanie.) "Obviously, stress isn't helping. But now it's definite—I'll never meet someone. And, if I do, I'll just be settling. The good ones are all gone."

She was sure she was a hopeless case, as she made perfectly clear in our first meeting. "I never thought I'd be in this

---

* Names and stories used as examples in this book are modified to protect privacy. My hope is that by reading versions of other people's experiences, you'll realize that you're not alone and that many of us share similar thoughts and feelings.

situation. Stupid antidepressants won't fix my life and I'm not really sure what you can do for me," she concluded, in soft, funereal tones.

Clearly, my new client was in mourning.

What happens when you worry continuously about ending up alone, the way Rachel does? The answer is that you actually lose your mind—or rather, your ability to think clearly. One of my favorite social psychologists, Roy Baumeister, has studied the effects of what he calls "anticipated aloneness," or imagining what it would be like to end up alone in life, and the experience of feeling rejected. As the author of more than five hundred papers, Baumeister is a leading expert on the very human need to belong as well as on self-regulation, or the science of managing emotions. He and his colleagues typically create experimental situations to tease apart exactly how feelings affect us. In one of his noteworthy experiments, his team gave subjects a baseline IQ test, followed by a personality test, after which they informed the participants that based on their responses, it seemed likely that they would end up alone. Ouch. After that harsh news, they were asked to retake the same test, and their performance suffered. As Baumeister puts it: "The prospect of social exclusion reduced people's capacity for intelligent thought." In other words, imagining that you will end up alone affects your ability to contemplate anything in a rational way, which makes it tough to cope with the tests that will inevitably arise in your life.

One thing you can do to help yourself when you're in the middle of one of those *I'll always be alone!* cycles is to remind yourself, compassionately, that your thinking is skewed. After all, there's no way to predict how your life will unfold or whether you'll meet someone, however sure you feel of your single fate.

According to renowned psychologist Marsha Linehan, who

developed Dialectical Behavior Therapy (DBT), all of us have a "reasonable mind" that's logical, as well as an "emotion mind." In wise moments, when we have perspective, we recognize that our emotions and our logic don't always line up. For example, we might freak out when we're on a flight and there's a sudden period of turbulence, though our "reasonable mind" knows that the plane will most likely land safely. One way out of panicked responses to judgmental conclusions like *This plane is going to crash and I'm about to die*, or *I'm doomed to live my life alone with a houseful of cats*, is actually labeling and acknowledging these as inaccurate messages from our "emotion mind." By paying attention, something I will talk about in the pages to come, you can see your thoughts and emotions for what they actually are, rather than mistakenly assume they are true.

The problem is, our emotion mind tends to be very quick to persuade us of its wisdom. As Baumeister discovered, just thinking about aloneness summons a reaction from the emotion mind, literally impairing IQ. And if a quick experimental suggestion persuaded people to anticipate loneliness and sent them down an irrational path, imagine how swayed we are when our own inner voice and life experiences, bad dates, or a string of failed relationships do the convincing. It's easy to forget that being single right now doesn't predict the romantic equivalent of solitary confinement for the rest of your life.

At times when we feel intensely, we may find ourselves captured by pseudo-logical thinking known as emotional reasoning. Thoughts like *I've been single for the last ten years; therefore, I'll be alone watching* Friends *reruns forever*, are definitely coming from your emotion mind. There is no realistic predicting when it comes to finding a partner or how you will feel in the future. Many people in good, stable relationships talk about how they once thought that they would never meet anyone and experienced unnecessary hurt as a result. Our emotions are often a helpful guide. But there are also times when our feelings don't serve us because they're based on problematic thoughts. The only thing that preparing for possible future pain does is ensure that we'll be in pain at that very moment, though it can be hard to see that when we're hurting and not thinking clearly.

In addition to anticipated aloneness leading to distress, the act of dating, an activity that inevitably involves some rejection, taxes us further. After going out on an initial date with a guy that she wasn't all that "into," then not hearing from him again, Rachel panicked: "Even loser guys don't want to see me again," she said. "This isn't my anxiety, this is reality." Rachel is not alone (no pun intended) in linking her self-worth to any rejection she experiences. Research spearheaded by Tyler Stillman, one of Baumeister's colleagues, demonstrates that people who feel rejected (either by a stranger of the same sex or while playing an online game) are more apt to give up on seemingly frustrating tasks, make poor choices, and decide that life is less meaningful. Sadly, in a study with more than six hundred participants at the University of Florida, Stillman devised several conditions to induce a sense of rejection. In one, participants were told that they had enrolled in an experiment about first impressions, and were then paired with partners they met via video. Afterward, they were told, falsely, that their partner decided not to meet with them in person. Compared to a control group who wasn't rejected, people who felt rejected reported a measurably diminished sense of purpose and self-worth.

All of this seems like a milder version of dating apps, right? But of course, it's worse to go on an actual date (or three), have what seems like a great time together, then never hear from the person again, a trend commonly known as "ghosting." Ghosting actually reminds me of the famous "still face experiment" from the 1970s, devised by psychologist Edward Tronick and his colleagues, where researchers instructed a mother to first warmly engage with her baby, then to disengage. As you might guess, when warmth is suddenly removed, the child cries inconsolably. Human beings have an innate desire to connect, and it's maddening for someone to get close, then inexplicably pull away. (With a quick search, you can find a clip of this painful interaction online.)

Meeting someone promising who then disappears without apparent cause or explanation is the epitome of *invalidation*. Having your feelings dismissed, or being ignored, leads to difficulties in managing emotions, according to Linehan, the psychologist I mentioned earlier. When it comes to looking for love during a time when technology and new norms might trigger feeling like you don't matter, it's important to learn to treat yourself well.

After my initial meeting with Rachel, I thought of all the "Rachels" I've seen. For the last decade, I've worked with hundreds of people ranging in age from eighteen to eighty, in New York City and now in Los Angeles. As a clinical psychologist trained in mindfulness-based cognitive therapies, I specialize in teaching patients how to use evidence-based tools to help them think more clearly and live more fully. Though every person is different, I would estimate that at least half of my patients have struggled with worry, self-doubt, and sadness because they feel dissatisfied in relationships or are uncomfortably alone, co-dependent, or coping with feelings of rejection.

Now you may be wondering, *Wait! I'm single but I don't have any mental health issues. If I struggle with dating and relationships, does it mean I have psychological issues too?* Interestingly, many people I see have no psychiatric history; "This is my first time in therapy," I hear all the time. So if you find that worrying about your relationship status is stressing you out, despite other aspects of your life going well, that's okay. There's nothing wrong with how you're feeling. There's nothing wrong with *you*. And, there is a way to feel more content in your independent life. The tools in this book will help you get there.

The truth is, many of us struggle to find good guidance when it comes to relationships, especially single women. Unfortunately, much of what we see and hear ends up making us feel worse. Maybe your father, well intentioned, encourages you to try harder to find your Mr. or Ms. Right: "I want to live to meet my grandchildren!" he says, only half-joking. Perhaps a friend in the fashion industry suggests you wear uncomfortable sexy miniskirts in order to reel in the suitors. Similarly, reality TV, however entertaining, can derail us with its messaging that women today must compete, cry, and squeeze into heels to stumble toward a millionaire or beautiful bachelor to entice him to propose. The premise seems more like a setback for women than a lifestyle to aspire to.

If you do decide that you want some advice on dating, while well-intentioned, many popular books on the topic seem like they would work better on a *Saturday Night Live* sketch than on your nightstand, or worse yet, on your mind. There's a cover promoting the power of bitchiness, another claiming it has THE rules you need to follow to get a guy, and yet another with a prescription for settling. One client recently told me about a book that delineated why she needed to uproot her life and move to a new city to date. It feels sad to me that women are given advice like "Act like a lady, think like a man" to find a partner.

"Do you think I'm too picky because my parents have the 'perfect' marriage?" some ask. I don't think you need to endlessly analyze your parents, act in a way that feels fake, or move to another state to find a partner, much less peace of mind. It's possible to simplify your experiences without dissecting your personal history or accepting advice from anyone—or any book—that is making you feel worse. After all, more people are single than ever before. And with the rise of online dating, we have more ways to meet someone. Yet many single women tell me how stuck and disrespected they feel.

When I take a few minutes to think about my clients, certain conversations replay in my mind. I remember a woman in her mid-sixties who came to me after a suicide attempt. She explained that when her husband decided to marry his mistress, she concluded that her life was empty, and said, "The point of life is love." When I asked her about the prospect of future connection, she explained, articulately, that I may have missed a *Newsweek* article published in the 1980s warning that an educated single woman over the age of forty was more likely to die in a terrorist attack than marry. Much to her surprise, she started dating someone within six months of that thankfully intercepted attempt to end her life.

Actually, I see so many amazing people who seriously suffer with the anticipated aloneness that Baumeister and his colleagues documented in their studies. And it's more painful to witness personally than the studies read. I'm thinking of a beautiful eighteen-year-old in the throes of a college heartbreak. She was convinced that she would never find a partner again, and became so depressed she had to take a leave from her university. Then there's the twenty-four-year-old who recently told me that she'd scheduled a Botox appointment after being endlessly waitlisted from a selective dating app. "I didn't make the cut," she told me. "If no one wants me now, I'll look like a pathetic, wrinkled raisin at thirty!" She'd struggled with body image a bit in the past, but now, she couldn't stop wondering how to fix her appearance as she imagined men in her future who would similarly scrutinize her. Another woman, an immigrant in her early forties who grew up without running water and was the first person in her family to go to college, then graduated from Harvard Business School, told me she had "ruined" her life because she hasn't "gotten a guy."

For people who are driven, thoughtful, and looking for love, it may feel tempting to concentrate on finding a mate in a critical way. After all, for most problems, careful strategizing and planning often leads to the desired outcome. The challenge is, in situations that aren't entirely within your control—like relationships and dating—endlessly strategizing can be seriously depleting. You may even find that focusing on finding love, rather than loving your life, closes you off from great opportunities, or leads you to settle for something that doesn't feel right. Yes, it's a virtue to grow and improve, but it's important to remember that being single does not mean you're flawed and in need of fixing. Your relationship, or lack thereof, has little to do with your worth. I want to stop the cycle of loneliness breeding hopelessness. You deserve freedom from suffering, now.

♥

"You inspired my next book," I told Dr. Dan, a wise and kind psychiatrist with whom I often collaborate, after we sat down to catch up over dinner one night. As I thanked him for referring

Rachel to me, I said, "I see this issue everywhere, and I really want to write about it."

"I can't imagine you ever felt the way she does," Dr. Dan nudged.

A risk of dining with a mental health professional is a side order of analysis. My friend and colleague didn't know about my romantic history, but like Rachel, I spent about a decade feeling lonely and mired in rumination and self-doubt. I'd been primed by both my innate desire to build a family and incessant messages around me that I should focus on finding a long-term partner—neurotically so. Conversations with old friends always centered around who was still single and who might be close to the coveted goal of getting engaged. Even my fun hairdresser used to casually ask, "So are you seeing someone?" before moving on to how the rest of my life was going.

Since I was working on opening up more about my own struggles, I told Dr. Dan about Paris, when, illuminated by the lights of the Eiffel Tower, my boyfriend at the time had pulled out a seemingly flawless, emerald-cut diamond ring. It was a chilly December night, I was inching closer to thirty, and we had been together for almost a year. We'd met through my former college roommate, who had called to tell me that she had met "my future husband." "Can I set you up?" I agreed, and when I connected with him in person, I immediately liked his ruggedly preppy look. On our first date, I caught him parking his BMW motorcycle and adjusting his waxed Barbour jacket. A few months after we met, we were shopping for my helmet, though I never totally felt at ease weaving across intersections in Manhattan. But later, I loved that he asked "where I saw us" before I did and that he helped me move to New Haven,

Connecticut, for my doctoral fellowship without a hint of resentment, even when it meant we'd live farther apart.

Before this storied setup, from my twentieth birthday on, I'd probably spent an average of thirty minutes a day (with peaks around Valentine's Day and birthdays, and lows during fun-filled times) either thinking or complaining about my own anticipated aloneness and romantic rejections.

I went to an all-girls high school and anxiously wished there was some way to be sure that I'd meet a great guy when I graduated. Then I did meet someone I adored in college and I invested a lot in our relationship. But I actually always felt alone, even when we were together. It was like a marathon job interview where I couldn't quite grasp what I needed to do to prove myself. After being together for two years, my college love still refused to call me his girlfriend. I felt less-than because this guy who knew me well didn't know if he wanted to date me. Yet every time I committed to walking away from him, he moved toward me and began treating me like I mattered, until I seemed committed again. Once I was, he'd revert back to his flaky ways, forgetting dates and acting like he didn't care all that much, and the cycle continued.

Looking back, it may seem crazy that I put up with this for as long as I did. But I was in emotion mind, so I didn't see the situation clearly. Instead, I thought it was all my fault. "I love you but I don't know if I'm *in* love with you," he eventually confessed. I held back my tears and told him I was tired of us. Instead of agreeing to break up, he dismissed my feelings, trying to elicit my sympathy for the plight of his confusion.

We did eventually break up, and I invested years going on endless dates, wondering why I couldn't find a connection, or coping with feelings of rejection. Soon my closest friends were marrying their college boyfriends and post-college partners. When I went out or met people at parties, I fielded questions like, "You seem normal . . . Why are you still single?" which made me feel like I had to defend myself just for showing up.

By the time I met the guy my friend assured me would be my future husband, I'd estimate that I had amassed close to 1,600 hours of undue stress worrying about my appearance, personality, fertility, and frustrating dates that went nowhere or disappeared. I compared myself to friends and strangers and replayed conversations I had, wishing I could edit them to seem *better*. A committed relationship seemed simpler than the nightmare that was my mind—I was an outlier, fodder for a mix of gossip and pity. I was tired of watching other people travel to Thailand and expand their families via social media as I lay in bed alone in my studio apartment with an old laptop and a bad Internet connection.

So when I started dating "my future husband," I seamlessly filled in any questions I had about him with positive assumptions. I also quickly minimized any potential red flags. I posted our travel pictures and before I knew it, I was living what Facebook depicted as a dream life. Except like most staged photos, they didn't capture what was going on in my real life (leading to my theory that the prettier the picture, the less truth it tells). Regardless of how perfect everything seemed in my online feed, I wasn't happy.

The problem was, he was actually attractive, generous, and loyal, everything I thought I wanted, which made it harder to accept that he and I actually wanted entirely different lives, lives that weren't compatible together. My vegetarian diet alone was an ongoing argument. "It's just not classy," he whispered loudly, when we were alone. When he brought me home to meet his parents, they mocked me, repeatedly asking me to explain the origin of what they insisted on calling my "veganism," as they sliced steak and I feigned fullness and finished a sweet potato. "I eat dairy," I offered, wondering if the anger I felt meant I was "too sensitive."

In emotion mind, I believed that we could make it work, given our attraction and shared desire to commit. When he proposed in Paris, I felt elated and jumped into wedding planning.

But getting what you think you want doesn't guarantee happiness. Even with a ring on my finger, "my future husband" called me "too independent," and confessed that he found my quest for spirituality "naive." He wanted me to fall into his life like someone surrenders in that team-building trust fall. I was never good at that game. I questioned myself and went to therapy, worried that my parents' divorce was impairing my ability to commit. Yet I also believed the people who warned it was "impossible to meet someone." I was about to finish my doctorate in clinical psychology and I believed them (thank you, anticipated aloneness). More than anything, I wanted my beloved dying grandmother to think that I was happy and secure.

Secretly, I wasn't at peace. I painfully started to realize the truth in the axiom "love isn't enough." When I found the courage to question our relationship, I didn't know what to do. Stressors that came with ending an engagement, like losing the wedding deposit or having weird conversations at work, terrified me. My life appeared fanciful on the outside; I had a fiancé (even the word sounds glamorous) and a meaningful career as a therapist. In fact, I was teaching chronically suicidal patients strategies to get out of their heads and take courageous steps to build a life that was worthwhile. I also taught relatively content people ways to live better. Increasingly, I noticed the discrepancy between my recommendations for others—trying to be mindful of thoughts and feelings, practicing self-compassion, and accepting the pain and challenges that arise when living according to your values—and my own struggle.

After advancing in my work, and really practicing the advice I was giving to my patients, not just preaching, I decided that I was willing to go through pain, guilt, and loneliness to act courageously. I realized that I could sit with thoughts of anticipated aloneness if it meant I would be able to live my life in a way that fit with my most cherished values. I had been practicing yoga for a decade, but it was my professional training that made my mind more flexible and less seduced by my emotion mind. I do want to acknowledge that my ex-fiancé was the first partner to make me feel worthy and I will always wish him well. But finally, with a clear sense of what we wanted our respective lives to stand for, "my future husband" and I broke up.

Afterward, I felt both miserable and relieved. I created a schedule filled with goals linked to higher values that I hoped would bring me fulfillment and contribute to others as well. I brought ice cream to a dying woman in my neighborhood, wrote a book, worked on being a good friend, invested in religious practices, practiced yoga, and went on mindfulness retreats. On one of those retreats, newly single, in Maui, as I sat in front of meditation masters Ram Dass, author of the celebrated *Be Here Now*, and Sharon Salzberg, who has also written practical books on mindfulness and whose compassion is contagious, I noticed that for the first time in a while, I wasn't lonely.

Of course, there were hard times. I went on dates and experienced plenty of ghosting. I sometimes envied couples who seemed compatible. At times, I wondered if I was just "too picky," which led me to worry that I had blown my best chance with my breakup. But through these ups and downs, I tried my best to recommit to letting go of unhelpful thoughts and feelings, to remind myself that I was trying to live according to my values, and that I needed to focus on what I could give (e.g., openness), not what I could get (e.g., a fourth date with someone *amazing*).

Most mornings before I went to work, to enhance my sense of discipline, I practiced Mysore, a type of yoga that requires you to memorize a sequence of postures in an hour-long routine guided by breath. Mysore wasn't as fun as my power yoga classes, yet I found the regimen—moving through poses I didn't like, and focusing on my breath count, one breath at a time, instead of the teacher's words, therapeutic. I had to practice being non-judgmental of my body when my neighbors sat comfortably in graceful lotus positions that I could never manage. I worked through twists, developed my core, and, though scared, learned the "king of yoga poses," *sirsasana*, headstand. (Much to my surprise, I discovered that this liberating and confidence-boosting posture requires engaging your core strengths, rather than bearing too much weight on your head.) I grew to appreciate being part of this community. "Where have you been?" my Mysore classmates would ask when I missed a few days. I loved that I counted and that all I needed to do was show up.

Outside of the studio, in my life, I delved into the trickier parts of my prescription. I tried to stop complaining and instead focused on building a balanced life. I repeatedly tried to embrace acceptance: If I met someone, I did, but that would be because of a mix of effort and luck, not a rigid plan. I retired from ruminating (thousands of times). I told myself that what was in my control was being kind, patient, present, and grateful. Yes, I wanted to meet someone, but that wasn't my sole reason for living, and this quest wasn't going to ruin me the way it had seemed to for years. I realized that I didn't deserve to feel ashamed about being single, and stopped acting embarrassed.

Eventually, I met a man I'd been introduced to years earlier, at a lecture Senator Cory Booker gave on *tikkun olam*, the Hebrew phrase for building a world of kindness. A friend had awkwardly introduced us, we spoke briefly, and he quickly wandered off. Several years later, we met again. He didn't remember me, but this time, something clicked and our relationship evolved without much stress. I was curious about him, but not attached to an outcome, and I was committed to my life. As we sat sharing drinks on our second date, I realized that a sample copy of the first book I wrote was arriving at my door that night. I was dying to see the galley and excused myself early. He cheered me on.

"It's hard to imagine meeting someone who is smart, sensitive, driven, warm, funny, athletic, handsome, spiritual, and easygoing. You are," I told him at our wedding four years ago. We named our daughter, Sylvie, after my beloved grandma, and our son, Eli, after my inspirational grandpa.

I realize how lucky I am to have my family. But I also know that if I hadn't met Adam, I could still build on my grandparents' legacy and emulate the values they embodied. Life has joy and purpose, and it's possible to feel whole and happy, shame-free, without a person by your side.

I wish I hadn't wasted precious years doubting my future and myself. Studying clinical psychology, especially my science-based specialties, helped me break that cycle and change my life, showing me what participating in living is, regardless of whether I was sharing my time with a romantic partner or enjoying it on my own.

♥

AND SIX WEEKS after I met my patient Rachel, she began telling me that she felt more energized and hopeful than she had in ages. Though she sometimes feels annoyed after a bad date, she isn't feeling the way she once was: sad, worried, hopeless, or afraid she will have to settle, leading to despair. Instead, she is building a life she loves. "Music is amazing," she noticed when she came to see me after going to a concert, something I'd "prescribed." She seemed relieved that her therapy homework wasn't to sit quietly in meditation but rather to engage actively in her life and the things she enjoys, without getting sucked into the emergency warnings that her mind launched.

Think about how much time you might be spending predicting anticipated aloneness or processing perceptions of rejection. Now think about this: Every minute you get stuck in unhelpful thoughts and feelings is time you're not spending experiencing the moments of your life as they happen right now. I know you've probably heard about the idea of being present, another way of talking about mindfulness. When you are mindful, thoughts and emotions still arise, but you move away from what mindfulness expert Jon Kabat-Zinn calls "full catastrophe living," or the emotional avalanche that once haunted me—and Rachel. The diagram on the next page sums up the process:

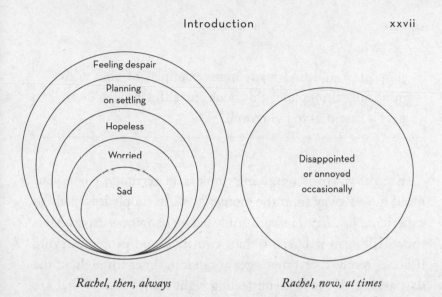

Rachel, then, always   *Rachel, now, at times*

WHAT IS MINDFULNESS?

Throughout this book, when I use the term "mindfulness," I'm referring to the practice of learning to pay attention with an attitude of acceptance so you can live with more clarity. That might mean instead of getting hijacked by thoughts, feelings, or physical sensations, you notice them, acknowledge them, and continue to pursue what's meaningful to you. More broadly, mindfulness is living your life in a way that's deliberate and effective. If you're trying to meet new people, for instance, and have the thought, *There is no point in trying since I'll end up alone*, the mindful thing to do would be to notice the thought, without assuming that it's true, and continue trying to connect with others. Or if you feel lonely one late night, a mindful way of dealing with that emotion would be to acknowledge it in the moment rather than judging, *I'm so pathetic*, which will only make you less likely to reach out to friends for support. You'll find many more examples of how to live mindfully throughout this book since this type of awareness is essential to living well.

Even if you're not entering unpleasant territory, when your mind moves away from the moment, you're simply less likely to experience joy. In a Harvard study led by happiness expert Matthew Killingsworth, more than two thousand people carrying iPhones received text messages at random times throughout the day, asking, "How are you feeling right now?" and "What are you doing right now?" and "Are you thinking about something other than what you're currently doing?" In monitoring people's happiness in real time, the researchers learned that participants' minds wandered frequently, and that *people were less happy when their minds wandered*, even if the content of their thoughts was something pleasant. In other words, you will ultimately feel better if you focus on the *now*.

Incidentally, the happier you are, the more likely it is that you will find a partner. Sonja Lyubomirsky, a psychology professor at the University of California, Riverside, and her colleagues have studied whether people are happy because they're successful or successful because they're happy. Lyubomirsky's team concluded: "[There's] compelling evidence that positive affect fosters the following resources, skills, and behaviors: sociability and activity, altruism, liking of self and others, strong bodies and immune systems, and effective conflict resolution skills." This makes sense. When you're in a better emotional space, you're more likely to pursue hobbies and spend time with people who bring you joy. Also, positivity is endearing. A study at the

University of California, Berkeley, run by two psychologists, LeeAnne Harker and Dacher Keltner, found that when people looked at yearbook photos of women with genuine smiles versus those who looked less happy, they perceived them as productive and having a good sense of humor, even when controlling for attractiveness. I want to highlight: the point of feeling joy is not to attract others, but to live well, because *you* deserve that.

IN THE CHAPTERS to come, you'll learn just how both to enjoy the present moment and to feel like the hopes you have for your future are within your reach. To sidestep hopelessness, we all need wisdom. Just like it's smart to take a list to the store so you don't forget what you need when you're exhausted, *How to Be Single and Happy* is a validating reminder that you can pick yourself up when you feel alone. You don't need to live in a fantasy—but you surely don't deserve to prepare for tragedy. A soul mate is just that, a mate. You are whole; a person is a "+1." Now, to quote Mary Oliver, "Tell me, what is it you plan to do with your one wild and precious life?"

PART 1

The Misery Formula

Why Looking for "Mr. (or Ms.) Right"

Is Making You Feel So Wrong

DATING IS CHALLENGING enough—you don't deserve to feel any worse. But there may be certain ways you are torturing yourself that are guaranteed to make anyone hurt. For example, does a part of you believe that a relationship is the only way to feel complete or ultimately happy in life? Are you worried that maybe you're not as likely to find love as others are? In the first part of this book, I will help you take inventory of unhealthy psychological habits, which is the first step to living a more fulfilling life, whether or not you have a partner. If you find yourself dwelling on unhelpful self-critical thoughts (possibly exacerbated by scanning your ex's social media), or you're drowning in regret, or feel as if you're settling in some way, stop beating yourself up. Many of the people I talk to in my practice initially believe that analyzing, venting, regretting, or avoiding their feelings will help them somehow. If you've tried these tactics and they aren't working for you, I hope you will discover—as my clients have—that there's a freer way to think, live, and love. As you read, my wish is that you come to realize that it's not *you* that is getting in the way of finding love and happiness—it's these soul-shattering psychological traps you've been caught in that you need to break up with.

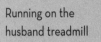

Running on the
husband treadmill

Ruminating

Regretting

Settling, suppressing,
and other
avoidance
moves

CHAPTER 1

Happiness and
the Husband Treadmill

*He who is not contented with what he has would not be
contented with what he would like to have.*

—SOCRATES

I'M ASSUMING THAT you're reading this book for one of two
reasons:

1. You're single and you're feeling disappointed by dating or
   convinced you'll never meet "your person."

   OR

2. You're unhappily coupled but you dread being single again.

Over the years I've spent as a clinical psychologist, one thing
I've learned is that many of my clients are pretty much convinced that when they meet someone, they'll finally feel happy.
I definitely empathize. Women get the brunt of this pressure to
couple up; there's still no acceptable female equivalent to a "confirmed bachelor" in our culture. Ages ago, older women who
weren't married were looked upon as "old maids," a concept

that's never entirely left our psyches. Even the most well-intentioned family members and friends can make uncoupled women feel like there's something wrong with them with comments like, "Don't worry, you'll meet someone" (as if that is the only way you'll be okay) or "He doesn't seem so bad. Maybe you're being too negative. Why don't you just give him a chance?"

I know the fear and sadness that being single can bring. I also know how disappointing it can feel to stay in less-than-optimal relationships because it seems too scary to risk being alone in case you never meet someone else. My goal, as I said earlier, is to show you that you can live with happiness and fulfillment, with or without being in a committed relationship. After all, over the course of life, most people will spend time in relationships and also experience periods when they are single. Once you get to the end of this book, you will feel liberated by a new approach to being single, one that will allow you to find more satisfaction.

For a long time, I certainly believed that meeting my soul mate was the key to my contentment. And it's true that finding someone wonderful *might* increase your joy, though perhaps not as much as you might think. In the pages ahead, you'll learn more about what psychologists know about love and how it relates to happiness, but first, I want you to take a moment to come up with your best estimate of how much *you* believe that meeting your dream person might increase your joy. Five percent? Fifty percent? One hundred and fifty percent?

Now hold on to that number as you read this next sentence: *The belief that your happiness hinges on an external circumstance that you can't control (i.e., meeting a romantic partner) not only makes it harder to find love, but it also sets you up for unhappiness.* Letting go of the maddening myth that happiness comes from coupling up is the first step to freedom. Stressing out about meeting someone will not help you meet that person any faster. The healthiest way to increase your chances of finding love is to increase your happiness, right now.

That's what my client, whom I'll call Juliana, ultimately discovered. Sweet, funny, with lots of freckles, this forty-three-year-old stay-at-home mother was an only child whose parents divorced when she was in middle school. She told me that her childhood was "lonely," and that ever since she was a young girl playing with figurines in her dollhouse, she was convinced that a fulfilling marriage ensured happiness. As a young adult, Juliana attributed her mother's sadness as a by-product of divorcing her father years before.

In her late twenties, Juliana met George, the man who ultimately became her husband. "Right away, I felt like, if he's with me, I'm good," she told me in one of our early sessions. The start of their relationship was "insanely blissful." Juliana described herself as introverted and a bit nervous in social situations. George was extroverted enough to be a talk-show host or comedian. Juliana also told me that she'd struggled a lot with dating. "I'm not in the lucky gene pool," she told me, explaining that she wasn't trying to sound negative, but that she was acutely aware that she was "below average" in looks and didn't consider herself to be particularly smart. She'd been anxious about dating and eager to find someone and felt lucky that George, someone she adored, reciprocated her feelings.

By the time Juliana came to see me, she and George had been together for thirteen years. Her marriage, she told me, was "pretty much over." George wasn't attentive and she explained that they'd "failed" couples counseling. She told me that their therapist had agreed with George that her wish for ten minutes of nightly conversation was "too much" to expect, which left her wondering if her nudging about anything had been unreasonable and exacerbated the tension in their marriage.

The problem was that their needs were at odds with each other. Juliana, who left her job in advertising after she had a baby, craved adult companionship after spending her days with their four-year-old daughter. George was bored in his work as an accountant and exasperated by their New York City bills. When he came home at the end of the day, the last thing he felt like doing was talking. "He's not the kind of guy who does things he's not in the mood to do," Juliana said. Recently, he'd mainly connected with Juliana when they were out in a big group and he was drinking.

After years of feeling they like were in a rut, George and Juliana decided that they couldn't continue living together in their small apartment. But they couldn't agree on what to do about their challenges. Juliana hoped to improve the relationship; George thought it was too late. He didn't want more "work" in his life. While George checked out, Juliana was increasingly absorbed in reminiscing about their early years. "We clicked so well," she gushed. She was also anxious about the prospect of returning to dating, which she remembered felt like a constant stream of frustration. Reflective and growth-oriented, Juliana continued to assume, "I could've been better and it's my fault." Instead of mourning George's lack of commitment, Juliana was doing something I've seen many women do in the midst of a breakup. She kept telling me how great he was, seeing George through a cognitive distortion called the *halo effect*, attuned to his virtues and disconnected from his flaws.

After hearing for months about Juliana's begging George to try a new couples therapist with her and his continuously refusing, her mother told her to quit pushing and go to therapy on her own. "Honestly, a part of me hopes that maybe if I fix myself, George will change his mind," Juliana told me when we met.

Happiness Studies and Love Stories

Juliana assumed that repairing things with George would provide her with joy. Let's see what research says about marriage and happiness. Given we're all unique, every relationship is an incomparable creation. Rather than sensationally promising simplifications that reduce the complexity of what we know about connections, I want to share a few broader findings on the topic of happiness with you.

According to the classic *hedonic treadmill* theory, everyone's happiness seems to hover at a fairly stable set point throughout life. What that means is that neither hugely wonderful nor painfully tragic life events affect our well-being as much as we think they will. We get used to jewelry (including a big ring), a new house, and a promotion at work. We adjust to bad things too. After a breakup, we spend time with friends. We laugh and smile again. Generally, we recover. When it comes to happiness, the good news—and the bad news—is that unless we practice specific skills to alter our happiness level, we tend to bounce back to our baseline no matter what happens. (We will cover these skills in part 2.)

What creates happiness, anyway? According to positive psychologist Sonja Lyubomirsky and her colleagues, happiness stems from three factors: our genetics (e.g., that happiness set point), our circumstances, and our activities. What's noteworthy is that Lyubomirsky believes that circumstances, like finances or relationship status, generally account for a smaller slice of the happiness equation than our deliberate behaviors. What this means is that your actions matter—which is hopeful since it's usually easier to change your behaviors than to create your ideal situation. In case you're feeling discouraged by the thought that you might have a low happiness set point based on your genetics, as a behavioral therapist, I'm pretty convinced that it's possible to stretch your "set point" and that you are more in control of your sense of well-being than you might assume.

Yet many of us chase a partner, running for years on the "husband treadmill," in the belief that finding the right person (i.e., changing your circumstances) will mean a permanently elevated mood and a happier life (I'm naming the husband treadmill as a riff on the hedonic treadmill, though this concept is directed toward any coupling). While happiness may surge after a great date and nosedive after a breakup, research suggests that eventually, it will revert to your mean, sort of like your weight after either a strict diet or an indulgent vacation. Despite what experts say about adaptation, running on the husband treadmill, like Juliana was doing, remains insanely popular.

Clearly, there's a chasm between what experts say about joy and what the average person thinks about coupling. Juliana wasn't alone in her theory about love. In a 2012 Reuters global poll of more than twenty thousand adults, two thirds of those in relationships said that their partner was their greatest source of happiness and 45 percent of single respondents assumed that finding a partner would grant them bliss. This raises the question: Are people good at knowing what makes them happy?

Juliana, for one, looked skeptical when I explained to her that despite what people assume, experts like Barbara Fredrickson, a psychology professor at the University of North Carolina, Chapel Hill, who specializes in researching positive emotions, don't glorify coupling. In fact, Fredrickson says that the Reuters

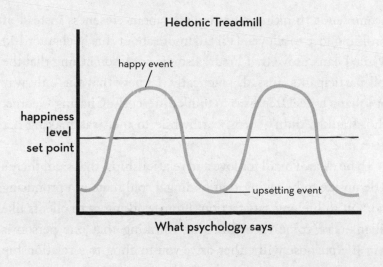

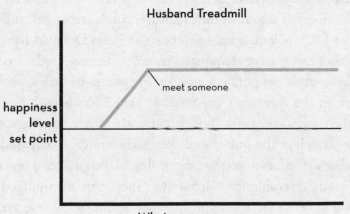

poll reflects a "worldwide collapse of imagination." She warns: "Thinking of love purely as the romance or commitment that you share with one special person—as it appears most on earth do—surely limits [your] health and happiness. . . ." She recommends thinking more broadly about closeness instead of confining love to a lover. (I'll talk more about this in chapter 10.) While I can't prove that Fredrickson is on to something that the poll participants missed, practically, I knew that the only way for Juliana to feel freer was to think differently. Chasing George, who, frankly, didn't seem worthwhile to me, was making her miserable.

To be clear, I'm all for love and relationships; that said, there's little upside to believing that finding a soul mate is a promising shortcut to lifelong satisfaction. From working with clients like Juliana, I've come to realize that thinking that one person is your life purpose will either drive you to cling to a relationship or make you unhappy if you're single.

Beyond Juliana's dilemma, why do so many of us maintain these miraculous views of coupling? One reason is that even as the numbers of single women increase, single status still suffers from a PR problem. Social psychologist Bella DePaulo has devoted her career to studying stigmas around being single. In one of her studies, researchers asked participants to rate a person based on the following description: "Anna has been living in Munich for some years. She is currently single. In her spare time, she plays the guitar and goes swimming." Compared to those described as in relationships, singles were rated as less extroverted, agreeable, and attractive. They were also judged as having lower self-esteem and life satisfaction. Are these prejudices accurate? While the single people described did feel less satisfied with their relationship status and lonelier than those who were coupled, their satisfaction with life, self-esteem, attractiveness, and extroversion were comparable to that of people in relationships. It turns out that not being in a relationship isn't a good predictor of someone's personality or happiness, despite prevalent stereotypes.

Aside from the risk of loneliness, which we may remedy by thinking more widely à la Fredrickson, global negative ideas about single life might be more of a spinster fable than a reality. It's hard to remember this fact in a world that adorns women's fingers with expensive diamonds like trophies earned. But keeping this research in mind can prevent you from the unnecessary torment Juliana was experiencing. Plus, believing that you will be lonely actually predicts feeling lonely later in life, according to a study led by Jitka Pikhartova, an expert on aging and well-being.

The combination of buying into cultural stereotypes about what it means to be single and *affective forecasting*, or predicting how we'll feel in the future, keeps many women stuck on the husband treadmill. Back to a question I posed earlier: Are we actually good at pinpointing what will make us happy? The answer is an unqualified no. In a study spearheaded by Professor Daniel Gilbert at Harvard, researchers asked more than five hundred college students to predict how happy they'd be two months after a breakup. The researchers found that the students' bleak predictions of how they'd feel after ending a relationship were way off. Happiness levels of partnered and recently single participants didn't differ. Gilbert and his colleagues explain that we routinely overestimate our negative reactions as well as the depth and longevity of our good feelings. Our ability to anticipate how we'll feel in the future is imprecise, at best.

When we imagine meeting someone, for example, we may myopically focus on the positive details, like cuddling or kissing, and forget the potential difficulties that arise from adding someone significant to our lives. Even the most amazing person typically comes with a few annoying friends and family members, not to mention bad habits, like forgetting to replace the toilet paper after using the last square, or snoring. I'm not recommending that you dwell on the endless ways that finding love may ultimately cause you stress, or making a case for staying single. My point is that everyone can benefit from the reminder that our unfulfilled fantasies, like our stereotypes, are just *thoughts*. My prescription is for you to start practicing joyful living *now*.

I know this from personal experience. When I look back on my life, especially my single life, I notice that I was miserable because of what was going on in my mind, not my actual life. I'd routinely imagine that a birthday or a pleasant Sunday would somehow be better with a boyfriend and then my mood would plummet. It's easy to forget as we scroll through photos of couples at brunch in coordinating cozy sweaters that Instagram isn't instant truth.

In case you're worried that I have some bleak take on marriage, I do feel lucky to have met my partner. The key wasn't getting married, though. What helped, really, was learning how to practice mindfulness. The more I worked on entering the moment without wishing things were different, the less I worried about my future, criticized myself, and replayed various bad dates—and the more comfortable my life felt.

Of course, when I met Adam, it felt easier to dwell in the moment. I wasn't tested as much by situations like hoping for someone I liked to express interest, or worrying about having a child, as I listened to friends debate over which high-end stroller, a Bugaboo or an UPPAbaby, was best. Yet while I no longer get dragged down by some of the triggers that once upset me, as affective forecasting studies highlight, there are also times my mood drops in ways I wouldn't have predicted. On a recent

Friday night, I was lying on the couch wearing sweatpants, immersed in a page-turning story in the *New Yorker*, sipping mint iced tea. Adam, however, was bored. "Next Friday, we should have my friends over," he said. Suddenly, I was stressing about having to prepare for a party I didn't want. I also watched myself worry, *I'm not good company.*

On the baby front, while I daydreamed of blissfully holding a cherubic infant, I never envisioned how I might feel returning home from work at 9 p.m., six weeks after giving birth, to unsuccessfully console a colicky baby who cried for hours in our one-bedroom apartment. As I tried to analyze whether my misery was sleep deprivation or postpartum depression, I thought about how poorly I'd predicted my feelings (and also tried to remind myself that emotions pass, as you'll read in chapter 9).

Whether I was single or partnered, during stressful times, it was mindfulness that offered me a way to reengage, and to escape the pain of imagining that my negative thoughts and feelings would last forever. Mindfulness is about fully participating in activities instead of letting past pains or future worries contaminate your moments. Being present in your life is the opposite of waiting for love, and research suggests that the more present you can be, the more fulfillment you will experience. Supporting this theory, researchers at the University of Wisconsin, Madison, deem the "happiest person in the world" a Buddhist monk named Matthieu Ricard. After examining neural correlates of joy in hundreds of people, the scientists discovered that Ricard's bliss was off the charts. As Ricard explains, training the mind is the foundation for happiness.

Learning to refocus your mind can also alter your brain, shifting your happiness set point. Going back to Juliana, she was convinced that her family history and her parents' divorce tainted her capacity to feel content. She was excited to learn about a brain study led by neuroscientist Britta Hölzel that examined people before and after they practiced mindfulness. Hölzel and her team found that eight weeks of mindfulness training resulted in neural changes associated with managing emotions. Remarkably, researchers have also discovered that present-focused attention reduces the risk of depression.* Even people who have repeatedly struggled with depression can reduce their risk of relapse by learning to notice their thoughts and feelings. Juliana was surprised to see firsthand what researchers promise: Behavioral efforts can remarkably impact our biology.

The Magic of Mindsets

Why is it essential to rethink what brings you happiness? For a moment, imagine that you are spending a couple of weeks working in the housekeeping department of a hotel. The hours are long, your pay is low, and you have limited time and money to go to a gym, so you don't think of yourself as someone who is especially fit. But what if you changed your thinking?

In a remarkable study, Stanford psychologist Alia Crum divided eighty-four women who cleaned hotel rooms for a living into two groups. In the experimental group, she told the women that the Surgeon General recommended thirty minutes of physical activity every day for a healthy lifestyle, then congratulated

---

* Throughout this book I'll mention psychological problems, including research on suicide prevention, given this is something I specialize in treating. But I'm not implying that you're struggling with debilitating sadness or any other disorder. My intention is to offer you hope that if these techniques work for people who feel seriously stuck, you can infer that they'd certainly help in coping with circumstances you don't like. That said, if you are in crisis, a self-help book is no substitute for therapy in person with a professional. To find a behavioral therapist near you, visit www.abct.org.

them on meeting, and likely exceeding, this guideline. She and her team also gave the women estimates of the calories they burned for all the various tasks they performed (e.g., 15 minutes of vacuuming = 50 calories). The control group, in contrast, wasn't given this information. After four weeks, the women in the experimental group showed reductions in weight, blood pressure, body fat, waist to hip ratio, and body mass, *without* changing their exercise habits. How did this happen? Once the women believed they were doing something healthy, their bodies responded. This finding wasn't a fluke; decades of research by psychologist Carol Dweck demonstrate that believing can create real change. Which is why I really want you to shift from thinking your happiness is in a person when social science says there is more to enduring satisfaction.

What we tell ourselves can also change our behaviors. One study led by psychologist Lisa Blackwell found that when twelve-year-olds in New York City public schools are told that they can improve their intelligence rather than believing that their IQs are unchangeable, they actually enjoy learning, feel more driven, and perform better. In another study on the power of mindsets, Crum and her colleagues introduced a short video to employees at a financial institution that conveyed that stress is performance enhancing. Reframing stress as adaptive improved both their work performance and their mood. Shifting our thinking powerfully impacts our body, mind, and emotions.

When it comes to finding love, while you may not be able to conjure up the right partner instantly, you can change your mindset on what being single means. According to Roy Baumeister's research on happiness, *believing* your life is relatively easy correlates with happiness, while *thinking* your life is difficult predicts unhappiness. Letting go of assumptions, stereotypes, and affective forecasts and adopting a more hopeful perspective can increase your happiness.

A More Mindful Mindset

Mindfulness offers us a powerful way to shift our mindsets in a useful direction. So in order to show you how to apply it to your single life, I turned to the experts. One Sunday morning, I felt like a nervously excited star-struck fan. Famed mindfulness teacher Sharon Salzberg had invited me into her light-filled apartment in New York City to learn more about her experiences helping others navigate relationships using mindfulness. Sharon's teachings have impacted me personally, and I love relaying her wisdom to my clients. As one of the leading teachers of loving-kindness meditation in the United States, she perfectly embodies a unique combination of authentic New Yorker laced with over forty years of spiritual practice. She's down-to-earth, funny, and profound at the same time.

Sharon explained that when we learn to focus our attention, we're able to think more expansively instead of sinking into narrow judgments. This makes a lot of sense, since mindfulness actually enlarges the parts of the brain that help us align our behaviors with long-term goals. Sharon went on to clarify that when we're mindful, instead of chasing something like money, we ask ourselves: *What would I do if I had more money?* Maybe we'd travel more or spend more time with loved ones. Ironically, by focusing on a goal like "more money" we may shut out opportunities for adventure and fun with friends. A more mindful mindset in looking for love might be considering: *What would I do if I had a partner? How would my life be different? And how can I do some of that now?* If you are someone who relies on someone else to feel loved, how else can you feel appreciated? Is there some way you can start to add more self-care, now? (We'll cover more on self-compassion in chapter 7.)

Before meeting with Sharon, I debated whether I could respectfully ask her about her personal life. Sharon's parents divorced when she was four, her mother died when she was nine, and her father left, returned, and then permanently entered the mental healthcare system when she was eleven. I'd read that by the time she was sixteen, she'd lived in five different family configurations all ending in loss. I wondered how she'd survived to create what seemed like a remarkably satisfying life. She told me that at age sixteen, through an independent study program at the State University of New York, Buffalo, she studied intensive meditation in Burma and has been practicing since. One of her most influential teachers, Dipa Ma, also experienced great loss, the death of two children and the sudden death of her husband, and found solace in meditation.

Given Sharon's openness, I continued to wonder: Is it a faux pas to ask your mindfulness teacher about dating? I respectfully went ahead. "May I ask if you're currently in a romantic relationship?" I asked. Sharon looked completely at ease as she explained that though she was not in a relationship, the door was open to one in the future, and she felt fulfilled in the present. "If you have a sense of being deeply connected to yourself and deeply connected to your life through the bigger picture of life, then you don't have a sense of, 'I have to find a best friend by Tuesday!' or 'I have to find someone to fill these empty hours to make up for all that I'm lacking.'" I can hardly imagine anyone having a richer life than the one Sharon's created. She radiates love, lacks shame, and has both an incredibly meaningful career and rewarding personal connections. You too can experience profound fulfillment and feel receptive to a relationship without attaching your happiness to that outcome.

Marriage Doesn't Guarantee Happiness

Back to the question I started with, just how merry does marriage make people? Let's step back from our biases and look at how marriage affects happiness on a larger scale. In a remarkable study looking at more than twenty-four thousand people over the course of fifteen years (utilizing data from something called the German Socio-Economic Panel Study), Michigan State University professor Richard Lucas and his colleagues noticed that on average, most people reverted to their happiness baseline after an initial emotional uptick following marriage. (More support for the hedonic treadmill.) Lucas and his colleagues concluded, "On average, people only got a very small boost from marriage (approximately one tenth of 1 point on an 11-point scale)"—that's a mere 1 percent! The authors share the unsexy finding that there were as many people who ended up *less* happy after marriage as there were people who reported being more content. All of which means that running on the husband treadmill can end up propelling you into a less-than-satisfying union. My hope is that these facts free you to think more clearly about relationships and your current ability to experience joy.

Not that marriage doesn't have its perks. Married people tend to experience improved health and longevity. But it's tough to tell if that's because of the marriage itself or the improved economic situation and health insurance that often come with it.

Here's another thing to keep in mind when you find yourself equating marriage with happiness: Research led by sociologist

David Johnson, at the Pennsylvania State University, suggests that people who marry and stay married tend to report feeling above-average life satisfaction *before* they wed, which again supports the idea that marriage arises from happiness, not the other way around. Positive affect, or feeling grateful and acting upbeat, is not only related to feeling happy; it's also strongly associated with living a longer life. In case you're skeptical that you can feel positive and remain uncoupled, in a fascinating study spearheaded by epidemiologist David Snowdon, 180 nuns were followed for several decades, beginning in 1986, to learn more about aging and Alzheimer's disease. Among other things, researchers analyzed handwritten accounts of the nuns' lives and discovered that a woman's description of her life at twenty-two strongly predicted her risk of dying early. Women who included positive emotional content (like love, gratitude, and hope) in their autobiographies lived an average of nine years longer than women whose stories lacked positive emotions. Given that positive feelings extend our lives and also make our lives worth extending, it certainly seems worthwhile to purposefully cultivate them.

Close to a year after we first met, Juliana and George divorced, yet she was surprised that she felt happier than she would have predicted. Of course, there were times when she missed the connection she'd experienced at the beginning of their relationship, especially as she approached dating apps for the first time. "I wish I could hire someone to message people for me so I don't have to deal with all the back and forth," she said. Moving apartments and setting up more childcare for her daughter was also stressful. But over time, she created a meaningful routine for herself. She is working part-time in real estate and embracing the vulnerability required to get close with someone new. "I'm shocked, but I'm less lonely than I've felt in years, and maybe 35 percent happier," she told me. The same way many of us overestimate the joy of marriage, Juliana underestimated the toll of living with a partner who didn't share her definition of closeness. She had hoped that marriage would make her feel important and seen. When that didn't happen, she ultimately heightened her joy by changing her activities and adding mindfulness to her life. We worked on ways to help her worry less in social situations which allowed her to enjoy conversations. She made plans with parents from her daughter's school and attended networking events. These new behaviors and relationships helped her feel validated. In the same way, I hope that by replacing the husband treadmill with a more mindful mindset, you can build what Sharon Salzberg describes as "a heart as wide as the world."

CHAPTER 2

Ruminating Will Ruin Your Life, If It Hasn't Already

There is nothing either good or bad but thinking makes it so.

—WILLIAM SHAKESPEARE

WHY AM I still single?

I'll never meet anyone.

I shouldn't have to spend my Saturday alone.

People don't even date anymore, so how am I supposed to find someone?

It's ridiculous that I have to go to this event next week by myself. Again.

Do you obsess about not being in a relationship? If you've ever felt like you're playing the emotional equivalent of that whack-a-mole arcade game where thoughts erupt and hijack your peace of mind, you're not alone. This mental habit is called *rumination*—obsessively dwelling on certain thoughts and symptoms, and it is the *worst*. Unlike other behaviors, rumination can be so subtle we often don't notice we're doing it, and it's completely portable. So we can practically ruminate constantly, even in yoga classes (as I once did—more on that later). This chapter will help you free yourself from overthinking so it doesn't stand in the way of your happiness.

Frankly, it's hard enough to cope with romantic disappointments without replaying them in your head, as my client, Emma, tended to do. A passionate and petite thirty-nine-year-old who works in politics, Emma was an experienced ruminator and one of the smartest women I've met. When I asked her about her therapy goals, she said, "I want to stop being crazy in relationships, and move on more easily after a breakup." She went on to describe her experience with Nina, her most recent ex. They'd dated for eight months and had split up about a month earlier. But Nina was still almost constantly on Emma's mind, a spiral I could see in my office: "If Nina meets someone, I'll definitely feel jealous. But I find her pathetic in so many ways. Maybe that means I'm codependent?" As she spoke, going through countless possibilities and catastrophes, it was clear that Emma was obsessed with thinking about love. She couldn't tolerate the uncertainty of not knowing when she'd find her next partner, which she thought was the only way to exit her stressful existence.

Compassionately, I asked Emma to estimate how much time she spent ruminating. "Since the breakup, probably half my waking hours," she told me. She noticed that the obsessing was getting in the way of her productivity, and that she had to work extra hours to compensate. Even when she walked down the street, she found herself imagining bumping into Nina, which prevented her from enjoying her beloved neighborhood.

Emma isn't an outlier. Many of us are prone to overthinking. On the positive side, analyzing, anticipating, and predicting challenges can help us prepare for and solve future problems. One study found that 73 percent of young adults and 52 percent of middle-aged adults describe themselves as overthinkers. The trouble comes when you start thinking compulsively about issues you can't control in the moment or when your analyzing morphs into damaging and inaccurate assumptions you start to believe. That's when rumination can leave you stressed and unhappy.

Why, then, do we ruminate? One cause is when we're facing a goal (like finding a relationship) that can't be readily achieved. Instead of moving on, we fall into dwelling on it, and the more importance we place on the goal, the likelier we are to ruminate. So many of us ruminate on the topic of relationships that psychologists have even developed the *Relational Rumination Scale*, which includes items like: "Thoughts about how to find a partner plague my mind" and "I think about how I should have prevented the breakup with an ex."

Unfortunately, just as it's impossible to solve certain problems instantaneously, like finding someone to love right this minute, we also can't choose our emotions. And when we're in a negative mood, we're that much more likely to get sucked into thoughts that maintain how we feel. To help break the cycle, it can be helpful to appreciate this idea:

Feelings ⟷ Thoughts

As I mentioned in the introduction, when we feel intensely or notice that we're in emotion mind, it's much harder to access our ability to think reasonably. And again, anticipated aloneness and facing the feelings that come with that gloomy prediction renders us less able to perform tasks we're capable of, like solving math equations. Yet ironically, people prone to ruminating (and the intense emotions that result) assume that they're working to understand and solve their problems. But we need to remember that overthinking ruins our mood and drains our energy, making it that much more difficult to actually fix anything.

With this in mind, Emma and I worked on noticing the intensity of her emotions (e.g., "My anger is a 9," on a 1 to 10 scale) and reminding herself that she needed to postpone thinking about a hot topic and instead do something to take a small break until she felt more clear. "This is like taking an exam and realizing that the more you reread a tough question, the less sharp your mind feels. If you can step out to get a drink of water, you'll not only feel refreshed, you'll also think better," I explained. Again, when you're in emotion mind, overthinking only leads to more intense emotions.

Ruminating Actually Causes Psychological Problems

Decades ago, Susan Nolen-Hoeksema, a psychology professor at Yale until her death in 2013, wanted to understand why women are twice as likely to suffer from depression as men. In her quest to make sense of this puzzling gender difference, she discovered that women are more likely to overthink, a habit that significantly increases our incidence of debilitating sadness. So if you notice that you ruminate, remind yourself that you're not alone, and that the habit might be the culprit of feeling badly, not your single status. After extensive research, Nolen-Hoeksema discovered that if you want to create depression, anxiety, and a host of other emotional ailments, in one word: ruminate.

Given the problems overthinking can create, it's important to learn how to stop an upsetting event, like a bad date or a breakup, from creating a lasting bad mood. There's no way to prevent upsetting experiences but you can limit the duration of your pain by managing your mind. In fact, in a study led by Jessica Genet at the University of Miami, college students were asked to keep daily diaries to track events in their lives and their moods. They also answered questions on ruminating. On days when they ruminated less, unpleasant events didn't spiral into negative moods.

Maybe you're wondering how it's possible to pinpoint rumination as the source of a bad mood. Couldn't a bad breakup make you miserable, not overthinking that breakup? In 1989, when a large earthquake shook San Francisco, Nolen-Hoeksema was a professor at Stanford. As it so happens, days before the quake, she asked nearly two hundred students to answer questionnaires measuring their propensity toward overthinking, depression, and anxiety. In the days and months after the terrifying event, she tracked down most of these students to see how they were managing. Were any of their close friends or family injured? Remarkably, ruminating predicted both short-term and long-term reactions to the earthquake. The students who were more vulnerable to obsessive thinking were more likely to feel depressed after the event and develop symptoms of post-traumatic stress, even if they hadn't been depressed before or personally affected.

Life is hard enough without your mind ringing with nasty thoughts. Imagine, for example, that you've received an invitation to a party where you don't know anyone but the host. For weeks, you anticipate the event with dread. Then the night of the party comes, you reluctantly attend, and you discover that though there are moments of awkwardness, the party isn't as bad as you'd feared. What a waste of worrying! When you let yourself be a pessimistic forecaster or your own private bully, it's hard to find inner peace.

Social Networking ↔ Ruminating

It can feel so tempting to distract ourselves any way we can. Timothy Wilson, a social psychologist at the University of Virginia, and his colleagues devised a study that asked college students to sit alone for fifteen minutes. During this time alone, they had the option of giving themselves painful shocks. If you had the choice to sit alone or receive electric shocks, which would you choose? When given this choice, 67 percent of the men in the study and 25 percent of the women administered shocks to escape time in their head. I don't know what to make of that gender difference—maybe men are more likely to take physical risks or women are accustomed to overthinking? Either way, given that the mind can feel so dreadful that people are willing to resort to physical pain to distract themselves from thoughts, it's easy to imagine that we'd pursue more enticing escapes, like surfing the Internet.

While rumination can haunt us when we're alone, we're also vulnerable to falling into this habit when we're attached to our screens. Social networking and ruminating can feed off each other. While there are certainly lots of perks to our online communities, ranging from experiencing a sense of connection to learning about meaningful causes, we need to practice noticing when our feeds lead to upsetting thoughts. Snapchat texts evaporate on our screens but they can easily marinate and multiply in our minds. Since social media is often a passive form of surveillance and we tend to observe more than we post, it can become a forum to get in our heads, in full color. We need to remember not to jump to conclusions as our fingers jump around our screens. After all, we have access to filtered and staged "news" that we'd never otherwise see, stories that may enhance our worst fears, giving us lots of inaccurate ideas that everyone else is happier, more successful, more interesting, or having more fun than us.

Substantiating my concerns, Emma told me, "I feel exhausted and totally stressed, but I can't stop looking at her Facebook and Instagram, even though it makes me edgy and gives me insomnia." Every time Emma noticed that Nina had added another "friend," she felt a pang. "Why is she moving on and I just can't?" she wondered. Gently, I told her, "She is moving on and you're leaving your life to watch hers."

Emma was doing what comes naturally. It's so instinctive to compare, to think, like Emma did, *I'm so much better*, or *She's prettier than I am*, especially when browsing social media. Judging is one way we ruminate and find ourselves in unsettling permutations. In reflecting on her experience, Emma noticed that both positive and negative conclusions were equal opportunities for feeling badly. Researchers at the University of Miami who studied how people adjusted after a breakup found that rumination was associated with increased Facebook use, and the more people logged on to Facebook after they split up with their partners, the more they ruminated—and the harder it was for them to move on.

One of the first things Emma and I worked on was her social networking. At first, she told me that she had "no self-control," but eventually, she let a friend reset her account passwords until she learned to be more mindful and willingly agreed it was time to "unfriend" Nina. Understandably, she was itching to keep up with her, but ultimately she found that getting some social media distance was freeing. "It's true what they say about ignorance and bliss," Emma said.

Venting Isn't Guaranteed to Help

When I asked Emma how she might cope with her breakup stress, she predicted, as many of us do, that talking to a friend would help. She had some amazing friends whom she could text, even at 2 a.m. While it sounded like a decent plan, her friends were bluntly impatient. It's natural to want to reach out to friends and talk through details of our experiences. The sad reality, though, is that when we start ruminating, our loved ones may start to burn out. After a weekend visit with her mother where Emma talked endlessly about her misery, her mother was frustrated. "You're only as happy as your unhappiest child," she told her.

Besides her mother, Emma connected to friends who cared and wanted to listen as they poured her a glass of her favorite rosé. But after a few weeks of ongoing texts and in-person complaints, one assertive friend acknowledged that he found Emma's relentless self-focus "selfish." Ruminating isn't only depressing for the person doing it; it upsets others. Emma wondered if she should look for new friends, but I didn't think that was in her best interest. A study following people struggling with mourning found that those who continue to talk about their loss and its meaning for many months after the event notice that others get frustrated with them. "If my friends don't have the patience for me, obviously, no one will want me," Emma said.

I sympathized. But when I tried to explain that *co-rumination*, or excessively discussing problems and rehashing details, won't lead to relief, or bring you closer to another person, Emma felt hurt and accused me of taking her friends' side. "My girlfriend left me and now my friends are flakes," she said. But as we continued to talk, she had the courage to notice that her play-by-plays were making her feel worse.

Speaking of venting, Emma and I set up a system where she was allowed to briefly update me for a few minutes at the start of our sessions, then we'd shift into using the rest of our time rehearsing ways she could cope when she was tempted to ruminate. At first, she resisted the structure. "I need five more minutes, this is my time," she begged, tempted to continue endlessly venting. I pointed out that she'd already noticed that voicing her unhelpful thoughts made her feel worse and affected her friendships and used the analogy of a person who finds himself on a losing streak at a casino yet can't stop gambling. "Sure, there's a tiny chance that you'll hit a jackpot solution. But it's more likely that you'll actually lose more than you anticipated." I cared too much to allow Emma to feel worse. Though she agreed, very reluctantly, eventually she thanked me.

Of course, friends can be great sounding boards during tough times. The trick is to learn to feel unburdened without burdening yourself further or shifting your unhappiness onto others. I encouraged Emma to apologize to her friends for her recent self-absorption and hyperfocus on her breakup. To try to reconnect with them, I suggested that maybe she could start by asking them more about how they were doing. We also worked on her adopting the outlook that get-togethers with friends could be a "vacation" from her overthinking. Instead of replaying the same things again and again, she could participate in new conversations, look beyond herself, and listen deeply to the people she cared about.

At first, Emma was skeptical. "Isn't that suppressing?" she asked. I agreed with her that pushing aside thoughts and feelings wasn't the point, and would inevitably lead to rebound thoughts. (We'll cover more on suppressing in chapter 4.) After all, "Don't think about dating" has *dating* in it. As an alternative to shutting her negative breakup dialogue down, she could compassionately notice whatever thoughts came up and choose not to pursue them—like seeing a doughnut, thinking it looks good, and opting not to bite into it—and fully partake in doing something else. What helped was engaging in activities, like going to trivia night or a movie, which made it easier to stay in the moment than lingering at a café.

Obsessing Steals Your Willpower

Emma was worried about sticking with her plan to participate with her friends without ruminating aloud. "The best way to do this," I explained, "is to not ruminate when you're alone." When we first started meeting, as I mentioned, Emma hadn't thought of herself as someone with much self-control. It's hard to muster the energy to manage your behavior when you're depleted by upsetting thoughts. Besides struggling with redirecting her mind, Emma also texted compulsively, overate, and occasionally drank too much when her thoughts and feelings felt too overwhelming to handle. That didn't surprise me. Nolen-Hoeksema found that rumination predicts binge eating and drinking. Not only are we more emotionally distraught when we ruminate, we're also less healthy.

Together, we looked at how learning to stop ruminating would enhance her willpower and also bring her closer to her ultimate goal of improving relationships. After all, to manage relationships, we need to manage ourselves. Emma once thought that Nina and her friends should accept her unconditionally, but the fact is, we're most likable when we can take care of ourselves.

I told Emma about a landmark study by psychologist Walter Mischel, who gave preschoolers a marshmallow and asked them to wait to eat it, promising a second marshmallow for those who were able to sit patiently. Mischel's daughters were the ages of the young participants, so he had the unique opportunity to watch these children grow up. Over the years, the five-year-olds who were able to accept the craving and not eat the marshmallow were significantly more likely to have strong social relationships at age fifteen.

In case you worry that self-control just isn't you and that you'd eat the marshmallow in seconds, there are some tricks that helped children delay gratification. One proven strategy that increased their willpower was telling them to imagine that the tasty treat was a cloud. In other words, they practiced getting unstuck from taking their enticing thoughts seriously—which is what you'll learn to do too.

Ruminating Isn't Romantic or Attractive

Ruminating can make you feel worse, as we've learned. And it certainly takes you out of the present moment. But it can also taint your romantic relationships. Repetitive thoughts can skew your perspective, for one thing. For another, if you can't break up with rumination when you're single, you may increase your risk of ruminating in a relationship, and research shows that overthinking increases conflict and unhappiness in couples. Studies have shown that people who tend to ruminate are less able to recall a partner's positive qualities, and feel more negatively about the relationship. This makes sense: Rumination gets in the way of our ability to shift our attention.

When we angrily obsess, we're prone to impulsively snap with people we care about. Emma told me that it was hard for her to stop overthinking and discussing how her partner hurt her. "Isn't letting go of that anger sacrificing my self-respect?" she asked. I knew where she was coming from. I've often struggled with the desire to ruminate my way to justice, both in my head and aloud. Eventually, I decided that I wanted to be the sort of person who embodies kindness and forgiveness rather than litigiousness.

Emma and I reviewed the facts, and it didn't seem as if ruminating had worked well for her self-respect. She also noticed that asserting herself (which we will address in chapter 10) was a nice alternative to obsessing alone. "All of us have a choice," I told Emma. "Do we want to be right or do we want to be liked?" Of course, we can take action and walk away from people who hurt us without brooding. But if we want to stay in a relationship, studies confirm that obsessing interferes with our ability to move forward.

Emma shared with me that she habitually went through mental checklists of her grievances with Nina, easily accessing a list of all the times she'd made more effort than her ex. As you can imagine, Emma's thoughts led to critical words and grouchy behaviors. Some people are more *rejection sensitive*, or worry and perceive rejection easily, and this mental risk factor, like rumination, ensures disappointing outcomes. Emma came to expect that Nina would disappoint her, which she did. Expecting rejection leads us to act in ways that elicit rejection, becoming a self-fulfilling prophecy. Emma, so busy ruminating on all the ways Nina had disappointed her, wasn't exactly fun to be around, so both she and Nina were suffering. Nina, understandably, began to withdraw, which led Emma to increase her angry analyzing until Nina ultimately decided she didn't want to stay in the relationship. While rumination wasn't the only cause of their conflict, neither Emma nor Nina deserved all the stress they experienced.

When Emma was finally able to step back and think less emotionally about their partnership, she could see that despite their chemistry, she and Nina didn't have much in common. Emma was career driven, and always rushing into my office from work in her suits with ID badges dangling. Nina, on the other hand, was younger, right out of college, and less focused. Emma knew she wanted a partner who was passionate about politics. Nina wasn't. While Emma wanted kids in the next couple of years, Nina wanted to put that decision off for a decade. Ruminating on small details took Emma away from focusing on the concrete realities of why their relationship wasn't working. Now that she could think clearly about it, she was in a better position to move forward with her life.

Idealizing Isn't as Fun as It Seems

So far, we've talked about how harping on upsetting thoughts affects your mood, behavior, and relationships. But what happens when you linger on more positive thoughts? Do you ever find yourself glorifying someone you don't know well, for instance? According to some theorists, ruminating isn't always negative; it also encompasses dwelling on thoughts that aren't immediately necessary. "But what about if I'm thinking about something happy?" I often hear. I routinely explain that in addition to noticing when we get the urge to mull over painful material, we also need be on the lookout for fantasizing so we don't let ourselves wander away from the freedom that comes from experiencing reality in this moment.

When I was in college, my now close friend, Sarah, whispered

before yoga, "You seeing anyone?" I shook my head as we un-
folded our mats. "I'd like to set you up with my ex," she continued.
Before Sarah could furnish details, class started. I noticed that as
my body moved through downward- and upward-facing dog postures my mind similarly wandered in downward and upward directions. *Why was my new friend introducing me to someone she
dated? Would he like me? If he wasn't good enough for her, why would
he be right for me?* In my mind, Sarah seemed more desirable than
me—she was in medical school, cute, and charismatic. *Should I
stave off rejection by saying no?* I wondered.

Weeks later, after her persuading, I finally met Sarah's ex.
Our date lasted about an hour, at which point, he excused himself to meet up with a friend. I didn't want our conversation to
end—this guy was hilarious and seemed to have his life together.
He worked in finance and compared to the guys in my dorm
who could barely shower and get to class, he seemed like a mature mensch. A few days later, as I was leaving for vacation, he
texted me and I found myself replaying our date in my mind.
While I was away, I imagined how great he was and how I'd
amusingly describe aspects of my travels. But when I was back
in town weeks later, Sarah's ex was seeing someone else. What a
waste of precious time.

Years later, I noticed that technology enhanced my ability to
waste mental space and create emotional highs and lows. At a
friend's New Year's party, I met someone who seemed perfect.
When I got home, Google substantiated my imagination. I
couldn't believe that a quick search led me to discover that this
guy had literally won an award for being a good person. *This is
like a Modern Love column*, I thought. Obviously, I was thrilled
when he asked me out on several dates and sent flowers to my
office. But as my roses bloomed, I bumped into Mr. Good Person

canoodling with someone else on a New York City sidewalk. We'd never discussed being exclusive, but seeing him with someone else stopped me in my tracks. I mean, why send a gift for my colleagues to ask about when you just reserved a table for dinner with another girl? I had wasted weeks deciding he was perfect for me, despite having little firsthand information about him.

The Mindful Solution

Whether you're lost in painful obsessing, like Emma, or, like I used to do, you find yourself creating idyllic futures, ultimate peace of mind resides in being in the current moment. I feel lucky to have discovered that, to know that I couldn't find serenity through a person, as my husband treadmill–fueled rumination sessions had once convinced me, like a chauvinistic cult leader. I also discovered that developing tools to get unstuck from my mind would ensure more enduring freedom.

So far, we've talked about how believing you can't feel happy without a partner dampens your joy. You've also seen how rumination creates misery. If our problem is not living in the present, the solution is jumping right in. Mindfulness is the opposite of rumination. When you keep your mind in the moment, with acceptance, you're less likely to get lost in nightmares or daydreams. (You'll learn how to do this in part 2.) The more aware you become of your thoughts and feelings, the more perspective you'll have and the better you'll feel. Promising research suggests that developing the ability to practice mindfulness reduces rumination and allows us to more effectively approach our lives. In a study led by Roselinde Kaiser at the University of Colorado, Boulder, people listened to recordings of someone they loved saying something that started with, "One thing that really bothers me about you is . . ." Understandably, those who ruminated about the critical words weren't able to recover and perform as well on a follow-up task as those who were more mindful and acknowledged their thoughts as mere thoughts (you'll learn to do this in chapter 8).

Emma's mind continued to generate content, but she also started to see her thoughts without acting on them. Creating distance helped her meet her goal of feeling more at peace with herself, as well as with others. At this point, your job is to catch yourself ruminating like you'd catch a thief, and name it so it doesn't run off with your precious life and well-being.

Breaking Up with Rumination

At times, we forget how much pain this mental habit has caused or forget the details of how we got there in the first place. If you take a few minutes to track what happened a recent time you found yourself unproductively ruminating, you'll have a clear incentive to try a different approach. You might observe that certain situations, like coming home from a date, or like Emma, following a breakup, leave you feeling especially at risk. If you know when you feel most vulnerable and specifically strategize ways to escape the minefield during those times, you'll likely feel more prepared. Edward Watkins, a psychology professor at Exeter University, has developed a treatment called Rumination-Focused Cognitive Behavioral Therapy that's been found to curb this depressing problem. He considers rumination to be a type of avoidance and recommends connecting with your life as a powerful remedy. For example, if it's typical for you to start replaying and analyzing a night out when you come home, devise a competing activity that's captivating and meaningful (e.g., picking up a great book, listening to a podcast, or working out, instead of the less stimulating things like Web surfing or tidying up). To best help you enter the moment, make a list to motivate you to let go.

Reminders to Help You
Move Away from Ruminating

1. What happened the last time I got stuck ruminating?
2. What warning signs do I notice before I fall into ruminating?
3. What actions most absorb me?

You can find a freer headspace. To quote Steve Jobs, "Simple can be harder than complex: You have to work hard to get your thinking clean to make it simple. But it's worth it in the end because once you get there, you can move mountains." If you're convinced at this point that you want to break up with rumination but still don't quite know how to move away from this tricky habit, in part 2 you'll learn more about how to become unstuck.

CHAPTER 3

Regretting the Rock Star

*Finish each day and be done with it . . . To-morrow is a
new day; you shall begin it well and serenely, and with too
high a spirit to be cumbered with your old nonsense.*

—Ralph Waldo Emerson

My client Casey was filled with regret. Over a decade ago
she had broken up with her high school boyfriend because
she didn't think his rock star fantasy was ambitious enough.
Now that he's actually living his dream, she can't stop wishing
she could go back to him.

When they first connected, they were fifteen and shared a
passion for smoking pot. After dating for a few years in high
school, Casey moved from their town to a big city for college
and he stayed behind to play with his band and attend classes at
a local community school. Their relationship fizzled when Casey
decided she wanted a "normal college experience" and didn't
want to feel tethered to her first love. "I figured that he would be
living with his parents and struggling financially," she said. "I'm
anxious. I didn't want to worry about crap like my partner not
having health insurance."

When she came to see me, Casey was twenty-eight and she
and the rock star hadn't been in touch much over the years.

Once she started college, she threw herself into her life and didn't think much about him. "I thought a clean break would be best," she said. Then, a few months before we met, she stumbled upon a celebratory social media post from a high school friend: Her ex would be the opening act on a major artist's tour. Casey felt sentimental and immediately searched Google images to discover that he'd grown "hotter" with age. Lonelier now that she was out of school, with fewer opportunities to meet new people, she quickly reached out to him, confident that they'd rekindle and get back together. They exchanged sentimental messages, which buoyed her hopes. She learned that he'd signed with a major recording label. Bored, doing temp work in a frigid cubicle, and entranced by his success, she let him know that she wanted to see him when he played in her city, and held out hope that would happen, repeatedly checking her inbox, waiting for his reply to her flirty invitation. As she was refreshing her Gmail, she fantasized about locking eyes with him as he performed. She'd always liked his music—she just didn't predict he'd actually find fame and financial security.

The rock star returned her message days later, saying he'd happily comp her tickets to his show but that he was seeing someone so wouldn't meet her. That's when she descended from feeling somewhat unhappy with her life to miserable. She felt guilty that she hadn't had more faith in his dreams and that her pragmatic sensibilities clashed with his unlikely stardom. "My life is s**t and it's my fault," she told me. Casey had recently left a design position after her company downsized and she was working on various projects until she found something permanent. Outside of work, she was sick of sharing an Ikea-furnished walk-up with a roommate who left dishes in the sink for weeks. She had some good friends but they'd been weaving in and out of her life as their priorities centered on building careers and finding love. Casey herself hadn't met anyone she found exciting. "I get that you have to invest in coupling, but it's so banal," she told me, after sharing a weak beer with a bland boy.

The more she thought about it, the more Casey couldn't accept the gap between what she thought she was missing (passion, joy, and a rock star) and her sense of dull aloneness. People joke about "FOMO," the fear of missing out, but she felt that intensely and constantly. "He's the 'one who got away,'" she cried one day in my office.

Regret, one of the most frequently mentioned feelings in our everyday conversations, often arises when we believe that a different path might have led to a better outcome. Understandably, the more something matters to us, the more we mourn making the "wrong" decision. A random telephone survey asked a diverse group of respondents about their regrets. When prompted, women most regretted their decisions around love, as Casey could vouch for, while men struggled most with work-related decisions. Given that we're social beings and want to connect, regrets on the topic of love are not only felt intensely, but also the hardest to overcome. If you struggle with regret, letting go of your incriminating story and forgiving yourself is a liberating choice. In these pages, you'll learn how.

Even after Casey found a stable job that she liked and upgraded her apartment, she struggled to get past the bitter feeling that she'd misplaced her one pass to bliss. On some level, she was acting as if the more that she grieved, the more the universe might conspire to help her. But like the husband treadmill or the act of ruminating, if we don't accept our situation, we'll never feel good. While Casey felt stuck, according to her ex's Instagram account, he was on a tour bus in Toronto, oblivious to her misery. As she studied his concert photos, she decided that she needed help managing the feeling that she'd made a mistake and wouldn't recover. "All I want is an exciting life with someone familiar," she told me.

Mind Games and Heart Pains

While Casey's story is unique, regrets haunt many of us in different ways. One reason the emotion can be so painful is that in contrast to disappointment that arises when we blame circumstances, when we feel regret, we blame ourselves. For example, if you meet someone newly out of a relationship, and he isn't ready to date you, that's frustrating. But if you decide that he isn't available because you "screwed up," that's so much worse. It's especially hard to sit with the one-two punch of pain mixed with self-blame, which is why drowning in intense regret can take such a toll on our well-being.

Just as it's difficult to rally your strength and rational thinking when you're anticipating aloneness, when you feel regret you're also less able to manage. In a study where researchers asked people to think about a situation they regretted, participants had a hard time solving math problems and tolerating their frustration This makes sense when we remember, again, that we have limited bandwidth. If we're stuck in regret, we don't have resources left to invest elsewhere.

I thought of this when I got an e-mail from my friend Danielle, a usually carefree and competent thirty-three-year-old architect, who was seeking dating advice. She wrote: "Hooked up with this guy on a first date. Kept hearing from him, but he wasn't asking me out. So finally, I said to him, 'I'm not looking for a pen pal so if you're interested we should hang out.' After that, we semi–hung out one night for a few hours. He got drunk and nothing much happened, though he texted me the next day. But he wasn't saying, 'Let's hang out again soon.' So, I said to him, 'I'm not going to make an effort to talk to you anymore. Good luck with everything. Bye,' and he didn't respond. Then I realized that I had made a mistake so I texted him saying, 'I freak out when I see potential, but I would want to hang out if you're interested.' He responded to me a day later, saying something like, 'You come on very strong.' Should I accept this guy as a lost cause and walk away—or say something?"

When I first read Danielle's message, I couldn't understand why she was beating herself up for asserting herself with a person who left her feeling uneasy. Also, I hadn't known her as someone who ran away from relationships, so I didn't grasp why she was taking all the blame for things not working out. Danielle's regret didn't make sense to me, but then again, intense emotions, including regret, confuse us. When I asked Danielle why she thought this person was worth her time, she couldn't pinpoint any specifics. Yet despite the fact that most of their time together was interlaced with a sense that she couldn't capture his attention, she got caught up in the story that his rejection was all her fault.

I excitedly told Danielle, who specializes in logical foundations at work, that researchers label our urge to categorize *what might have been* and *if only* ideas as *counterfactual thinking*, since imagining other possible outcomes is inherently imprecise. If Danielle played it "cool," would this guy offer his loyalty and prove wonderful? Based on her descriptions of his behavior, I'd say: doubtful.

Back to Casey. I wanted her to look at the rock star situation more realistically and tried a tactic to help her broaden her thinking. I asked her to consider a wider range of possible realities than that dating the rock star would have worked out perfectly. "How do you know that he isn't loading up on cocaine, the way he did when you knew him in high school?" I asked.

At first, Casey was taken aback, wondering why I, a cognitive behavioral therapist focused on mindfulness and compassion, would encourage her to think about what might go wrong with the rock star. She wanted to cultivate good karma and didn't like thinking unkindly. I entirely agreed with her and clarified that we weren't judging or wishing him unwell. "At times, it can help to remember that thoughts are simply thoughts, and that one thought isn't a fact. It can feel freeing to introduce other outcomes to get unstuck," I explained. Nodding, she grabbed a pen and jotted down a few less-than-ideal scenarios, such as "he could cheat on me," or "he may have a drug problem," to balance her fantasy. Eventually, she generated a real list that helped her remember that there is more to reality than what we see with our emotion mind. She sounded convinced as she told me that if they'd stayed together, she likely would have "missed out on my education" and also acknowledged, "enduring success isn't a guarantee."

After she worked on thinking more flexibly, Casey seemed less devastated. I wasn't surprised that the list-making exercise helped. Hongmei Gao, the same researcher who discovered that regret affects our ability to solve problems, found that this simple tool also improved performance. When study participants read the following statement—"Everything can be viewed from different perspectives. There is positive value in every experience."—and were then asked to recall at least one benefit from a regrettable event, their smarts resurfaced. Adopting a more flexible attitude, like Casey did when appreciating her decision to embrace academics, can also help restore your mind and your peace.

The "Soul Mate" Risk

Practically speaking, my goal was to help Casey shift her idea that she was destined for a single soul mate, and instead, consider that there are many people we may appreciate for a variety of reasons. But initially, when Casey felt less stuck and downloaded a few dating apps, she was disappointed. "These guys are either physically attractive, but a pain to talk to, or nice to talk to, but unappealing," she complained. Maybe the men she was meeting weren't right for her, but research suggests there may have been more contributing to her disinterest. When we fixate on the idea that there's a *best* option, we find ourselves feeling dissatisfied with any alternatives, and less able to commit to our existing choices.

However, the more Casey practiced thinking more flexibly, the more willing she was to let go of the idea of a perfect soul mate. We spent time together noticing how every person (and every decision) has both positives and negatives, so that she would be less prone to considering her current situation subpar. And while it was hard for her to come up with any negatives associated with living like a rock star, she did begin to notice that there was something comforting about the routine in her life and that no relationship is entirely #luckyinlove.

There are more reasons to let go of perfectionistic standards when it comes to relationships. If you face a challenge in a relationship you considered flawless, it will be harder to cope with the inevitable conflicts. In a study spearheaded by Spike W. S. Lee and Norbert Schwartz, researchers at the University of Toronto, participants who were in a relationship for at least six months were quizzed about their familiarity with common expressions that alluded to the idea of a soul mate, like "made for each other." In a second group, people were tested on expressions that suggested that love is a journey ("look at how far we've come") rather than something perfect. Afterward, people in each group were asked to write about good and bad memories with their partner, then rate their relationship satisfaction. Notably, the people who'd been primed to think about love in an idealized way were less happy in their relationships. When we glorify relationships and assume that a person completes us, it follows that if that person disappoints us, we are apt to feel especially pained.

Moving Forward by Replacing Rumination with Self-Compassion

Casey and I also worked on noticing that much of her regret was fueled by rumination (which we explored in chapter 2). That's not surprising since regret itself is a type of rumination. Relatedly, the more that she searched for stories about her ex on social media, the more upset she felt. "I like to just chill out and relax at night," she'd told me, explaining her browsing. But we noticed that looking at him wasn't actually helping her unwind. We decided that following @thewaywemet and @humansofny instead of her ex's new love on Instagram could also satisfy her voyeuristic urges and help her swap desperation for hope and inspiration.

Of course, it's possible to also feel regret spontaneously, as Casey often did after an uneventful date or when she'd unexpectedly hear her ex's songs on the radio. But most often, regret comes from a mixture of thoughts, like affective forecasting. Regret also shows up when we judge ourselves, as we touched on earlier in this chapter. To help Casey stay strong, we broke down her struggle so it felt less personal and more like a universal phenomenon:

$$Regret = rumination + self\text{-}blame$$

Casey learned to take a step back when she caught herself in that equation. To remedy these traps, we explored ways for her to treat herself with more self-compassion, like she'd treat a friend. (We'll cover the specifics on how to do this in part 2.) Casey acknowledged that the idea of being good to herself seemed nice in theory, but worried that letting go of self-blame meant she'd never learn from her mistakes and potentially walk away from someone incredible, again. (I was happy that she was no longer calling the rock star her soul mate.)

As Duke psychology professor Mark Leary reports, self-compassion actually leads to taking *more* personal responsibility after a negative event. If we're too burdened by regret, we may feel so overwhelmed that we can't think through opportunities and grow after our perceived setbacks. With a dose of compassion, we may have more faith in ourselves and feel hopeful that we can actually improve. In studying regret, researchers Jia Zhang and Serena Chen at the University of California, Berkeley, examined entries on the blog www.secretregrets.com and rated them for compassionate content. Their analyses found that regret stories that included compassion were more likely to result in self-improvement. To further test the theory that self-compassion is helpful in growing from regret, the Berkeley researchers also asked four hundred students to write about their biggest regrets. The students were divided; in one group, participants were asked to imagine that they were talking to themselves about their regret from a compassionate and understanding perspective. Compared to the people who weren't asked to practice compassion, the experimental group experienced increased acceptance, which led to more personal improvement.

The takeaway is, we don't need to run from regret. Rather, we can learn from our past and treat our mistakes and ourselves with kindness. Researchers Abigail Stewart and Elizabeth Vandewater, who followed women decades after they graduated from the University of Michigan, found that regretting life choices in middle age was likely to lead to setting goals. Yet those whose regret led to rumination struggled with actually implementing those life changes. In contrast, women who utilized the feeling of regret to take actions, like improving their careers, enjoyed a heightened sense of well-being.

As Casey practiced getting unstuck from her mind, she gradually stopped believing that her life would always be "less than" because she was "an idiot." "I made the best decision I could at the time," she says now. She is optimistic that there are other romantic options out there for her and is clear from her first love experience that she values someone creative and brave. Just a few weeks after we talked about letting go of the rock star story and giving herself the gift of self-compassion, she met someone through a friend. "He's fun," she told me. But best of all, "I feel like a much happier person."

When Regrets Are Life-Changing

Sometimes we face situations when our regret is unquestionably real and the impact of our action endures. One afternoon, a woman called my office and asked my assistant if our office suite was handicap accessible. The following week, Greta arrived for an evaluation to join my Dialectical Behavior Therapy (DBT) group.

For a moment, I'd love to share a bit more on DBT, a treatment developed by Marsha Linehan, the psychologist you met in the introduction who coined the term "emotion mind." Her strategies brilliantly synthesize behavioral therapy and mindfulness, creating an approach comprised of useful, practical tools for optimal living. A lot of wisdom in this book stems from Linehan's curriculum of skills on managing emotions, entering the moment, communicating effectively with others, and coping with crises. (You'll learn a lot of these skills in part 2 of this book.) It moves me to tears to think about the lives Linehan has touched since many help-seekers turn to DBT when nothing else works and describe the approach as lifesaving. Courageously, Linehan acknowledged that after spending years in psychiatric hospitals, she changed her own life using elements from the approach she empathically created to empower others.

When I met my new DBT client, Greta, a notably articulate former school administrator in her fifties, wearing a bright floral-patterned shirt and sitting tall in her wheelchair, I was immediately touched by her kind manner and enthusiasm. As we talked, I learned that several years earlier, feeling utterly hopeless in the aftermath of a divorce, she jumped from the sixth floor of her apartment building. Her suicide attempt left her paralyzed from the waist down, leaving her with endless medical complications and chronic pain. After expressing concern for her ongoing struggle, I asked, "Is suicide on your mind now?" Greta answered, confidently, "Not at all." She went on to tell me that she wanted to join my group to enhance the life she was committed to living but that now felt harder to manage.

I was so moved by the fact that she once found her life

intolerable, and now, in the context of so much discomfort, she was resolved to live. How did she do it? She explained that she found meaning in her survival and her regret led her to a renewed commitment to self-care. She also noticed that life is challenging enough without pummeling herself with *If only . . .* thoughts. Instead, her attitude was: "I made a mistake, and now I need to take care of myself." Meeting Greta inspired me. Especially when we face serious consequences as a result of our actions, we need to let go of our incriminating stories, release our regret, and turn toward not only coping, but to embracing our life.

How to Navigate Regret

1. Is my regret based on actual facts or obsessive thinking (like Casey)?
2. What are some productive actions I can take (e.g., join a therapy group) versus staying stuck (e.g., venting and trolling social networks) in the bad feelings?
3. How can I show myself some self-compassion?

Fear Regret? Choose Courage

It may sound crazy, but besides regretting events in the past, we can also struggle with worries about regretting the future, which is known as *anticipating regret*. This category of regret—I'm personally familiar with it—often causes people to stay in unhealthy situations or not take useful risks because they fear they will regret them in the future.

When I was with my ex-fiancé and started to question our relationship, whenever we moved toward ending things, I'd begin to worry that I'd regret my decision and freeze. One weekend, in a period of intense ambivalence in our relationship, I'd spent time with a close friend who was married with children and had this sense of clarity: *I want a family life like hers.* I was envious, and as uncomfortable as envy feels, the emotion was tugging at my leg saying I cared about something and that I'd regret proceeding without it.

My fiancé and I had gone back and forth on our values a lot and struggled to find a mutually respectful middle path. It became pretty clear that a lot of what I deeply cared about he couldn't stand and vice versa. Clear on my concerns, when my ex and I sat down for dinner soon after that moment of wisdom, I shared (again) what mattered to me and why. He explained that my hopes were impractical. This hadn't been the first time I'd directly confronted the fact that he and I couldn't agree on certain significant decisions, especially ones that impacted our future.

After he spoke, I felt so conflicted. There was so much attraction between us and I felt so grateful for him. But I had to ask: "Do you think we want different things? Maybe this isn't fair to either of us." He said something like, "So you want to break up?" And I said, "I think . . . we keep getting stuck." How, he asked, could I not be flexible if I loved him? Couldn't I have faith that everything would work itself out? Finally, he warned, "If we break up, you'll regret this." Those were the words that made me want to erase the whole exchange. I hated the idea that I could make a decision today that would torture my tomorrow. A client once described good planning as a gift to her tomorrow self. I didn't want to sabotage my tomorrow. So for months, I was stuck between noticing we had differences and thinking I'd make a mistake I'd never get past. I was in limbo, questioning either my wants or my relationship, which meant doubting myself, constantly. It was awful.

As I mentioned, I also spent a lot of time really practicing mindfulness and considering what I wanted most deeply (which you'll do in chapter 5). Finally, it became clear that our fears were driving us to stay together, and that neither of us deserved to sacrifice our life vision. And so, we broke up.

Then, one afternoon, I was lying on a close friend's couch, telling her about feeling sad after my breakup. Like me, my friend happened to pursue a doctorate in clinical psychology and she told me she thought that if I was so conflicted, there must be a reason for it. "Could your feelings be telling you that there's too much in your relationship you don't want to lose?" Now, I absolutely love my friend; we've been close since the third grade. I knew that she was trying her very best to patiently support me. This feels embarrassing to share, but I think it's a common experience worth admitting: I totally rationalized what she said as permission to run to my ex's incredible apartment for a dose of security and to ease my fear that I'd be alone forever. But as we once again spent time together, our differences resurfaced. Which meant instead of either of us peacefully moving on, we were stuck in a prolonged purgatory.

Finally, we decided we needed to just sit with our respective thoughts and feelings and use our values to drive us. That meant facing my fears of regret and ultimately of being alone. It wasn't easy, but I'm so grateful that we circumvented the bigger regrets we'd face in the future had we ended up getting married. Now, when I get lost in fears of regret I try to remind myself of what I value, rather than let worry overtake me. I am confident, these days, that following what I value will always steer me in the right direction.

So many women who come to my practice share similar worries: "Will I regret not staying in this relationship?" or "What if

I regret this for the rest of my life?" I remind them that we all prefer certainty to uncertainty and explain, "If your concerns are based on your values and inner wisdom, allow fear of regret to be there, and act courageously, anyway." I don't think any of us is trying to obstruct our joy. Psychologist Daniel Gilbert, whom you met in chapter 1, has found that people often mispredict the experience of regret. In a paper on the topic, Gilbert references a dramatic scene in *Casablanca*, quoting, "If that plane leaves the ground and you're not with him, you'll regret it. Maybe not today. Maybe not tomorrow. But soon and for the rest of your life." After researching regret and its longevity, Gilbert concludes, adding science to the scenario, "Ilsa could not face the possibility of looking back in anguish and so reluctantly boarded that plane, but had she stayed with Rick in Casablanca, she would probably have felt just fine. Not right away, of course. But soon. And for the rest of her life."

Of course, when we face a significant decision, like choosing a partner, we shouldn't just assume, *It doesn't matter, I'll manage.* When doubts are based on valid concerns, we'd best see our emotions as powerful informants and have faith. As it so happens, once Casey didn't feel as burdened by regret, she decided to grab lunch with her ex when they were both in their hometown for the holidays. As they sat down, she saw clearly that they had both changed over the years and there was no spark between them. She regretted all that regret—which inspired her to keep practicing thinking more effectively and acting with self-compassion.

CHAPTER 4

Settling, Suppressing, and Other Avoidance Moves

Your task is not to seek for love, but merely to seek and
find all the barriers within yourself that you have built
against it.
                                                    —RUMI

LET'S TAKE A moment for you to check in with yourself. Have you ever found yourself in any of these very common situations?

a. Having a best (platonic) friend you actually wish you could marry
b. Waiting to date until a specific thing happens—like losing weight, getting a better job, or feeling more confident
c. Continuing a romantic relationship with someone you're not sure you even like
d. Casually hooking up with someone you actually have serious feelings for
e. Feeling frustrated because no one meets your standards

If you said yes to any of these scenarios or if any of them sound familiar, I hope this chapter will inspire you to reconsider whether they are working for you.

So far, we've talked about letting go of some of the ways we invite misery into our lives, including running on the husband treadmill, ruminating, or getting mired in regret. As you let go of these habits, you'll inevitably face emotions you may not enjoy, emotions that aren't about your headspace but that arise from situations in your life. Noticing mental traps is a great way to start living a happier, more fulfilling life, but sometimes unpleasant experiences pop up and prompt feelings that you can choose to either notice or overlook. I suggest you notice them, since that's an essential part of being mindful.

Even when they're uncomfortable, noticing what you're feeling is key to moving toward pursuing what matters to you, as my client Annie learned. I always appreciate the courage it takes to tell a relative stranger your struggles and especially felt moved by Annie, who explained that this was her first time confiding to a therapist. On the first morning that I met her, she smiled as she told me that she needed help managing "stress." In her mid-twenties with an impeccably polished outfit and way of expressing herself, she told me about her grueling hours working in finance, then looked away as she told me that a couple of times a week, she found herself overeating after work. "No one knows I do this and everyone sees me as together," she told me.

To get a better sense of her, I asked Annie about her relationships, which she hadn't mentioned. "I don't have a lot of time [with you] and just want to focus on stress and food," she said. Still, she politely gave me a quick overview. Her relationships were "good," she said, explaining that her former boyfriend had moved to Seattle about a year earlier and they remained best friends, though it was hard to stay together romantically long distance. "But it'd be too terrible to break up."

Her solution: a mix of Tinder and the telephone. She used the app to meet guys for physical relationships but called her ex when she needed emotional support. "I get what I need," she told me, explaining there wasn't much downside to substituting a relationship with a partner with a mishmash of its parts. "It works for me, especially with my career," but she fidgeted as she said it, and I suspected she worried I was judging her.

The last thing I wanted was for Annie to feel analyzed by me; she already had enough stress. I hate the idea of judging. I explained that I wanted to honor her request to focus on her eating issues and stress. I also asked her permission to address how she manages emotions, so she could feel less overwhelmed and more confident in her ability to manage. Details like whether or not her relationship with the guy in Seattle was helping her weren't as important to me as how she was navigating her feelings.

A Huge Problem You May Not Even Know You Have

What heightens your risk of suffering? If you could pick one habit to work on, which would you choose? Would it be eating mindlessly, like Annie, or procrastinating, like Erika, another client you'll meet later on? What do you typically do when you face an uncomfortable emotion?

a. Notice and accept the feeling
b. Try to rid yourself of the experience
c. Indulge the emotion (e.g., if you're sad, you lie down and listen to sad music)

As you might have guessed, cathartic as it may initially feel, option c. will prolong suffering. Option b. may seem appealing since it's instinctive to try to dodge things that are uncomfortable. But if you revisit your own history, you may see that past efforts to escape difficult thoughts and feelings (by eating, or procrastinating) often backfire. Trying to escape feelings is no escape. (After all, it's not exactly helpful when someone says, "Don't worry!") Which brings me back to the sneaky issue at the root of most people's distress: It's a behavior known as *experiential avoidance*, first described by psychologist Steven Hayes, and it's defined as coping by running away from unpleasant thoughts and feelings. While it's true that overthinking and venting aren't the best strategies for dealing with difficult emotions, that doesn't necessarily mean that doing the opposite, stifling your feelings, is the way to go. Like an unwanted credit card bill, stuffing your sorrows in a drawer guarantees greater costs in the future. Hayes is one of the founders of Acceptance and Commitment Therapy (ACT), one of my favorite types of therapy, and one that's moved me personally. Briefly, this approach teaches people to take courageous steps to build their lives, independent of how they feel or their circumstances. After decades of research, Hayes and his coauthors put it this way: "Many forms of psychopathology can be conceptualized as unhealthy efforts to escape and avoid emotions, thoughts, memories. . . ." In other words, many of our problems are actually caused or exacerbated by the imperfect solution of trying to avoid our pain.

After seeing Annie for several weeks, I noticed that she often avoided talking about or focusing on her feelings. "Don't we all have to?" she wondered, when I mentioned it. It's natural to distract ourselves from distress, and in some situations, we can evade pain with no real consequence. My dentist, for instance, keeps a bulky pair of video-projecting glasses so patients can watch a comedy while getting a cavity filled. I can tell you, watching a *Seinfeld* rerun is a great way to drown out that drilling noise.

In most situations, however, trying valiantly to escape your feelings can lead to serious consequences. Initially, it may feel good to avoid or postpone something unpleasant, which means it's tempting to keep on avoiding. But sooner or later, you're likely to face emotions that are even more uncomfortable. When you interrupt a big project at work with an online shopping spree, after you've punched in your credit card and see the time you've wasted (and the money you've spent), it's likely that you'll feel even more anxious and on top of that, you may feel guilty too.

Annie was stressed, but she wasn't a procrastinator. Her tactic was to push away thoughts like, *This isn't what I want to be doing with my life*, and instead, stay at the office after hours, producing exceptional financial models and presentations. Raised to "put on a happy face," she'd been taught that most people "have it worse," and that she "should" feel grateful.

I understood that to excel professionally, Annie couldn't mope about how unhappy she was in her work life. Yet her general strategy of trying to control and ignore her feelings was backfiring, in terms of her happiness and satisfaction in life. She lacked joy and felt like she had no options other than to feign passion at work (and on dates) and then comfort herself by misusing food. This didn't sound very appealing. By continually dodging her feelings, she was also hindering her ability to change the circumstances that were making her miserable. If Annie couldn't acknowledge that she didn't like her job, it'd be extra hard for her to justify going elsewhere. Plus, not communicating when she felt overworked led to her landing even more assignments, increasing her feelings of hopelessness.

In short, Annie suffered from a need to appear like she had everything together, even when that wasn't necessarily true. Studies show that people who struggle with perfectionism avoid their emotions and face increased risk of sadness. This makes so much sense to me. To seem "perfect," we have to dismiss our reasonable feelings and limits, to worry more about how we perform than how we truly feel.

I had a hunch that Annie's friendship with her ex also had to do with her urge to avoid. As I promised her, instead of just assuming this, I put this on our therapy agenda and she agreed to discuss whether staying emotionally linked to her ex stemmed from her not wanting to miss him and deal with a painful, imperfect goodbye. ("I'm not going to end this relationship abruptly on the phone," she'd once said.) Once Annie bought into the idea that avoiding her feelings was hurting her, she acknowledged that her current situation wasn't working, took off her blazer, and let herself cry. She confided that she recently called her ex and he hadn't returned her call until the next day, which was unusual for him. She'd spent the night tossing and turning, clutching her iPhone, worried and jealous that he was "sleepless in Seattle" for other reasons. Meanwhile, she didn't feel attracted to anyone since no one could compete with her ex, who was moving on. "Do all women like Lululemon?" he asked Annie one night, unknowingly torturing her by asking for help getting a new woman a birthday gift. *Annie's on Tinder, so we're cool*, he probably believed.

It took Annie awhile to see that she could actually manage uncomfortable emotions that might arise from talking honestly with her ex, or saying goodbye. Together, we reflected on the fact that rather than pushing away her sad emotions, if she could sit with them and let them guide her (as you'll learn to do in chapter 9) she could get a better sense of what she needed and wanted.

Choosing Wisely

By acknowledging her feelings, Annie was taking the first step toward taking space from her Seattle friend and, eventually, finding a job where she didn't eat dinner at her desk every night followed by a binge later. Instead of waiting to feel ready, or "sure," as she put it, we worked on looking at the pros and cons of staying in close contact with her ex, compared to a list that described what could happen if she said goodbye to him and accepted her sad feelings. To further clarify her options, I had her star any items on her list that might affect her long-term.

Take a look at what Annie discovered, below.

Decision	Pros	Cons
Stay emotionally connected to Seattle	♥ Good to have support ♥ Don't have to sit with immediate loss ♥ Hold on to hope we'll rekindle ♥ Maybe we can be friends and I'll get over him	♥ Likely miss him more* ♥ Hold on to false hope* ♥ Don't give others a chance* ♥ I'm staying in the habit of avoiding my feelings*

Decision	Pros	Cons
Goodbye, Seattle	♥ May find more peace* ♥ May find more fulfilling relationship with someone nearby* ♥ Prove to myself I am strong* ♥ Won't compulsively check my phone* ♥ Won't feel as jealous*	♥ Will feel sad and lonely ♥ Will wonder a lot about him ♥ Won't have the immediate dose of love

Now, try making your own lists. If you're currently feeling conflicted about something, this might be the time to consider weighing your options. In applying reason to emotional decisions, you might notice that it's worthwhile to get face-to-face with a difficult reality, instead of lingering in avoidance.

After reflecting on the pros and cons, and seeing how the status quo was hurting her, Annie decided to make the break from Seattle. Initially, she worried that because she missed her ex so deeply, she was a weak person, and we worked on normalizing and accepting her experiences. Ultimately, she noticed that she began to feel less anxious and more capable of enjoying the moment, and to gain control of her eating. This wasn't a coincidence. Believing you can't sit with your emotions often leads to using food as an escape.

Many people get trapped by what economists call *sunk costs*—essentially, once we invest in something, we don't want to walk away from the commitment, so we mistakenly continue to put our efforts into a money pit. Annie had once ruminated, *We've been close for years, he gets me, I can't lose him, I'll feel so alone.* With the help of her pros and cons list, she realized that she was investing her energy into the romantic equivalent of a sunk cost. Given her career in finance, the concept resonated with her and she saw that more contact with her ex brought diminishing emotional returns. It takes so much awareness to notice when a relationship that once felt nice no longer does. Annie felt empowered once she decided to stop their "friends, with limited benefits" setup.

I wonder if you notice that there are ways that you are trying to dodge discomfort that won't work in the long run? If you tend to believe that emotions cause problems, you're more likely to avoid them. You're also more likely to try to avoid your feelings when you assume that you won't be able to cope with them. While a trusted friend or therapist can point out what you're trying to overlook, I also think *you* can choose to get real and notice if you've been putting off normal human experiences, like loneliness or sadness, by staying in suboptimal relationships or avoiding connection to prevent possible rejection. The fact that you're reading this tells me, and should tell you, that you're the sort of person who values growth. I have full faith that you can check in with yourself and acknowledge whether you're avoiding something. If you are, I hope you'll think through the pros and cons of staying in limbo and choose to embrace a courageous, and ultimately liberating, path.

Procrastinating = Avoiding

When I first met Erika, a graduate student in her thirties, she explained she was struggling with her dissertation deadlines. "I'm like the biggest mystery to my advisor. Everyone knows I'm capable and smart and seem like a decent person, then I just don't meet deadlines and seem like a flake," she said. As the first person in her family to go to graduate school, she wanted to excel. Plus, she knew that if she didn't complete her assignments on time, she'd feel buried under more student loans. Once Erika fell behind, the quality of her work dropped from meticulous to below average, as she rushed to turn in overdue assignments. One of my goals was to help Erika turn in work that was "good enough" instead of panicking around the prospect of needing to churn out perfect papers. As you'd imagine, once she lowered her standards, she had the time to revise her drafts and the quality of her work improved. We also focused on not waiting to feel "motivated" to do something, but to stick to a schedule. (You'll read more on this concept in chapter 6.) That meant learning to sit with feelings of boredom and allow for insecurities, like *I'm such an imposter*, without letting those distractions take over.

As awful as procrastinating feels in your professional life, postponing what you want in your personal life can feel even worse. Like Erika, many of my clients have a difficult time understanding why they delay acting on their deeply cherished goals, even when it's clear that working toward those aims will make them feel better.

One reason people stall is to avoid stress or other difficult emotions in the interim, like Annie. Yet as much as you think that you're putting off the hassle by avoiding taking an effortful action, it's hard to fully relax when you're not moving toward fulfilling your needs. In the long run, it's impossible to ignore your feelings, your desires, or the pain that comes from not meeting your needs. Emotions have a way of stalking you.

I ended up seeing Erika for about a year, and she did eventually complete her doctorate and move on, so I hadn't seen her in a while when her name popped up on my appointment schedule.

When she came in, we caught up a bit, and she explained, "So, I'm trying to apply acting independent of your feelings, like we did with my work, with this dude, Teddy. Remember all those jerks I complained about? He's actually super sweet." About eight months ago she'd met Teddy on a location-based dating app; he lived in her trendy Brooklyn neighborhood. They quickly fell into a routine, which she said felt so much easier than the vague, tentative texts she'd been exchanging with other guys, which she understandably hated.

When I'd last seen Erika, she expressed her concerns about finding a partner as a woman of color. "I get lots of dates but 70 percent of black women are single," she told me, insisting that her dating worries were reasonable. I encouraged her to let go of thinking in terms of statistics. Possibilities aren't guarantees and this sort of thinking wasn't enhancing her wellness. Now, she appreciated that Teddy was kind, smart, cute, and committed. She was invested in seeing her relationship with him as an opportunity. In the same way that she tried to keep moving forward when she didn't feel driven in grad school, she tried to act lovingly toward Teddy, even when she wasn't feeling totally enthusiastic about their relationship. Many couples therapists recommend this strategy, since giving love can lead to feeling love. Erika liked Teddy and hoped that with the right approach, she'd start to love him and achieve her goal: a great relationship.

Yet despite her resourcefulness and determination to apply what worked for her dissertation to her dating life, she felt stuck. As she sat across from me, advocating for Teddy, she started to tear up. "This is awkward to say, but we don't have sex, and when we do, it's not good," she confessed. "Do you think I'm depressed?" she continued, trying to find a way to solve their sex life. From what I observed, Erika didn't seem clinically depressed, nor was she taking medications with libido-dampening side effects. I wondered why she blamed herself.

Before I continue with Erika's story, I want to explicitly say that different people attach varying degrees of importance to physical chemistry. For Erika, passion was a priority, and trying to tamp down this innate yearning wasn't working or consistent with treating herself kindly. Their first kiss was "weird." She tried to be patient, since she'd never faced this challenge in a relationship, and appreciate the good about Teddy instead. "He's cute and my best friend," she'd tell friends, hoping they weren't seeing her distress and skepticism. Meanwhile, she and Teddy got more serious. At his brother's graduation party, she won over his family; then, a couple of months later, at his sister's wedding, she seamlessly played the part of his fiancé-to-be, even dancing with his grandfather. This wasn't a testament to her acting prowess; Erika liked Teddy and appreciated that he was loyal and future-oriented. She wanted to get married and have kids. Her younger brother was married with a child and she regretted not giving a guy she'd dated a few years earlier more of a chance. To sum it up, Erika was extremely driven to put in maximum effort with Teddy.

Prioritizing Isn't Settling

I appreciated that Erika was trying techniques that worked in graduate school to feel more invested in her relationship. But clearly, she was in a bind. She was in her late thirties and she wanted a baby, Teddy was "nice," and great company, but something was missing. What should she do?

This probably sounds hard to believe, but many of my clients who dreamed of pursuing motherhood but ultimately didn't have a child discovered that they managed to adjust to this loss (especially when they practiced letting go of rumination and regret, and added self-compassion and values-oriented actions to the mix, like mentoring kids or doing other nurturing, maternal activities). In some situations, like Erika's, women may have more time to meet people than they assume. But the reality is, in dating, as in the rest of life, we have to weigh our options and accept uncertainties.

Choosing a mate, especially when you feel as if your biological clock is ticking, can feel extremely conflicting. One could argue that it was reasonable for someone like Erika to accept motherhood as a top objective and choose to sit with the romantic disappointment that arises when you're with a mate who doesn't feel "right" but might be a good-enough parent. (In chapter 5 you'll read more about identifying and prioritizing your values.) I've met many women who have entered relationships because they wanted to start a family, and seen scenarios where couples can respectfully collaborate in raising a child, even without experiencing passion. But I've also seen clients who partner to build a family and struggle to conceive. And there are also times, especially in the midst of contentious custody battles, where women tell me they wish they had gone to a sperm bank, though not all of us can afford the expense of raising a child on our own, much less pricey fertility treatments. (You'll read more on these topics in chapter 6.)

It's hard to predict what will prove to be the most meaningful path in life but prioritizing your values can feel clarifying. It also helps to remember, again, that no one person will create enduring happiness for you, that no person is perfect. I'm an optimist, yet I still can't imagine meeting a neurosurgeon who looks like Leonardo DiCaprio, shares Will Ferrell's humor, and has a heart as huge as a special needs teacher. Still, I would never prescribe settling. Instead, I encourage the more proactive, accepting practice of deciding what matters to you (which includes making space for another person's imperfections) without ignoring your needs.

Erika and I worked on replacing settling with scheduling. We worked on picking a time to talk to Teddy instead of ignoring her feelings and hiding the truth from everyone. We also decided that Erika should choose a date to decide if she could embrace Teddy's character alone and feel satisfied without sexual chemistry. When Erika spoke to him, honestly and kindly, he was receptive, and even suggested a romantic weekend getaway. Erika felt hopeful, but when they checked into a hotel a few weeks later, she had to turn on the shower to muffle the sounds of her crying. She just wasn't feeling it; she never felt it with him.

After the hotel weekend, I asked Erika if she'd thought more about her decision and she panicked. I wasn't surprised. In a study using the "Fear of Being Single Scale," people considered whether statements such as "I feel like it is close to being too late for me to find the love of my life" applied to them. It turns out that one consequence of worrying about being single is settling for someone you're not actually happy with simply to not be by yourself.

Erika and I spent a lot of time noticing her fears of being alone instead of avoiding those fears (and the risk of ending up unhappily settled). We also worked on how she could put more space between herself and her fears. (More on this in chapters 8 and 9.) Eventually, she felt willing to sit with sadness and anxiety and broke up with Teddy. He actually took the news graciously, and Erika was also surprised to find that she coped better than she'd predicted. Not too long after that, she enjoyed better chemistry with guys who were good people. She recently wrote to tell me that she had moved in with someone.

Honesty: A Better Game!

Like Annie and Erika, many of us seem to have decided that it makes sense to act differently from how we feel inside. Personally, I find it disturbing that some dating books advise women to feign a perky yet unopinionated persona. People often then regurgitate some version of: "I can't act too into it. I have to play 'hard to get.'" In many ways, games and rules are prime examples of the avoidance tactics I've been talking about. Sure, initially you might get more dates by making guys "chase" you, and you may prevent conflict at first when you present a blank, emotionless face to everything. But in the end, people don't want to constantly be chasing someone; they get bored or they decide you're not worth it. And if you never show your emotions, others will find it hard to become intimate. Plus you're likely to become so stressed from suppressing all your feelings that you'll either make yourself miserable or blow up eventually when you can't hold your emotions in any longer. In a study led by psychologist Sanjay Srivastava that explored students transitioning to college, the tendency to suppress emotions actually predicted having a harder time getting close to others. Studies similarly confirm that there's a close connection between avoiding in our relationships and feeling hostile and anxious. Honesty is what allows for authentic bonding and brings about the relief we experience from supportive relationships.

Too many women follow conventional dating guidelines rooted in deceit: saying we're busy when we're not or waiting to respond to a call, e-mail, or text when we watch it arrive. There's nothing wrong with taking things slowly and not giving a stranger your soul on the first date, but since when is enthusiasm a character flaw? Research seems to contradict these sorts of dating tips. In another study on suppression, by Allison Tackman and Sanjay Srivastava, people watched videos of others either reacting naturally or suppressing their feelings to an emotional event. The psychologists found that suppressors were judged as less extroverted, agreeable, and less compassionate, and were viewed as more avoidant and anxious. Interestingly, when the person suppressing was masking their amusement (vs. sadness), they were rated as especially unlikable.

Even worse than others finding us less appealing, suppressing emotions diminishes our joy. In a study designed by Stanford University professor and emotion regulation expert James Gross, women were told to hide their emotions while watching film segments (including sad, funny, and scary clips). The researchers discovered that this rule led participants to feel less captivated by what they were viewing. Even before watching the scenes, anticipating having to mask feelings created physiological stress, as compared to women in the control group who didn't have to follow rules.

Do these lab studies actually mean anything when it comes to romantic relationships? In a study of eighty couples led by social psychologist Emily Impett, suppressing feelings was found to increase negative emotions and decrease positive emotions. Interestingly, in daily life, when partners made sacrifices for loved ones, like running errands for them, when they suppressed their feelings, their relationships were seen as less satisfying and their sense of conflict increased. Suppressing also predicted more thoughts about breaking up. This makes sense when we remember that hiding feelings intensifies them, so looking tired and asking for a hand when you come home with groceries is better than powering through and gritting your teeth.

Fun Doesn't Equal Happy

As a psychologist, I've thought a lot about avoiding and suppressing emotions in my own life. Years ago, I decided that I wanted to stop following dating "rules" and start living according to the science of managing emotions. One example of how that played out was when I was single and visiting L.A., and ended up at an event talking to a guy I'll call Jordan. I hadn't had a boyfriend since my ex-fiancé and I found Jordan attractive and endearing. He sounded smart, spent weekends running on the beach, and seemed down to earth. I couldn't stop smiling when he asked me for my number, but when we texted, I realized that he didn't remember that I lived in New York City. (Clearly, he'd met a lot of people that night.) I was disappointed and worried he'd delete my number so I let him know I'd be in town again the following month and we made a tentative plan to grab a drink. In the meantime, we exchanged a few "Hey, how was your weekend?" messages.

It may seem crazy to start a bicoastal texting exchange, but I grew up in L.A. and I'd been planning to move back. Instead of an obstacle, I considered Jordan living there to be a perk, since I visited often to see family and friends and explore job opportunities. Weirdly, when I next visited, Jordan was harder to reach than when we were in different time zones. "What's up?" he'd write. (I felt relieved to know I wasn't alone in finding these exchanges ridiculous when reading Aziz Ansari's *Modern Romance*.) I'd reply and he'd respond a solid eight hours later. I felt disappointed, but also told myself that we'd met once; he didn't owe me anything. Still, I also felt jerked around. Why text me for weeks, then not set a time to see me when I was actually in town?

The day before I left, he asked me to meet at the last minute and we got a drink. He enthusiastically asked, again, how long I'd be in town, convincing me to join him for a late dinner and directing me toward his Jaguar convertible. People joke that pets resemble their owners, and Jordan reminded me of his mercurial car. He made a puppy-dog face and hugged me tight when we said goodbye and promised we'd talk before I left the next night. You've probably guessed by now that he didn't text for a week, though when he wrote, he said, "Amazing seeing you!!!!!" The next few times I was in town were basically a repeat. He sparkled, revved up, sped through some terrain smoothly, then slammed on his solid brakes—and I ended up carsick.

As a behavioral therapist, I know a lot about the impact of erratic contact. People are more responsive to *intermittent reinforcement* (someone who is available, then not) than they are to *continuous reinforcement*. There's something about not knowing when we'll receive the next reward (or text) that makes us stay focused and excited. Inconsistency keeps us attentive and trying. But I didn't want to sit around salivating; I'm not a dog in training. I decided that part of my mindfulness and self-compassion practice included honoring my emotions, not dropping everything when a guy I'd seen five times in as many months finally decided that he was ready to make a plan. I was sure that I wasn't going to let "winning" him trump my self-respect.

Life is too short to play games. That was my motto in my new dating life, and I told myself that I was willing to do what worked for me. With that in mind, I called Jordan, and keep in mind this was the first and only time we'd ever spoken by phone. "Hey Jordan, it's Jenny, hope you had a nice trip. Call me when you have a sec." A few hours later, he texted back the hackneyed "Hey, what's up?"

I surfed my urge to succumb to the safer, random texting ritual and instead I wrote, "Wanted to catch up. Call me when you have a couple of minutes." To cheer myself on, I reminded myself how unsettling it feels to have a prolonged text message conversation. It was especially insulting to feel like I was his person-on-demand; I told myself that I had a life and people routinely made appointments to see me. Finally, hours later, now past my bedtime, Jordan called. It was awkward. We made some small talk, my heart raced (*that's normal, of course you're nervous*, I reminded myself). Then I stammered a bit and said, "I was thinking, I've never asked you and we've been in touch for a couple months, are you looking to meet someone to date or for something casual? I know we're still getting to know each other, but I was thinking I really want to spend time with people looking for a relationship rather than looking to hang out. I don't want to put you on the spot but wanted to see what you were thinking." By this point, I wasn't even sure I wanted to date Jordan. I didn't know him that well and his hot and cold behavior was distracting. But I did know that I wasn't interested in a texting pal. I find ongoing "Hey ☺" messages annoying. Why should I let someone interrupt my workflow or my walk? I put a premium on entering the moment and don't want a text from anyone if it's not significant. So while I didn't even know if I wanted a commitment from Jordan, I did know that if a charming restaurant didn't have an open table, I wouldn't hang out there waiting for hours, just in case.

"I had fun with you," Jordan answered, politically. I'd had

"fun" with him too. But, as I often reiterate to my clients who struggle with substance abuse, fun ≠ happy. I thought about this as I sat with my elevated pulse, enduring the silence instead of rushing to fill it. Eventually, Jordan stepped in: "I'm not really looking for anything serious." My heart sank and I felt rejected; I wondered if I should be embarrassed. Then I reminded myself I wasn't an avoider.

"You just don't do that," a guy friend admonished. "You can't ask someone point blank what they want—the guy has to ask you," he warned. I'm sure lots of dating coaches would concur. But the next day, I felt relieved. I had clarity and peace knowing that I had informed consent in my personal life.

A few months later, I was surprised to see Jordan at another L.A. party. At first, I felt awkward, then I reminded myself that I had no regrets. Smoothly, he cruised over and offered me a fruity cocktail. Later, as I saw him flirting around like an exotic butterfly, I realized how silly it was to personalize other people's personalities.

A little more than a year later, I met Adam in New York City. We hadn't explicitly addressed our relationship status, but he was reliable and respectful, and I didn't feel like we were playing hide-and-seek. At the time, I was studying for the California psychology boards, seriously planning my move, when, over dinner at a Thai restaurant, he said casually, "You seem like you're moving."

"I really want to," I acknowledged, though we'd been seeing each other for a few months and I was happy with how things were going.

"I like seeing you," he told me. He'd said as much in his actions, but never expressed this in words. "How soon do you want to move?" At that moment, a version of my guy friend's words replayed in my ears. "Do *not* say you're moving or it's over. If you like him, keep your plans to yourself. He's not moving across the country so that's a deal breaker." Yet I knew that avoiding isn't just hiding emotions; it's also about keeping secrets. I took a breath and told Adam that I loved my job but that in the long term, I saw myself living somewhere more relaxed than Manhattan, closer to my friends and family. He didn't flinch and casually asked if I'd give things more time or whether I had a departure date. We agreed that we'd get to know each other and revisit the topic in a few months.

That night, I fell for Adam. He got real, I got real, and it felt exciting to openly talk about our future hopes. Adam works in a pretty New York–centric career, so I had to accept the frustrations and stresses that came with delaying my move. But like the husband treadmill, I don't think a city is the key to happiness. Now, five years later, as I write this, we're getting settled in Los Angeles. While I'm thrilled, I was also pretty nervous about wrapping up my career in New York to start my therapy practice from scratch in a city I hadn't lived in since high school. But I know with certainty that avoiding unpleasant feelings ensures missing out on a better life.

The only way to reliably feel best is by learning to sit with feelings, even if they are painful. No matter who is around, you can never break up with your emotions. That's a good thing, since they have a lot to teach us.

PART 2

The Sane Solution

Living Freely in the Times of Tinder, Ghosting, and Exes on Instagram

Now that you're more aware of the ways in which you might be making yourself struggle, are you ready to maximize your quality of life? The strategies described in part 2 of this book, "The Sane Solution," are derived from well-researched behavioral therapies proven to help people build meaningful lives, independent of painful circumstances. The concepts that guide the chapters ahead arise from some of my favorite therapies, ones I use with my patients all the time—many of which I've mentioned in these pages already: Dialectical Behavioral Therapy (DBT), Acceptance and Commitment Therapy (ACT), Mindfulness-Based Cognitive Therapy (MBCT), and Cognitive Behavioral Therapy (CBT). They've been game changers for my patients—and for me. I can't wait to delve into them with you.

Running on the
husband treadmill

Ruminating

Regretting

Settling, suppressing,
and other
avoidance
moves

Watching
your mood

Focusing
on your values

Building
your community

Participating in activities
and living in the moment

Giving to others

Accepting your
emotions

Seeing your
thoughts

CHAPTER 5

What Do You Want? Whatever It Is, Cupid Doesn't Have to Say Okay

Life is never made unbearable by circumstances, but only by lack of meaning and purpose. —VIKTOR FRANKL

FROM AN EARLY age, most of us are taught to master *getting*. We try to *get* happy, *get* on the team, *get* good grades, *get* the cool stuff, *get* the guy or girl, and *get* the money. It may even be true that getting what we want makes us feel happy, at least momentarily. The thing is, the getting quest can also guarantee misery. Setting a goal and working to achieve it doesn't ensure success, no matter how diligently we try, and that leads to disappointment, one of the most depressing emotions. Disappointment can make us feel powerless, and psychologists actually talk about two different types: *outcome-related disappointment* (when things didn't go as we'd hoped) and *person-related disappointment* (when people let us down). Dating can deliver a double dose of disappointment, since most of us are looking for both a wonderful person and an idyllic future. In this chapter, you'll learn a practical and hopeful alternative to feeling confined by circumstances that you wish were different.

A Better Way to Measure Your Worth

Chelsea, twenty-three, was sick of feeling like she was chasing her ambitions and not reaching her goals. She'd recently moved to New York City from Tennessee to follow her dream of pursuing a career in publishing. By the time she came to see me, she'd been in the city for a year and hadn't gotten any job offers. Plus, she'd gained more than thirty pounds from binge eating when she felt stressed. Her struggles with her body made her feel uncomfortable and embarrassed to see friends, so she rarely left her apartment. She worried that her excess weight was also keeping her unemployed, and that prospective employers were judging her. She also criticized herself: "My parents can't keep supporting me. I'm worthless," she said, dropping her head to hide her tears.

She also felt lonely. When I asked her about dating, she predicted: "That's never going to happen." In terms of the getting quest, Chelsea wanted to get a job, get thin, and get love. "I'm at my breaking point," she told me, consumed with shame and self-hate.

Yet despite Chelsea's despair, I sensed there was a stockpile of enthusiasm resting inside of her. She had a sweet voice and an edgy haircut/color combination. But life was disappointing her, though not for her lack of trying. If we hacked Chelsea's laptop, we'd see that each day she diligently pursued her aims—applying for jobs, tweaking cover letters, and researching the publishing industry. She also maintained food logs and looked up calorie information until her frustration got the better of her. At that point, usually around 8 p.m., she'd give up and spend the rest of the night comforting and torturing herself with Netflix and Seamless.

Chelsea assessed herself and defined herself, as many do, by her work, her weight, and her relationship status. It's not that it was wrong for her to want those things, of course. They're important goals, and not achieving important goals, especially ones we have sacrificed for, is brutal.

But there's an alternative, a way to shift how we measure success. I experienced this firsthand last year, when I learned that a writing opportunity I'd yearned and labored for fell through. I pouted and ruminated for a while, then realized that I needed to attend to bigger aims to gain perspective. So I deliberately focused on a photo of my late grandmother, Sylvia, on my iPhone. Purposefully looking at her moved me to think about the character traits that made her so endearing. She was consistently grateful, positive, and wholeheartedly focused on others. Thinking about her led me to recall a *New York Times* opinion piece in which David Brooks differentiated résumé virtues (the strengths we bring to the workplace) from eulogy virtues (the attributes that illuminate the lives of those around us). "The eulogy virtues are the ones that are talked about at our funeral—whether you were kind, brave, honest, or faithful," he wrote. Brooks prescribed prioritizing our "moral bucket list" over the drive for getting.

I couldn't bury my bad news—trying not to think about something upsetting just leads to rebound thoughts, as we've discussed. But I could switch my focus to tracking my eulogy virtues, which include being a great listener (complaining, incessantly, isn't what I ever want to be known for, as tempting as those words feel at the time) and working hard. I also made a conscious effort to practice acceptance and to think about gratitude (my health, my family, my mindfulness practice). It took a lot of willingness to get out of the free fall that is *it's not fair* thoughts. I did some moping, but I also caught myself, which allowed me to choose to do better.

Looking at the photo of my grandmother reminded me of my larger life picture—the greater purpose I was aiming for. We all need a clear sense of purpose, one that comes from our values, not our goals. Values aren't the same as goals. With a goal, we win or lose, get it or not. With values, if we're *acting* (not just thinking) consistently with our aims, we can cherish a sense of mastery, independent of the end result. Values aren't measured by what we *get* but by what we *give*. We can wait a long time to feel better or to find luck, or to meet that good-enough partner. The alternative to focusing on that kind of potentially disappointing uncertainty is to purposefully start living better, right now, by focusing on what lies within our control.

It would take time for Chelsea to get a job, lose the weight, and find a romantic relationship. But in the meantime, she didn't need to live a life of heartbreak—or hell. First, however, she needed to change her focus. "Can we focus on how you show up, instead of whether you've accomplished your goals?" I asked her one morning, explaining, again, that our new metric system was what she brought to her life (e.g., effort) rather than the results she achieved.

I was overjoyed to see her shoulders soften and her smile emerge. "I like that idea," she agreed. She had been living as though she had committed a crime; now, it was as if she'd been exonerated.

With her buying in, we worked on creating her personal life mission statement, what I think of as a kind of cheerleading mantra she'd tell herself. Our new way of describing her focus was both authentic and aspirational: *Chelsea: kind, courageous, healthy, and hardworking*, which felt more useful than: *Chelsea: single, overweight, and unemployed.* We weren't sugarcoating: as a therapist, I try to balance optimism with realism in my work with my patients. Instead of replacing truths with wishes, we were focusing on more workable tactics. Chelsea could choose kindness, courage, and health. After all, weight, jobs, and partners fluctuate, but a life based on meaningful values is a constant option. Chelsea knew that she was an exceptional friend, that she was smart, and that she had a passion for animals and social justice. She had been so distracted by her setbacks that she let them overshadow her inner strengths. Her sense of failure led her to abandon aspects of her life that mattered to her—aspects she *did* have control over. In recent months, she'd been flaky with her friends, often canceling on them at the last minute, and avoiding exercise. She was willing to try a different approach when she realized that focusing on outcomes, instead of processes, was backfiring. With outcomes, she could either succeed or fail, and she felt as if she were constantly "failing," which was wearying.

Chelsea's initial dilemma reminded me of a life lesson I learned from my friend Chris. Not too long ago, while waiting in line for water at a spin studio, I started chatting with my fountain neighbor. He said he played the trumpet. You don't hear that every day, and I said I'd love to hear him. A few months later, I ended up going to one of his shows at the Blue Note, a celebrated Greenwich Village jazz club. Initially, I thought it would be great to support an artist and hear live music. Little did I know from our water-break small talk, this humble man was a celebrated Grammy-winning musician. As you can see, I'm not a huge jazz fan, but that night I became a huge Chris

Botti fan. Chris isn't merely a performer—he's valued action in person, at spin and onstage. At his concerts, he shows up in a buttoned-up suit, bursting with energy, despite playing an instrument that leaves most people breathless. He's generous, and seems truly eager to touch hearts, from those of his bandmates as he steps back to complement their talents, to the girl from Italy who was celebrating her seventh birthday that night. His presence gave me awe-inspiring chills.

Though Chris isn't struggling with feeling less-than due to his relationship status, I wondered how he mustered the resources to consistently give in a life that seemed potentially depleting. He's on tour for more than 275 days a year, to the point that he found it impractical to keep a permanent home, possessions, or even have a partner. I couldn't imagine how he maintained his drive without the comforts that sustain many of us. I had to know how he embodied joy and generosity in circumstances that led many to substance abuse and debt. How did he find bliss? Was fame fulfilling him? Not exactly. "My commitment is to my instrument," he explained, with a quality of surprised gratefulness. Even with a brutal schedule, he continues to practice for hours each day. And if you're thinking, "Of course he's happy, he's lucky, he's famous," he humbly told me that he hadn't really been "successful" until he was forty-two (he started playing at nine years old). Yet his life rules have always been the same: work hard and act positive. "Practicing is a meditative journey; it's all about breathing. And I'm not one to sit on my hands," Chris said.

Chris spent several decades singularly invested in playing the trumpet and focusing on his breath, moment to moment. His measure of success was himself—was he doing his best? He didn't compare himself to others or yearn for a world tour. If he had, I doubt he'd be in Dubai with Sting today. We can't persist or feel consistently satisfied when we're looking outward. "What about when you're not feeling it?" I wondered. He told me about performing at a concert two hours after his father had died (which he knew was the way his father had wished to be commemorated). His commitment to his valued routine transcends his emotion. Chris's words nicely illustrated how Chelsea could move from misery to freedom.

Persistence was one of the first things Chelsea and I focused on—sticking to her plans even when she wasn't in the mood. After all, most of the time, we're not in the mood to do what will leave us most fulfilled, long-term. Generally, it requires more effort to pursue actions that are ultimately the most meaningful for us. At one time, psychologists used to promote building self-esteem. Now, the wisdom in the field is that self-control, doing what we know is wise, even when we aren't in the mood, is the key to evolving and growing. "Self-control is not just a puritanical virtue. It is a key psychological trait that breeds success at work and play—and in overcoming life's hardship," according to Roy Baumeister. When we depend on external factors, including other people, to live well, life feels risky.

That's why I ask my clients, like Chelsea, to start focusing on their values. The first step to feeling empowered in life is to define your values. Initially, I was so enthusiastic about values—and the eulogy virtues idea—that I did things like run to a wedding of a distant friend the week after I ended my own engagement. I had RSVP'd weeks prior and I didn't want to cancel. I convinced myself that it was noble to celebrate my friend's joy, but sitting on a two-hour party bus, alone, for the wedding of someone I hadn't spoken to for years didn't exactly leave me glowing in generous feelings. As I sat at an empty table watching the other couples slow dance, I realized that I was torturing myself. I was attempting to be a good friend, but not to myself. In living a life based on values, we need to make room for self-care too.

As for Chelsea, she and I came up with a month-long plan of action based on the values that mattered to her. In addition to writing her daily to-dos on Post-its (e.g., work on cover letter, meet a friend for a walk), each week, she'd deliberately consider which values mattered to her, whether being active or strengthening her connections. Chelsea had mentioned that she wanted to contribute to causes, prioritize her health, and pursue closeness with others, so she began researching opportunities to follow her passions. She couldn't cherry-pick a perfect job, partner, or physique, but she would have a say in her day-to-day. She started volunteering at the ASPCA, walking more, attending book readings to network, and downloading dating apps.

Paradoxically, like my jazz friend Chris, she discovered that the less she focused on achieving certain goals, the greater her sense of accomplishment. "Action is the way out of anxiety," she noticed. Today, she has an internship at a magazine, works as a college essay advisor, and has lost fifteen pounds. She is dating, and most important, is kinder to herself. During one especially discouraging week, when she was rejected from what she considered to be her dream job and a date stood her up, she was "bummed," but she wasn't broken. "It sucks but I'll survive," she said in my office, as she committed to continuing her job search the next day.

By choosing values first, then selecting goals linked to her personal mission, Chelsea felt freer and stronger: her fate *wasn't* beyond her reach. Instead of feeling limited, it's possible for all of us to feel empowered. What it takes is reflecting on what matters, then shaping your day so that you can achieve your personal best.

Choosing Your Life Purpose

Sit with a notepad and pen or just quietly with yourself. Ask and answer the following two questions. The intention is to access your wisdom and values. If your mind wanders away into worries about whether you'll be able to take action or you feel guilty over past setbacks, just notice your emotions, and come back to these questions:

♥ What do you want your life to stand for?
♥ How do you want to live your life?

Having a Say in Your Life Is Liberating

Chelsea's newfound resilience isn't a one-off success story. Research suggests that feeling as if you have a sense of purpose in your life builds emotional and physical well-being. Scientist Stacey Schaefer and her colleagues at the Center for Investigating Healthy Minds, a wellness research institution at the University of Wisconsin, Madison, conducted a large, multiyear study of adults aged thirty-six to eighty-four as part of the U.S. Longitudinal Study of Health and Well-being. At one point, the participants were asked about their purpose in life. Several years later, they were shown unpleasant photographs, such as a reddish newborn baby crying in pain, while their psychophysiological responses were recorded. Incredibly, having stated a clear sense of purpose two years earlier predicted a faster recovery from the disturbing photos. The more meaning you feel your life has, the better able you are to regulate negative moods and emotions. And once you cultivate a strong personal sense of meaning, the benefits are enduring.

Beyond recovering quickly in an experimental situation, feeling as if you have a purpose in life is a protective factor for one of the greatest health burdens, the decline of the mind, as well as overall well-being. Aging expert Patricia Boyle and her colleagues from Rush University Medical Center in Chicago followed a sample of more than 1,200 adults, assessing them six times over eighteen years. People with a stronger sense of purpose reported lower levels of disability and fewer depressive symptoms. They also lived longer. Even in adults with Alzheimer's, a strong sense of meaning seemed to slow cognitive decline.

Why is this? In a famous study in the 1970s, psychologists Ellen Langer and Judith Rodin divided nursing home residents into two groups. One group had their furniture arranged for them, a preset schedule, and a plant that a nurse came by and watered. In the second group, residents were able to decorate their rooms, plan details of their days (e.g., select dining times, which movies to watch), and care for their own plants. Just three weeks later, the group with more autonomy experienced significant improvements in health and emotional well-being; the seniors with diminished freedom either declined or showed no improvement. *Autonomy* literally refers to regulating yourself. Having some freedom to choose what matters, from life values to design details, makes the rest of life feel full of choices too.

More recently, Google wanted to enrich the jobs of its employees in sales and administrative positions who didn't enjoy the lavish perks of the company's engineers. Adam Grant, a Wharton professor and bestselling author, was one of the consultants hired to motivate these employees. "We designed a workshop introducing hundreds of employees to the notion that jobs are not static sculptures but flexible building blocks." After the ninety-minute intervention, in which the participants were encouraged to think more creatively about ways of customizing their positions (i.e., adapt them so that what they did every day was aligned with their personal vision), these employees reported being happier and were 70 percent more likely to land a promotion than their peers who hadn't participated in the workshop.

Ready? Set? Act!

We can all feel happier and benefit in other ways by shifting our focus from the supposed limits of a situation (*The good ones are gone!*) and instead, think more about how we can meaningfully choose how we spend our days. One way to do this is to think about how you'd use your time if you felt as if you couldn't postpone living; as if you had very little time left on the planet. (I found *When Breath Becomes Air*, a memoir written by Paul Kalanithi, a young neurosurgeon with advanced cancer, a moving reminder of the preciousness of this moment.) It takes so much courage and strength to consider whether you're making the most of your time or whether you're waiting for life to go your way.

What Matters Most?

If you're willing and interested in going deeper into exploring your values and life mission, close your eyes and consider:

- ♥ If I had one month left to live, how would I spend it?
- ♥ If I had one week left to live, how might I spend that week?

> ♥ With one day to live, what would I do for that day?
> ♥ In the final hour of my life, what would I do?

What did you notice about your answers? What do they tell you about what you want to do *today*? Even if you can't quit your job to pursue political lobbying, it's possible to use your precious time in a way that feels, well, more precious. For example, maybe you can let go of overfocusing on your appearance to focus more on laughing with friends.

When I've really engaged in this exercise, I've become acutely aware that I often take detours rather than chasing what I feel is my life's assignment, to act in a way that might uplift people, especially those who feel discouraged. I've noticed that I spend too much time working and want to connect more with people who matter to me. Similarly, I realized that I tend to commit to seeing friends who are in town visiting but I am not as great at making time for friends who live locally, taking routine opportunities for granted. I observed that I complain too much about my struggles to my mother and don't ask her often enough about how she is doing. I appreciated how badly I wanted to strive to reach my grandparents' moral bucket list and how behind I feel. Taking a moment to sit with these reflections inspired me to take actions like reaching out to at least two friends each week.

Don't Let Your Mind Hold You Back

Some of us may think, *It's too late, why bother?* or *I've worked hard enough*. Recently, I met someone whom I now bring to mind when those sorts of thoughts get in my way. She is a fifty-something-year-old woman who is a medical resident in obstetrics. "Did you say medical resident?" I asked when I met her, that position usually being held by someone much younger at the beginning of their medical career. She explained, "I was a pilot for decades. Now I'm pursuing a new career." As I came to learn, Dr. Cholene Espinoza was a medal-winning Air Force U-2 pilot. After the tragedies of September 11th and Hurricane Katrina, she noticed that her life purpose was to offer direct care to people in need, and she did, offering incredible aid to Katrina survivors. Cholene also grew to care deeply about the people in South Sudan and decided she was willing to go through a decade of hard work and sleepless nights in medical school and residency to serve them. She easily could have retired, but in service of her value—offering medical help to women in need—she plans to move to South Sudan once she completes her training. Despite her incredible success in her first career, Cholene isn't basking in her previous feats or letting thoughts about her age and the complexity of her choices deter her. She's constantly and courageously moving toward her values. While she certainly looked tired, she also looked exuberant. I can't begin to imagine the profound joy she derives from knowing she is chasing her mission and that the world will be better for it.

Chelsea found that spending her days feeling helpless took an emotional toll on her soul. When it comes to your values, it's easy to think, *I have my whole life to think about this and figure it out*, but . . . why wait? For Chelsea, filling her time with things she cared about, like dinners with friends and Skype sessions with her family, gave her purpose. As we'd predict, in studying suicide prevention, researchers have found that people who believe their life is meaningful have a decreased risk of suicide and suicidal thoughts. Even *searching* for meaning predicts fewer thoughts of death. We may soothe ourselves with distractions, but asking ourselves what matters, and taking steps toward doing more of that, is ultimately the way to adorn our lives.

Many of us worry that starting to truly live today rather than focusing single-mindedly on goals means settling for being alone, or for a subpar job, or being ten (or fifty) pounds overweight. *But if I stop focusing on this goal, it will never happen!* I think there's a major emotional myth that accepting less than ideal circumstances prevents us from changing them. Investing in a solo trip (instead of waiting until you have a partner) isn't a waste of money, nor does it pave the way for a lifetime of tables for one. Taking a break from dating to focus on a passion project at work, for a couple of months, doesn't mean you're a workaholic who will never find a boyfriend. In fact, it may work for you.

When you add substance to your life, you might find companionship (though that's not the reason to do it). In a study conducted by social psychologist Tyler Stillman and his colleagues, students completed questionnaires on meaning in life and were also videotaped having conversations with a friend. Later, these videos were rated by independent evaluators who answered questions like, "How likable is this person?" and "How much would you enjoy a conversation with this person?" In a second study, the researchers filmed participants introducing themselves for ten seconds, then again asked evaluators to gauge their likability, as well as to predict, "How meaningful do you think this person's life is?" The researchers found that people with a strong sense of meaning were also perceived by others as having a meaningful life, which in turn made them more appealing. In other words, having a life purpose is beneficial for us, and can also facilitate closer connections with others.

Searching for Love ≠ Acting Loving

Dating for months and years can feel even more daunting than Chelsea's drawn-out job search. Some of my patients describe looking for love as the one to-do that seems out of reach. What is "looking for love," anyway? Finding a partner is a goal—not a value—so it makes sense we'd feel burned by this tactic. One of the most frustrating experiences is feeling vulnerable and dealing with uncertainty, an unavoidable part of dating. The only way to get through it with equanimity is to focus on more than just the *getting* goal, and instead focus on your values. Once you clarify your values, it's easier to move toward what matters, without focusing rigidly on any one outcome. In shifting your focus, spending a night out with friends is no longer "pointless" if you don't meet someone new; it's an opportunity for bonding, a chance to focus on the importance of closeness with friends. In the same way, a disappointing date doesn't have to be a dead end; it may be a time to get to know someone, offer a kind ear, or learn more about a topic that's new to you.

A meaningful alternative to finding love is giving love. In the classic book *The Art of Loving*, psychologist Erich Fromm writes about how love isn't simply a feeling, it's an action. One CBT technique used in couples counseling is to invite dissatisfied partners to treat each other to "loving gestures" instead of rehashing recent dramas. As hard as it seems, running to grab a soy chai for someone you don't especially cherish in the moment actually can produce loving feelings* when the action is done wholeheartedly. These gestures can teach us a lot about both how to discover and how to maintain love: it's not always about getting the buzz; it's about offering it.

Swipe Right on Shared Values

So how does this apply to dating? Instead of searching for the perfect person, it makes sense to consider how you want to approach relationships and also what virtues matter to you in a potential partner. Chelsea told me she wanted to feel liked and pursued; we replaced those understandable goals with the values of listening and opening up. It's nice when someone expresses interest in us, especially when we feel insecure. Chelsea much preferred when someone reached out to her first, but that passive approach limited her, as it would limit anyone. Gradually, on dating apps, she started contacting men who seemed like her type, and made a point of being open and honest, such as: "The job search is hard," instead of a vague "I'm in between projects." At first, Chelsea questioned my nudges for her to initiate and get real. But I wanted her to have a say, and women having a say works. In a survey done by the popular online dating Web site OkCupid, women who initiated contact with people they were interested in were 2.5 times more likely to receive a response than men who did the same. Once she learned that, instead of retreating from dating, Chelsea tried to courageously connect with

---

* In case you're wondering how this example is different from what wasn't working for Erika in chapter 4—that is a great observation. Acting loving can often enhance loving feelings. But in Erika's situation, she didn't feel a connection and was trying to force one, which felt more like suppressing her emotions and putting a relationship above her self-care.

others and put her wants out there, making suggestions of places to meet instead of waiting for the other person to decide, so she didn't have to trek out of her way in the snow. When things felt difficult, or a guy disappeared, she consciously went back to her list of what she aimed to give to others (e.g., vulnerability, openness) and to herself (e.g., self-compassion). After a few months, she met someone and they clicked. When she learned that he was a confirmed atheist (her family is Christian), instead of asking everyone what she should do, she concluded that she needed to be with someone who shared her faith. She felt sad about ending things, but also relieved to see that she could tolerate short-term pain in the service of living well.

Chelsea's decision reminded me of a date I went on with a man who had great résumé virtues and swagger. He invited me to a busy bar and I found myself feeling captivated by him. Then, toward the end of our date, someone accidentally bumped into him, splashing his pristine blazer with red wine. Most people would feel upset if someone's carelessness cost them, but this guy was livid. Later, I wasn't sure what to do—I certainly was attracted to him but was fairly put off by his unforgiving reaction. Using values as my guide and knowing I really wanted to be with someone more easygoing, I decided I didn't want to waste time getting closer to him when that kind of quick-to-anger reaction would be a real deal breaker for me in the end. As I continued to meet people using values as my metric, I felt like I was replacing first impressions with a sounder strategy that helped me stay true to myself. What dating values matter most to you? Do you want to show up as fun-loving? Or do you want to focus on understanding someone? Either strategy can work, as long as you clearly know what deeply matters, then follow your chosen course.

Below are some examples of values that may arise during dating, both within you and in another person. Take a look at these examples.

What values matter to you?	What values matter in another?
♥ Kind	♥ Respectful
♥ Enthusiastic	♥ Honest
♥ Open to new experiences	♥ Patient
♥ Loyal	♥ Generous
♥ Healthy	♥ Hardworking
♥ Responsible	♥ Open
♥ Affectionate	♥ Loving

Just as focusing on your own values can make you feel better about life, focusing on another person's values (e.g., generosity, loyalty) instead of their traits (e.g., looks, level of success) doesn't mean you won't meet someone who is attractive or accomplished. Settling is self-defeating, and it cements the idea that we're not good enough to keep trying for the possibility of reciprocal closeness. A huge part of self-care is being authentic and experiencing chemistry. But writing people off based on initial assumptions might lead to misunderstandings. Years ago, I was about to go on a first date with a guy when he contacted me at the last minute to push back our meeting by an hour. "I'm running late from the gym," he texted. Once we met, somehow the topic of fraternities came up, and he reminisced about his college fraternity. When it came time to part ways, he didn't offer to walk me to my apartment, just a block away from the restaurant. I definitely place a high value on chivalry and respect. But I was also really immersed in practicing a nonjudgmental stance. Despite those brow-raising moments (*Why didn't he walk me down the block?* and *I am not interested in frat boys!*), I noticed that I had a nice time. When I felt tempted to tell a friend about my reservations, I decided not to, thinking I'd be creating a story from inconclusive little tidbits, which was not in line with my intent of being open-minded and nonjudgmental. When he asked me out again, I went, and I learned that he was a really nice guy who loves a good workout and is always up for a good time with a group of friends. Months later, I sort of jokingly asked about why he didn't walk me home on our first date. "I didn't want you to think I was inviting myself over!" he explained sweetly. Now *that* is chivalrous and respectful!

I'm so happy I gave this person a chance initially, and I grew to discover that we shared similar values, so much so that I eventually wound up marrying him! We both cherish personal growth, spirituality, and independence. Yet we also have different priorities that help us facilitate balance in our relationship. I'm probably more focused on "doing my very best in my career," while he really focuses on "creating fun." This difference allows us to work toward a healthy middle ground. I keep him focused and he keeps me from taking myself and everything else too seriously.

"What should I be looking for in a partner?" patients ask me. Experts say it's helpful to choose a person who values being kind and respectful. "But I'm attracted to 'bad boys,'" I hear every so often. If you tend to write off "nice guys," there's some research that explains why that might prove problematic. In *The Science of Happily Ever After*, psychologist Ty Tashiro recommends choosing a partner who embodies values such as agreeableness and kindness. He explains that good relationships stem from choosing someone who cares about being a good person. John Gottman, one of the most celebrated marital experts of our time, has done extensive research on couples, filming them as they communicate, and has found that he can predict with amazing accuracy (94 percent of the time) whether a relationship will last based on a brief interaction. A key factor that predicts divorce, Gottman has found, is acting with contempt, or behaving in a superior, cruel way (the opposite of agreeableness). This means that respect is an essential ingredient in a successful partnership. Tashiro, Gottman, and other researchers are noticing that a potential partner's character matters more in terms of creating lasting love than having a big bank account or a full head of hair. And to be fair, consistent with the theme of giving rather than getting, while we're trying to monitor whether someone else is living according to universal values, like acting considerately, we also need to make sure we're doing our part to act that way too.

Finding Peace in Pie

What happens, though, when you feel as if you're giving, giving, giving, and not getting your goals met? It's exhausting to continuously give and we don't want to feel like the withered stump in the classic children's book *The Giving Tree*. To feel satisfied, we need to ensure that there are aspects in our lives that feel enriching. Chelsea noticed that cuddling with dogs in the animal shelter gave her a mood boost that cushioned the stress of her job search. She moved away from the all-or-nothing perspective ("I'm single so nothing's good") to a broader way of thinking. So much in our culture reinforces the idea that a relationship is everything, but just as it's financially smart to have a diversified portfolio of investments, the more you strive to make as many aspects in your life as meaningful as possible, the more satisfied you'll feel. Again, finding the right person is not the only path to joy.

Unlike Chelsea, my friend Sophia, who is forty-five, has what many would consider to be a dream life. Tan, blue-eyed, blond, and thin, she is also a doctor with the kind of professional success and physical appearance that inspires envy. Yet, like Chelsea, Sophia also struggled with dating, telling me that she felt like a "loser" because she was single. Her perceived problems tainted her happy moments. If you met Sophia, you'd be struck by her modesty and generosity. She's actually quite the match-maker too. Noticing her own struggles with loneliness, she's always trying to introduce friends to each other so they can avoid the same challenges she faces. Recently, we grabbed tea in her sun-filled office and I couldn't believe my friend had never described her orchid-lined penthouse medical suite. "You've made it!" I exclaimed, having seen how hard she'd worked to achieve this success in her career. But while she was helping heal others, we now needed to address what was making Sophia sick. I begged her to tell me what was going on, beyond her self-deprecating comments, and I learned that she'd been rock climbing, as well as volunteering at an inner-city clinic.

Sophia was so focused on what she didn't have, so caught in emotion mind, that she'd lost sight of the beauty she'd created in her life. She'd probably rate finding a partner and starting a family as her ultimate goals; she'd spent years on the husband tread-mill. I couldn't imagine she'd trade her life for a person. I knew she never dated people in other cities because she loved her medical practice. I wanted Sophia to remember in times of sadness that she did have autonomy in her life. Together, we worked on devising a life mission statement that would allow her to feel more fulfilled, whether she met someone or not. We came up with *Sophia: determined, grateful, and patient.* As we talked, she laughed a bit about the idea of focusing on values. "You're so New Age," she teased. I wasn't trying to teach her positive affirmations, and given her skepticism and our relationship (I can only push friends who didn't sign up for my services so far), I wanted to start small. We talked about little ways she could focus on appreciating moments and treating herself as though she mattered. Sophia cherishes aesthetics, and I imagine if she envisioned her last days, she'd fill at least some of her time appreciating beauty. Yet she didn't think she would eat off nice dishes until she had a registry on theknot.com. After our talk, she decided that she'd save the paper plates for work and invest in some nice dinnerware, one small step toward feeling like she didn't need to postpone living in the style she hoped to. When Sophia actively shifted her stance, she was able to notice that so much in her life felt fulfilling.

Now, if you'd like, you can experiment with this paradigm. You might notice, as Sophia and Chelsea witnessed, it's important to approach life holistically, rather than focusing on one thing, like work or finding a partner. Instead of overvaluing relationships, or making finding a partner a top priority, it's possible to create a pie chart (see the example on the next page) in which you personalize your values, then note how much each matters. The graphic can make it easier to take a mindful look at your life to make sure you have enough choice and balance. Keep in mind too that you don't have to write off fulfillment until certain things happen. If you value mentoring, instead of waiting until you're a parent you can seek opportunities to nurture people now, whether a nephew or through volunteer work. Once you brainstorm the values that matter to you, you can start moving toward them. Take a look at the example on the next page, then you'll have a chance to create your own graphic.

Make a Values Pie Chart

If you're a visual person, you may create a picture to keep your values in perspective:

- ♥ List what you know deeply matters.
- ♥ Graphically depict how much you'd like to prioritize each value.

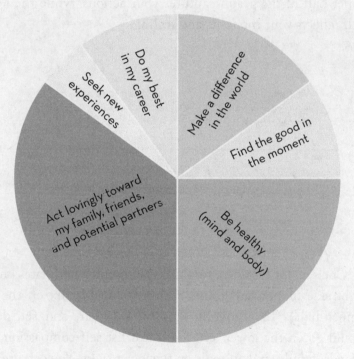

Now that you've learned the difference between *getting* and *living* according to your values, I hope you've decided that recalibrating your metric of success isn't just an interesting idea, but something that can practically guide you. To stay focused, in addition to seeing what you want to move toward with your pie chart, it's also helpful to notice what you want to move away from. To help you maintain your momentum, I like a matrix exercise that was developed by Kevin Polk, a psychologist in Maine. As illustrated in the sample diagram below, start with a bidirectional arrow, intersected by a line down the middle. On the right side of the arrow, list what you want to move toward; on the left side, write what you want to move away from. The upper half of the graph captures your actions, while the lower half reflects your thoughts and feelings.

What do you do to move away from what matters?	What can you do to move toward what matters?
← away	toward →
What thoughts and feelings get in the way of moving toward what matters?	Who's important to you?

Chelsea, for instance, might list: job search and dates on the right side (upper half), and Seamless and Netflix on the left (upper half). The thought *Why bother?*, fear, and self-doubt would go on the lower left, and she'd list self-compassion, her friends, family, and animals on the lower right. You can use this chart to address any areas in your life, from dating to working, so that you constantly have a clear visual plan and your urges or distractions don't sneak up behind you.

———

I GOT A call from Chelsea recently. I hadn't seen her in a while, and she told me that given how much her family matters to her and her preference for a quieter life, she'd decided to move back to Nashville, where she knew she wanted to live long-term. She's now balancing freelance writing with volunteering, and continues to date. As for Seamless and Netflix, well, she broke up with them.

Now we need to remember to let our values light up our lives like neon lights. As Aristotle put it: "[Happiness] belongs more to those who have cultivated their character and mind to the uttermost. . . ." One of my favorite stories involves three men who are laying bricks at a construction site. A bystander approaches and asks the men what they're doing. The first man says, "I'm laying bricks." The second man says, "I'm building a wall." Then the third man says, joyfully, "I'm building a church!" Just like a mediocre date, the task of moving bricks can either bore you or move you, depending on whether or not you have a larger vision of your life's aim.

CHAPTER 6

Happily Ever Now

Act as if what you do makes a difference. It does.

—WILLIAM JAMES

A NEW CLIENT of mine, Maggie, in her late thirties, had recently moved to Los Angeles for work as a production assistant for a new TV show. Initially, she felt excited by the opportunity and curious about how life in a sunny city would unfold. Then, a few months into her new job, the show she'd rearranged her life for was canceled. Stuck in a year-long apartment lease with no other semblance of structure, Maggie was justifiably unsettled and anxious.

When I asked about her situation before the move, Maggie told me that a car accident she'd been in years ago had left her in chronic physical pain. She had a couple of good friends but she'd never felt seen or chosen by men, which fueled a myriad of insecurities. "If a guy pays attention to me, he's usually trying to smoothly segue his way into talking to one of my friends," she said. After investing tons of hours over the course of many years on dating apps, she hadn't been on many dates. To her credit, she mustered the will to try her luck again in her new city, revamping her profile. But once again, she received few responses, and told me she felt overlooked. Initially poised when she mentioned her job loss, Maggie started to tear up as she confided that she always knew she wanted children. "I don't think that will happen now," she said. "I mean, I can barely get a date." On top of that, she told me that she had been diagnosed with polycystic ovary syndrome, a common endocrine disorder that can impact fertility.

Maggie wanted my help, but was worried about the cost of therapy after weeks of being unemployed. "If I can only afford to see you for just a couple of months, do you think you can make a difference?" she asked earnestly. Sitting across from me, she looked diligent yet defeated. I sympathized, reflecting on how life can feel incredibly hard sometimes, as if bad luck is piling up. Yet despite her many obstacles, I believed that two approaches, *adding positives*, or joy-enhancing behaviors, and *radical acceptance*, which is essentially an attitude of openness, would prove valuable. While I couldn't promise a complete life turnaround, I explained that together, we could work on improving her day-to-day moments. Over the years, based on research and my experiences with many clients, I've found that taking strategic actions along with shifting into a more effective stance can change your mood. In this chapter, you'll learn what I taught Maggie: how to live the way you would if you felt optimistic, however bleak your circumstances seem.

Expanding Your Life

Maggie assumed that unless something drastic happened to change her problems—loneliness, pain, and unemployment—there was really no way to improve her situation. I promised

Maggie that we could figure out ways to live better that weren't dependent on her circumstances. After all, we all need a sense of agency to feel hopeful. By moving past imagining how a person or conditions beyond your immediate control might enrich your life to, instead, plotting a course that allows you to honor your dreams more immediately, you'll feel happier.

We all know how disappointing it feels when plans diverge from our expectations. For me, I think of Thanksgiving ages ago when I decided that it would be cost-effective and different to spend the holiday on a yoga retreat with a friend rather than fly across the country to celebrate with my parents. Home wasn't as comfortable as it once had been, since my childhood friends were no longer as available given obligations to their burgeoning families—a situation that made me acutely aware of the fact that I hadn't started my own family.

Then my yoga friend canceled, and it was too late for me to get a refund, so I decided to work on my independence by going alone. Except instead of acting yogic, I kept obsessing over how awful the weekend was, barely tolerating the urge to text my friend play-by-plays of the strangers who told sad stories during the Tofurky dinner. I didn't want to feel ungrateful (after all, this was Thanksgiving) so I kept trying to rally to make the best of the weekend. But wandering around the rainy retreat center alone except for my phone, where I kept scrolling past other people's festive tablescapes, made it hard for me to get past the idea that what I was doing was pathetic and depressing.

Looking back on my weekend of misery at a place designed to bring inner peace, I've since realized that by not accepting the situation, I barely saw my surroundings. Even with a schedule of yoga classes led by a teacher I liked and who usually made me laugh, I felt as if I were being punished and certainly wasn't happy.

Speaking of happy, I think it makes sense to clarify that I'm not talking about the flashy sentiment captured in either a bright yellow smiley-face emoji or a quick selfie. Short-lived bursts of happiness that happen after an amazing date or fun night out with friends can't compare with the more enduring sense of meaning that arises when you live according to your values. That latter isn't always instantaneous—if you saw me sitting at the library writing this book at this very moment, I'd look more pensive than elated. Yet I know that long-term, I'd rather be here at my laptop than sipping a cucumber drink at a beach resort. Sharing teachings in psychology feels purposeful to me, and the opportunity to write this book is something I've strived for, unlike relaxing poolside.

Ironically, thinking about whether or not you feel happy can make you less so because it takes you out of the moment and pulls you toward instant gratification. For instance, just considering whether I feel happy now makes me want to leave this desk and rush home for dinner. Instead, it makes sense to reflect on whether you're doing the things you'd want to *do* if you were in an optimal state of mind, free of self-doubt.

Of course, as I've mentioned, doing what feels meaningful can feel difficult along the way. It can be tempting to give up. Psychologist and meditation teacher Tara Brach, author of *Radical Acceptance*, tells a story about Mohini, a white tiger who was enclosed in a 12' x 12' cage in a zoo. After many years, the zoo created a more liberating environment for the animal, allowing Mohini to wander through trees and a pond. Yet after years of confinement, Mohini habitually paced within a small slice of her now vast territory, just as she did when she was in her cage. As Brach powerfully describes, "Perhaps the biggest tragedy in our lives is that freedom is possible, yet we can pass our years trapped in the same old patterns. Entangled in the trance of unworthiness, we grow accustomed to caging ourselves in with self-judgment and anxiety, with restlessness and dissatisfaction. Like Mohini, we grow incapable of accessing the freedom and peace that are our birthright."

Planning Activities to Experience Pleasure and a Sense of Mastery

The truth is, even when you don't believe it's possible, you can find joy by expanding your range of actions and your thinking, starting with adding more positive activities to your life. If that sounds like some sort of superficial Band-Aid that won't actually make you feel more fulfilled, studies suggest otherwise: In one experiment, researchers assigned 241 patients struggling with depression either to a placebo or to one of three evidence-based treatment options: 1) cognitive therapy to target problematic thinking, 2) antidepressant medication to address biological vulnerabilities, or 3) behavioral activation (BA) to help people structure their days to engage in activities linked to their long-term goals.

At the time, medication was seen as the standard approach to managing depression. Cognitive therapy was one of the most studied psychological interventions. The behavioral approach, on the other hand, looked like the underdog. Here's what psychologist Sona Dimidjian, and her team at the University of Washington (she's now at the University of Colorado, Boulder), found: For those with more severe depression, antidepressants and BA were equally effective. Both outperformed cognitive therapy. But people tended to be more willing to stick with BA than to stay on medication. In patients with lower levels of depression, all three approaches worked equally well, but cognitive therapy and BA were more effective at preventing relapses. That a behavioral approach to treating depression proved so powerful is pretty remarkable and also highlights how the actions we take on a day-to-day basis aren't artificial—they're life-enhancing, as much as a potent medication. Positive activities aren't only for people who need a pick-me-up; they increase well-being and help prevent future psychological problems.

Understandably, when you start to feel stuck, it's easy to shut down, be a homebody, and withdraw from activities and life. For Maggie, simply going to work every day with her chronic physical pain had been a challenge; now that she didn't have an obligation to go anywhere, she wanted to curl up on her couch. She also told me that once her lease ended, she didn't expect to stay in L.A., so she didn't see the point in trying to make friends. "Why bother?" she said. "I'll just end up going out and spending money I don't have." I explained to her that in addition to having a clear sense of your values and a life filled with actions that align with those values (as described in chapter 5), it's also important to experience both *pleasure* and *mastery*. When I say *pleasure,* I mean activities that you passively enjoy, like going to a show, eating, or shopping. In contrast, *mastery,* a term described by one of the founders of CBT, psychiatrist Aaron Beck, involves doing activities that create a sense of accomplishment, like learning to cook, studying a foreign language, or practicing mindfulness, activities where you continually challenge yourself and grow.

In creating a meaningful schedule, it's important to find

balance. Just as you'll feel nauseatingly self-indulgent if you spend a long vacation tanning and napping, overworking will also deplete you—a middle path is key. That means indulging in an afternoon of pampering, but only after a productive stretch. Maggie wasn't doing much for either growth or fun; "I don't deserve to invest in myself," she lamented.

It made sense that Maggie was suffering, since avoiding activities and withdrawing from people creates long-term problems—that's one of the central tenets of BA. When you decide to melt into the couch in your apartment instead of going to a barbecue or doing another activity, you can't enjoy the naturally occurring rewards that arise from participating in your life, like bumping into someone interesting and having an unexpected great conversation.

Making Appointments with Yourself

One BA principle Maggie and I worked on together was to come up with activities that followed a plan, rather than her mood. I wanted her to become a scientist in her own life, tracking how much she enjoyed different activities and which ones made her feel accomplished. Like it did for Maggie, this knowledge allows you to design your best day instead of waiting for motivation to magically make an appearance.

During our sessions, Maggie and I spent time assessing her goals and brainstorming ideas about what she might enjoy, based on what she had enjoyed in the past. On the mastery front, Maggie told me that a physical therapist had mentioned that Pilates might help with her back pain. Before her job loss, she'd also considered trying to put money aside to eventually pay for procedures to help her get pregnant (more on this topic later in this chapter). In terms of pleasure, Maggie shared that before she'd moved, she'd imagined visiting different beaches and exploring neighborhoods she'd seen only in movies. On her coffee table, she had a copy of a local magazine with dog-eared pages of things she might like to try, like inviting old friends to visit and going to a bar she'd read about that featured classic arcade games.

Next, we strategized ways to make these ideas realities. First, Maggie found a Pilates class in her neighborhood. Then, since she was worried about money, she calculated that she'd save $8 a day if she gave up on a couple of fancy coffee drinks—not a lot of money but it felt responsible to cut her costs. Later, we made a list of things to do, like visit Malibu beaches, and we put these outings on her calendar, making sure to schedule them so she'd miss rush hour traffic and not end up exacerbating her physical discomfort with an unnecessarily long car ride. To help her get going, Maggie found two apps designed to help people stick with their plans: *SuperBetter*, which makes a game out of achieving goals and provides suggestions of things to try if you feel stumped, and *Way of Life*, which sent Maggie reminders and allowed her to keep notes on how she felt after various activities. One night, she even stopped by the bar she'd read about; they were having an '80s night with a DJ. She predicted that she'd feel happy playing Pac-Man while listening to Madonna, as long as the space wasn't too crowded with couples on dates or big groups of friends, and she did have fun. Maggie left her phone in her car and actually danced and sang like no one was watching.

If you're already doing a lot to create pleasure and build mastery, yet feeling like I did during my ungrateful Thanksgiving, make sure that you're mindfully participating by entirely throwing yourself into the activities you're doing for fun. If Maggie went to the bar but stayed glued to her phone or spent her time in the corner enviously people-watching wherever she went, she wouldn't have had the same uplifting experience.

Maggie was stunned to find that she was actually capable of enjoying herself, especially because she admitted that she'd only agreed to do these activities because I'd assigned them. But the more active she was, the more willing she felt to do even more, and we continued to expand her plans. As she tracked her activities, emotions, and physical symptoms, Maggie discovered that the more engaged she was in life, the better she felt, mood-wise and even physically. Not only is participating in life good for emotional well-being but researchers have also found that for people with physical pain, positive activities reduce discomfort.

Beyond pleasurable activities, Maggie also worked on increasing her sense of mastery by setting aside time each day to job hunt and network. Initially hesitant, she reached out to the producer who'd first hired her; to her surprise, again, this woman helped Maggie secure a job on another set. As her time filled up and she felt more productive, she remembered what she was once sure of: She had a good personality, a trait that was hard to detect in a dating profile picture, and she began to meet guys, not on an app but in person and at work.

On the topic of increasing activities and dating, if you're trying to meet someone, it might feel tempting to force yourself into activities that don't feel like *you* because they're socially prescribed ways to meet people (like going to bars or singles events). If you don't like clubbing at 1 a.m., that probably isn't a great way to meet a like-minded person. For years, from a place of desperation, I pushed myself to pursue activities that I found personally unrewarding because I thought that staying at home would sabotage my *slim chance of meeting someone*. I'm not a

late-night club person, but I'd stand around trendy venues struggling to hear people talk, straining my voice and accumulating
blisters on my heels, when all I wanted was to be in my bed
sleeping. Unlike adding positives to my life, those actions left
me feeling sad and anxious.

It's possible to stretch yourself without dismissing your legit-
imate preferences. Some of my friends now go to a grown-up
version of sleepaway camp where they play color war in skimpy
cutoffs and sip spiked Gatorade. I know I wouldn't like that, but
when I was single I pushed myself to do things that were out of
my comfort zone, like going to a dinner party where I didn't
know anyone except the gracious seventy-year-old host (and
where I ended up meeting people I liked). In contrast, scheduling activities where the only redeeming element was the possibility of finding a partner didn't build my self-compassion or
fuel my hope.

Creating Happily Ever Now

How might you enhance your life? If you're not sure, take a
few minutes to think about the following questions:

1. What gives you pleasure?
2. What actions might you take to increase your sense of
   mastery?

Once you generate ideas, start doing some serious
scheduling. (Personally, I like planning on paper with an or-
ganizer called Action Day. Many of my clients end up carrying these in their bags too.)

When Maggie and I started on our adding-positives journey, she initially felt overwhelmed. Many of my clients tell me that between working and trying to date, it's tough to find time for much else. Yet a calendar comprised solely of dates and to-dos is not the path to pleasure and mastery. I made the chart below (we'll cover connecting, contributing, and practicing gratitude in more detail in later chapters) for Maggie to use as a reference when she planned her days, so she didn't feel overwhelmed and also didn't miss any essential aspects of optimal living.

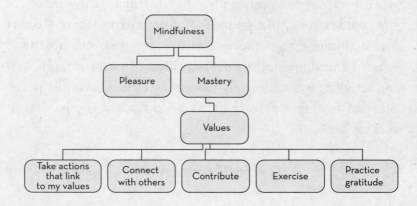

Why Is Exercise on the List?

We all know we should get to the gym, but it's easy to underestimate how powerfully working out will improve your day. Any client who sees me for therapy gets a workout pep talk—I would never want to shortchange anyone from one of the most effective therapeutic interventions. Like adding pleasurable activities to your life, it often feels easier to wait until you feel pumped to get going. (I can't tell you how many clients tell me that they want to lose weight before they start going to the gym.) And if you're not exercising enough (and only 20 percent of Americans do, according to the Centers for Disease Control and Prevention) know that you're not alone, and that now is the perfect time to get moving. If you're feeling depressed or anxious, exercise improves your mood as powerfully as medication does. It also improves sleep, reduces stress, and keeps your mind sharp. A study on hatha yoga found that people who engaged in the mind-body exercise felt more able to cope with distress and were less likely to turn to emotional eating than those in a control group. Personally, I need to do intense cardio for at least forty-five minutes, five days a week, or I don't feel as resilient. There's something about increasing the number of burpees you can do that makes you feel like you are up to facing any hurdle. I also know that I don't enjoy using machines by myself; I much prefer taking motivating classes with others. If you've been meaning to get moving but haven't made that a priority, I'd suggest you pencil in several workouts this week and track how you feel afterward. And if you're already working out, make sure that you're not hyperfocused on perfecting your body for your next date, but determined to invest in your health, since again, your aim is to feel empowered by your values, not depleted by the quest for approval. Needing to look good for someone else is dismissing your inherent worth.

Having a Say in Your Future

We've talked about things you can do to improve your day-to-day life and how you need to adopt a mindful attitude to enjoy what you're doing. But it's also important to consider ways to ensure a meaningful future. When I was in college, I went out with some old friends, and one of them noted that she'd never seen me so studious. In high school, I hadn't taken a single Advanced Placement course. In college, I was double majoring, double minoring, working on my honor's thesis, volunteering, and I had a job. My friend was perceptive. When I started at NYU, I had an epiphany that my life was officially in my hands. Unlike many who rely on eventually sharing responsibilities and expenses with a partner, I never assumed that was an option. My parents divorced when I was six, my mother remarried shortly thereafter, and when I was thirteen, in an unfortunate sequence of events, she had to give my now ex-stepfather my childhood home as a divorce settlement. It hit me then that you can't count on a husband for your security, a painful lesson but one I'm grateful for learning: I needed a plan; I couldn't assume that another person would be my life vest.

Weirdly, though I was reasonably confident that my professional life was within my control, I assumed that I needed a partner to have a fulfilling personal life. If I had known then what I know now, I would have made a list of how I thought my future would improve with a romantic partner. (I didn't do this until I'd been struggling with being single for a decade.)

Let's Talk About Babies (But Only If You Want One) . . .

Speaking of thinking about the future, for many women, that includes deciding whether or not they want children at some point. Since the goal of this chapter is to help you create the life you want, if parenthood is one of your goals, I want to offer you specific information to help you meet that goal, whether you happen to have a partner or not. (If you know you don't want children, feel free to skip this section. I'm not recommending motherhood if that's not one of your values.)

As I've mentioned, I was someone who worried a lot about having children. Yet when I was single, I lamented the prospect of freezing my eggs, assuming that it would be physically and emotionally painful, not to mention time-consuming and expensive. Rather than feeling liberated by medical advances, in anticipating aloneness I said things like, "Well, I guess I'll have to freeze my eggs!" like someone might describe getting a root canal.

Because of my own experience and the fact that many of my clients tell me they feel confused by their fertility options, I thought I'd try to relay some expert information here, especially since scouring Dr. Google for answers isn't a great way to gather wisdom that takes years of medical training to appreciate. One experience that confused me was when my client Alyssa decided to pursue becoming a single mother at forty-one. Years before we met, she'd had her eggs frozen. "If I meet someone, we can have a child together, even if I'm in my late forties. And if I'm still single then, I'll have the option to do it on my own," she told me. Then, when Alyssa's mother had a cancer scare, Alyssa decided to expedite her baby timeline. "I want to see my mother hold my child," she told me. She said she was worried about the costs and logistics of pursuing parenting alone, but decided that this was her priority and she'd make sacrifices. Alyssa went back to the reputable hospital-based program where she'd frozen her eggs in the first place, selected a sperm donor, and got started. One day, soon after, I noticed her crying in my waiting room. When we sat down alone she told me, "It's not good." Apparently, her eggs weren't surviving the thawing process. Each week, when she came in, I was on the edge of my seat hoping for good news. I'd always assumed egg freezing was like conventional banking, where you make a deposit or withdrawal at your leisure.

Ultimately, Alyssa pursued in vitro fertilization (IVF), a process that stimulates ovulation. And recently, she sent me a photo of her mother holding her two-month-old son. Alyssa said she felt fortunate she acted swiftly. If she hadn't decided to do IVF and become a mother when she had, it would have been too late to conceive, her doctor told her.

Alyssa's experience, and those of my clients who express uncertainty about when they should freeze their eggs, inspired me to try to find some guidelines about possibilities for conceiving. Dr. Richard Marrs, a reproductive endocrinologist who made history in 1986 by facilitating the first pregnancy from a thawed frozen embryo, is the founder of California Fertility Partners, one of the first and most respected practices in the country. As I sat in his Santa Monica waiting room ready to interview him, I noticed that the center looked more like a modern upscale spa than a medical practice, and was struck by the number of languages I heard spoken. People had traveled from all over the world for consultations.

When I met Dr. Marrs, in his mid-sixties with a Texas drawl, I found myself thinking that I'd never met someone kinder who had contributed more to his field. Even after decades in practice, he seemed truly elated when he told me about helping someone conceive—and heartbroken when the limits of nature prevailed. In the pages to come, I'll summarize what I learned from him. Sneak preview: Had Alyssa frozen her eggs using today's technology she wouldn't have experienced the months of anguish she'd faced.

How do you know if a fertility clinic is reputable?

Look at the history of a clinic and ask about their success rates. (A big caveat: It's hard to compare clinics because every practice sees a different population. A reputable program may see women who have tried multiple times elsewhere, which is a different case from a person who is trying for the first time. And while there is a movement to get the Centers for Disease Control to clearly report information on fertility center success rates, at this time, that information is hard to come by.) To be safe, make sure that the fertility group you're visiting does *at minimum* 100 to 150 cycles of IVF a year. If a program isn't doing that much IVF, they probably shouldn't be freezing eggs.

When is the best time to freeze your eggs?

Optimally, between the ages of twenty-eight to thirty-four and certainly before age forty (your body stops allocating eggs in menopause).

The younger you are, the better the outcome. A simple ultrasound (costing roughly $200) on the second or third day of your period can let you know the number of eggs in your ovaries and whether that number looks like egg freezing would prove promising.

To successfully freeze eggs, it's important to know how many eggs your body *allocates* or generates. In your twenties, you might allocate twenty-five eggs in a month; in your thirties, it might be around twenty eggs. Everyone is different. The older a woman is, the fewer eggs she'll produce; eggs also decrease in quality with age. For optimal freezing, you want about ten to fifteen eggs frozen in one cycle (which ideally gives you the option to have several children). If you're only allocating four to five eggs a month, or you're what specialists call a *low allocator*, you may need to do egg freezing twice, maybe three times, for the process to be a reliable insurance policy.

What does egg freezing entail?

If you decide that egg freezing is a good option for you, know that the process takes about two weeks and a handful of visits to a fertility practice. Beginning on day two of your period, you start a stimulation program, an injection of follicle-stimulating hormone (FSH) and luteinizing hormone (LH) to trigger egg production. The goal is to override what your pituitary is programmed to do, which is to grow one follicle which contains an egg cell; the drugs get all fifteen follicles to grow to produce more eggs. This takes about ten days and you can inject yourself at home, like administering a little insulin shot. Most of the time, you won't feel any side effects from the FSH and LH stimulation; in fact, many women report feeling good with higher levels of estrogen.

On days two, six, and eight (roughly), you visit your doctor for blood work and an ultrasound to make sure that the follicles are growing. By the tenth day of the injections, the follicles should be mature. That's when you receive a "trigger shot," a medication that tells your pituitary to release eggs just like when you ovulate naturally. Next, you wait a couple of days for the eggs to go through genetic divisions.

Finally, on the fourteenth day after the start of your period, a physician uses an ultrasound to ensure that the follicles have matured. An IV drip of medication (this doesn't require general anesthesia) is administered and a probe is used for egg recovery. Altogether, the process takes about ten minutes, after which you stay in a recovery area for forty-five minutes. Once the eggs are retrieved, you may have PMS-like symptoms (moodiness, breast sensitivity, and fatigue). After the procedure, you shouldn't drive because you've had narcotics, but you could work from home that afternoon or go out to dinner later that night. The next day, you can resume all normal activities. By the end of the day, your doctor will be able to tell you how many mature eggs were frozen that day (with ten to fifteen eggs frozen, a woman can rest assured she'll be able to conceive).

Long-term studies by the National Institutes of Health of more than fifty thousand women suggest that fertility treatments, full of high estrogens, *do not* increase the risk of breast, uterine, or ovarian cancer. Also, these treatments will not prompt menopause or reduce your reproductive lifespan. The one risk in fertility treatments, which applies to women pursuing egg freezing, IVF, or serving as an egg donor, is that if your body generates forty to fifty eggs a month (aka you're a high allocator, which you'd know prior to treatment), you'll need to be closely monitored and minimally stimulated to avoid hyperstimulation and fluid buildup, which results in your ovaries becoming painfully swollen. With advances in technology, this risk is less than 1 percent.

How much does egg freezing cost?

Treatments and medications are expensive, totaling about $10,000. Storing eggs can cost anywhere from $250 to $500 per year. Companies like Google, Yahoo, and Microsoft are providing insurance coverage for egg freezing. There are also programs for veterans to receive coverage for reproductive services. Despite the cost, many women across socioeconomic groups are saving to pursue this process.

What happens once your eggs are frozen?

With new technology known as *vitrification* (a snap-freeze process that takes milliseconds, unlike a slower-freeze process previously used) over 90 percent of eggs frozen end up surviving when thawed. They also fertilize as well as a fresh egg. If you have twelve eggs retrieved, you can expect ten to twelve of them to survive with this method. Eggs aren't at risk of "freezer burn" and can be stored without risk of genetic damage. In fact, in Australia an embryo frozen for sixteen years produced a healthy baby.

When you're ready to be pregnant, the doctor takes sperm (either from a donor or your partner) and fertilizes the eggs, letting them grow in a laboratory for five days. At that point, your doctor can perform genetic testing, then transfers the embryo into your uterus (and stores remaining embryos). To prepare for implantation, you take oral estrogen (no need for shots), and your doctor will monitor your cycle so that the embryo is painlessly transferred when you'd naturally ovulate (no sedation required). The process of thawing, fertilizing, and transferring the embryo costs about $3,000.

What about IVF?

If you're ready to get pregnant (as opposed to storing your eggs for a later date) and you're struggling to conceive naturally, IVF is another option. If you've frozen your eggs, you've basically done the first half of the IVF cycle (where you're trying to stimulate many follicles). But in doing IVF, instead of freezing the eggs, the doctor takes sperm, fertilizes the eggs, and allows the embryos to grow for five days before transferring the embryo to your uterus. Despite stories in the media, it's not advisable to pursue IVF after age forty-four, because the chance of pregnancy at forty-five is about 2 percent. (At age forty-three, your chance of having a baby from IVF technology is about 15 percent). If you're within the recommended age bracket, you should get pregnant within two to three IVF cycles. (Each cycle costs roughly $15,000.) All factors being equal, the success rate for IVF or egg freezing is about the same.

If you want biological children and you're not a great candidate for egg freezing, what are your options?

If you're not generating a lot of eggs, you're under age forty, and you want to get pregnant, you might consider if you're ready to go ahead with pregnancy now using a donor's sperm. Your fertility may be fine. Just because you have a low allocation program doesn't mean you can't get pregnant. With sperm donation, you'd ovulate naturally and then do an insemination each month (and IVF may not be necessary). If cost is a concern, using your natural cycle and a sperm donor is a lot cheaper than egg freezing or IVF. (Usually it's less than $1,000.)

Are men forever fertile?

Contrary to the idea that women age and men are always fertile, a man may have a low sperm count that requires his partner to seek IVF. And even if a man has an adequate count, sperm in men older than forty is correlated with an increased risk of autism and schizophrenia in off-spring.

How do women say they feel after pursuing becoming a single parent?

"I have never had a woman who said she regretted becoming a single parent," Dr. Marrs told me. "I can honestly say that."

After speaking to Dr. Marrs, I walked away feeling like egg freezing is a way for a woman to feel empowered, to feel as if she has options, albeit pricey ones. But if having a child is something that matters to you, there may be financially accessible ways to solve the cost problem. I've had friends and clients who have talked about bravely crowdfunding for this cause, and feel moved by the support they receive. A friend recently made a request that in lieu of wedding gifts, he and his fiancé were interested in checks to help them finance the expensive fertility process they hoped to pursue. He told me that initially he felt awkward telling friends, like me, how to spend their money—but it was worth it, and he was touched by how joyfully (and generously) people wanted to help. (We'll cover more on how giving to others brings you more joy than spending on yourself in chapter 7.)

For women who can't conceive or aren't attached to having

biological children, there are alternatives, like seeking an egg donor or adopting. With the help of an egg donor, women may have the option of carrying a fetus and delivering a baby, and I've had many clients who've spoken gratefully about being able to experience pregnancy using a donor egg (if their eggs aren't viable) with either their partner's sperm or a sperm donor. There are also options to use a surrogate so that another woman carries a pregnancy using either your egg or a donor's egg. Seeking an egg donor and/or surrogate can be pricier (upwards of $30,000) and require legal counsel. If you're pressed financially, there are lower-cost, meaningful alternatives, including becoming a foster parent or contacting organizations like Adoptions Together, which places would-be parents with special-needs infants and children. There's an incredibly moving Web site, Heart Gallery (heartgalleryofamerica.org), that shares information on some of the one hundred thousand children in the United States in need of homes.

How exactly do foster adoption programs work? I wondered. A lot of my clients tell me that they're eager to parent yet concerned about the cost and the prospect of raising a child alone. To learn more about opportunities to become a parent, I reached out to Sarah Boone, a social worker who runs Extraordinary Families, a nonprofit foster family and adoption agency in Los Angeles. Not only does Sarah have professional insight on the process, she's also a single mother who adopted through foster care.

"In L.A. County alone, there are more than twenty thousand children in foster care, ranging in age from two days old to eighteen years old," Sarah told me, poignantly. She is clearly driven by the mission to unite people who value parenting with children needing a nurturing home.

A quick overview of how Sarah's program (and programs

near you) tend to work: To start, prospective parents undergo a background check, attend a two- to three-hour orientation, then complete a five-week training that covers parenting skills, developmental milestones, trauma and loss, and legal information, including the fact that a child may ultimately be reunited with a birth parent. (Reunification happens roughly 50 percent of the time—say, for example, if a parent has struggled with substance abuse and is now doing well.) After that comes a home study, where a social worker meets you several times to learn more about you, so the best possible match can be made between you and your future child. Foster adoption programs take "extraordinary care" in connecting parents with children, Sarah was proud to share. For example, if you're a single woman working long hours who doesn't want to be up all night with a newborn, there may be a school-age child whom a social worker senses you'd absolutely cherish.

After learning about the prevalence of children in need of homes, I felt very moved, but couldn't stop myself from asking, "How can you love a child and potentially have to let them go?" Needless to say, this is a universal process all parents will experience, to some degree, and a perfect example of giving versus getting. "That is the biggest fear," Sarah told me. "And then there is a sense, after the loss, of what a gift I've given, both for another human being, and for society." Considering the number of children looking desperately for a family, offering your home and heart may nicely sync with your value of parenting. "And if your foster child is reunited with family, what do you do?" I wondered. Sarah said that many people foster again, and ultimately secure a permanent adoption, and find meaning in the entire process.

If you know that it would be too difficult to potentially have to part ways with a child whom you've grown to deeply care for, adopting a sibling set or an older child exponentially increases the chances that fostering will end in adoption. I was surprised to learn that there is no cost to pursue this process and that the state actually furnishes a stipend to parents interested in fostering and adopting. Also, unlike private adoptions which may take more time and can cost anywhere from $20,000 to $50,000, you can become a foster parent in as little as four to six months. If you pursue foster adoption, a perk to working with a nonprofit, like Extraordinary Families, is the ongoing help they offer, including counseling as well as activities and support groups to meet others in similar situations.

Once I learned some of the facts about the process, I was excited to hear Sarah's story. She told me that a decade ago, when she was thirty years old, she became a mother to three boys, who were each around fifteen at the time. Teenage boys are the hardest population to match with parents, and she was intent on becoming a mom to these guys. The experience wasn't always easy. Given the losses and traumas children in the foster adoption system experience, they may test parents, protecting their hearts until they know that their parent will be there. She told me that one of her sons called her "Bitch" for several months, then left her a note on her car windshield that read "Mom," and has treated her with love since that day. In reflecting, Sarah says becoming a mother is the most rewarding thing she has done. "My kids are my world," she told me tearfully. Today, she is very close to her sons, whom, despite the adversities they've encountered, she describes as "resilient, remarkable, and compassionate." In addition to relishing being a mother, Sarah also shared that she recently celebrated her engagement to the "love of her life."

Remember too that there are many paths to parenthood. In a BBC interview, Kim Cattrall, known for her role as Samantha on *Sex and the City*, explained, "I am a parent. I have young actors and actresses that I mentor. I have nieces and nephews that I'm very close to. I think the thing I find questionable about being childless or child-free is: 'Are you really?'" she said. "There is a way to become a mother in this day and age that doesn't include your name on the child's birth certificate. You can express that maternal side of you very, very clearly, very strongly. It feels very satisfying." To me, this statement embodies the theme of values being all about how you show up versus what you get (e.g., acting maternal versus having a baby who looks just like you).

I don't want to discount that for many women, egg freezing, adopting, and other fertility procedures are not their first choice; many of us would prefer to conceive at no cost with a lover, and the same holds true for pursuing activities to find pleasure and mastery—it's nice to do these things with a beloved person by your side, rather than alone. Moving forward with any of the options we've covered truly takes a tremendous amount of willingness and courage. I don't want to minimize that. And if you take steps to enrich your life, I hope you focus on celebrating your bravery rather than wishing reality were different.

Practicing Acceptance

For a minute, I'd like to invite you to try an experiment. Think of something you don't like, not something really terrible or something trivial, but a situation that falls somewhere in the middle. Now, for just a minute, while thinking of your selected challenge, tense your muscles, clenching your fists, raising your brows, and bringing your shoulders up to your ears while sitting with this source of pain. What do you notice? I've noticed that when I try this, I can almost give myself a tension headache with the fighting since it creates an additional layer of discomfort. And that's the thing:

The Difference Between Pain and Suffering

Pain = Pain

Pain + Nonacceptance = Suffering

The truth is, in life, there is pain we simply can't eliminate. Sure, you can skip something difficult and catch a quick escape, but then you might find yourself worse off later. Acceptance, while challenging, can also feel liberating. It isn't resignation—it's choosing to honor the pain that is there, a practice known as *radical acceptance*. According to psychologist Marsha Linehan, who describes the pain formula above, radical acceptance is being fully open to what is, just as it is, at this moment. It's not like walking through some magical doorway where you make the decision to accept and there you are, basking in the light. It's more like coming to a fork in the road where you have the option to choose openness rather than attachment to whatever it is that you want that isn't immediately available. That's hard, but you only need to accept *this* moment. And the door is always open to come back to acceptance, again and again. Acceptance makes pain more tolerable, and when things feel too hard to sit with, that's a sign that practicing acceptance will help. Some people assume that acceptance is the opposite of change—it's not, it's an attitude that allows you to change how you feel and can also improve your situation. When we let go of fighting reality, we have more energy to solve problems.

Why is this *radical*? To truly benefit from the power of

acceptance, you need to fully accept, in both mind and body. Accepting something partially is too hard and doesn't count as the therapeutic type of acceptance I'm talking about; that's like doing the splits and finding yourself uncomfortably torn between two territories. A good example of pseudoacceptance was me on my un-yogic retreat. I "accepted" that my friend wouldn't make it and chose to go by myself, but once I was there, I was full of judgmental thoughts, walking around ashamed and constantly debating whether to leave early. Now, I'm not equating my unpleasant couple of days with the tension of something more enduringly painful, like navigating chronic pain or deciding to have a baby on your own. What I want to show is how nonacceptance doesn't work, either with minor frustrations or with more significant ones.

For a moment, I'd like you to think about both a small and a larger source of pain that you need to accept, and consider what you'd do to practice acceptance. I'll share a struggle of my own, which I've mentioned, to illustrate that willingness to accept whatever the pain or frustration is doesn't mean you won't feel distressed, but that you can at least stop torturing yourself. When my first engagement ended, I had to keep focusing on acceptance while repeatedly explaining to people that I wasn't getting married after all (and having to awkwardly put them at ease when they inevitably felt badly for having asked). Doing this was hard, but I made sure I wasn't pouting. Then, when my younger sister got engaged a few months later, I gave her my carefully chosen wedding dress. She altered it dramatically, and it looked beautiful on her. It was painful *and* it was also freeing to contribute to her joy rather than letting that delicate lace gown torment me from deep inside my closet, a reminder of my ended engagement and the thousands of dollars I'd lost as a result.

Another way I accepted my situation was by hoping my ex found the joy he deserved rather than either carrying bad feelings or wishing things had turned out differently. As you'll notice, these are actions and mindsets. There were also times when nonacceptance felt enticing, and I had to recommit to practicing acceptance. I struggled with the fact that my recently deceased grandmother, whom I'd adored, wouldn't know my partner *if I ever found one*, and had to repeatedly remind myself that I wasn't marrying someone just because my grandmother approved or because he would know the beautifully kind woman she was. Since I'd struggled so deeply with my grandmother's death, I also decided to volunteer at a hospice center to get better at sitting with life's impermanence. Acceptance isn't easy, but it's less draining than fighting a battle you'll never win.

For Maggie to reap the benefits of her positive activities, she also had to fully accept her physical pain—notice it without judging it as *getting worse* or *being unfair*, and instead, focus on living well as opposed to waiting to take action until she felt 100 percent better. In fact, acceptance is a huge element in treatment for pain, both physical and emotional. Once she started her new job, Maggie decided she'd start saving money to freeze her eggs, which she told me felt more useful than worrying. She estimated that it would take about a year for her to save enough, and confirmed with her doctor that she could wait until then. Spending more frugally was annoying, but also gave her a sense of mastery.

When we first met, Maggie was full of *if only* thoughts (*if only I didn't have pain, if only I could meet someone, if only . . .*) which were completely unhelpful. Now, she's learned to let herself notice pain without prolonging it or fantasizing about how wonderful her life could have been *if only*. . . . Once you can live your life without *if only*s and instead fill your minutes, hours, and days with activities and people and goals you find meaningful, you'll find that you're able to do more, feel more, and surprise yourself by the joy and beauty you'll begin to notice all around you. It's time to start turning those *if only*s into a phrase I think is much more effective (and mindful): *If not now, when?*

CHAPTER 7

Give More to Feel More

Since you get more joy out of giving joy to others, you should put a good deal of thought into the happiness that you are able to give. —ELEANOR ROOSEVELT

A T A HOLIDAY party, Brooke, a friend of a friend, approached me. "I heard about your book idea. Do you actually believe it's possible to be *happy* while single?" she asked, skeptically. "My life is *so* much better with Trevor." (Brooke is not exactly one for insincere small talk.)

She did look pretty satisfied. The handful of times I'd spoken with her, I felt like I was standing alongside a celebrity. She's naturally pretty and lives lavishly—adorned with a Chanel bag and a rose-gold Rolex. Though she has worked in art galleries in the past, she's now mostly absorbed in traveling and supporting Trevor's endeavors. While money doesn't buy happiness, from what I could see, her husband looked at her dotingly. If anyone were to sell marriage as life-enhancing, it would be Brooke, and I was eager to hear her thoughts and share mine.

"Researchers who study happiness say that much of it has to do with our actions, not just our circumstances," I explained.

Brooke agreed that women today have more options, but

concluded, "I wouldn't feel content without Trevor." Then she sighed. "I feel sorry for people struggling to meet someone. Dating is awful."

I didn't entirely agree. "Dating *is* hard," I said gently, "but holding on to the idea that a person is your only path to happiness makes it worse. If you're not meeting someone, there's still so much to cherish, as long as you're able to let go of the idea that you're somehow less-than if you're not coupled. . . ."

At that point, Brooke interrupted to ask: "Do *you* get the stress of being single since you're married?" I told her that I'd spent most of my adult life single and could easily access that experience, even from my current vantage point in a satisfying relationship.

Though our opinions certainly diverged, I was moved by Brooke's authenticity. Truthfully, seeing Brooke did make me feel slightly envious. I love my career and don't think beauty or niceties can fulfill anyone forever, but she did seem to relish her life. And her days didn't seem as stressful as mine, which consisted of rushing to work, living in an apartment that seemed to have an unfixable mysterious stench, and generally feeling unglamorous. If I had to choose my life or hers, I'd choose mine, but there's something about appearances that stirs up craving.

So I was surprised to learn, just a few months after my debate with Brooke, that her beloved husband Trevor had been caught red-handed in a dramatic affair with someone else. I felt truly sorry for her, especially since it seemed as if so much of her existence centered around her marriage and her husband. It wasn't my place to reach out since she was a friend of a friend, and our shared friend warned me that Brooke wanted privacy. But I found myself picturing what I would say if I did talk with her. (I admit, I sometimes find it tempting to offer unsolicited input, as some of my family members will attest.) I imagined that Brooke might be questioning her self-worth, as I've seen many clients do, adding to the heartbreak of Trevor's infidelity. I wished I could somehow cheer her on and encourage her to practice self-compassion and expand her sense of purpose.

Watching one too many romantic comedies can drive us to look to fill our sense of worth and meaning through a relationship. Deciding to shift your approach to find appreciation intrinsically, rather than through external validation, can feel challenging, especially when you're in the throes of feeling betrayed by a person or exasperated by the process of dating. But while it's certainly nice to get adoration from others, especially someone you love, looking to another person for fulfillment leaves you vulnerable, robbing you of the essential life practice of good self-care. Taking care of yourself isn't about settling for being single. It's something you deserve whether you're in a relationship or not. In this chapter, you'll learn how to experience some of what people tend to long for from a lover, independent of one.

Why Do We Need to Do So Much?

In life, a long apology can't always cancel out a hurtful word. In Brooke's eyes, Trevor's years of generosity would never redeem him for his unfaithfulness. This phenomenon brings to mind a paper Roy Baumeister wrote titled "Bad Is Stronger than Good." Just like it sounds, the paper describes how upsetting events shake us more than good ones. From a survival perspective, it makes sense that pain persists in our memory—we don't want to get bitten by a snake twice. But since we're programmed to respond intensely to pain, for balance and life enhancement we also need to strategize ways to cultivate enduring positive emotions.

I've found that there are some effective, lasting ways to soothe yourself, which I'll sum up below.

If you are struggling with:		To cope, you'll learn to:
Self-criticism	→	Develop self-compassion
Feelings of worthlessness	→	Contribute to others
Believing that nothing is going well	→	Practice gratitude

How Self-Compassion Works

To start, let's talk about self-criticism and its opposite, self-compassion. When you feel rejected by others, it's tempting to look at yourself as though under a magnified LED-lit mirror, inspecting and poking at your perceived flaws while forgetting that these most likely aren't visible to anyone else and don't capture who you are as a multidimensional person. I've seen many women do this, including my client Rachel, whom I mentioned in the introduction to this book. Rachel, I noticed, spent a lot of time harping on what might be wrong with her, quickly listing off: "thinning hair, thick thighs, too stressed . . ." Like Rachel, many people assume that being self-critical keeps us motivated to meet our goals. As she explained, "If I can't manage to go on a few dates with even a mediocre guy, there's clearly something wrong with me. . . ." Yet, as we've talked about, research consistently confirms that it's self-compassion, not self-criticism, that keeps us growing and changing. Over time, by considering the pros and cons of being hard on herself, Rachel realized that it made sense for her to find an alternative way of being. She decided to try to catch these automatic judgments and replace them with kinder, more truthful words. "It can feel hard to meet someone you feel close to," she eventually said. I was glad to hear her speaking in a sympathetic tone since being overcritical increases the risk of facing emotional and psychological difficulties.

Self-criticism doesn't work in your relationship with yourself, or in relationships with other people; it's associated with heightened feelings of rejection and marital dissatisfaction. People who are better able to access self-compassion, on the other hand, are described by their partners as more emotionally connected. Self-criticism depletes us, while self-care makes us more endearing; the latter is associated with healthier romantic relationships and an enhanced ability to give to others. Just as it's hard to physically offer someone something you don't possess, some say, if you struggle with feeling compassion toward yourself, it might feel challenging to experience compassion for others.

So, what is self-compassion, exactly? Initially, Rachel confused it with self-esteem, assuming that our goal in therapy was to convince her of her strengths. "But that feels kind of fake," she told me. I agreed. Compassion, I explained, is more about accepting that all human beings are imperfect and will face pain. What I wanted her to try to do, specifically, was to practice the steps of self-compassion that expert and author Kristen Neff delineates. These include *self-kindness*, which means caring for yourself rather than judging yourself, seeing yourself as a part of a *common humanity* rather than as a woman alone. I also told Rachel that it was important for her to be *mindful*, to take notice of thoughts and feelings, rather than dismissing or exaggerating them.

Together, we worked on moving away from self-critical words and toward doing things to treat herself better, like responding as she would to a friend in need of support. Self-compassion isn't supposed to be a perfect substitute for love from others; I see it as a way not to feel *worse*. After all, going out with someone you don't see yourself with, then feeling snubbed when that person doesn't see himself with *you*, is sufficiently annoying without additional self-critical nit-picking. I went so far as to suggest that she rub her own tense-looking shoulders, and she shot me a sarcastic look. I rolled with her skepticism, knowing we'd have to take this step by step, and tried instead to focus on noticing that every person she'd ever come across had felt hurt by someone else at some point—a more realistic and less torturous perspective than feeling like you alone have been singled out for pain. We also worked on her letting go of the prediction that her bad feelings would go on and on, and instead to sit with her current experience just as it was in this moment.

A Cynic's Guide to Self-Compassion

At times therapy sessions can feel like an energetic tennis rally, with lots of shots back and forth, which was often the case with Rachel, who certainly added liveliness to my normally mellow office. "I'm not trying to seem rude," she said, "but this compassion stuff isn't me. I'm not touchy-feely and I'm not delusional so I won't be sitting alone in bed, surrounded by scented candles, pretending to experience inner peace and self-love," she said bluntly. In some ways, Rachel reminded me of myself. When I tried to practice loving-kindness meditation (a technique you'll soon learn), my initial reaction was something like *this is sweet but it won't really make a difference in my life*. I first learned Loving-Kindness Meditation (LKM) from Sharon Salzberg on a mindfulness retreat that was advertised to "Open Your Heart in

Paradise." I was there because my yoga teacher happened to be on the program. Since I was working on living my dream life single, I jumped at the chance to practice vigorous yoga and enjoy the beach. The other participants, many wearing tunics and beads, told me that they'd traveled for the lineup of spiritual gurus, and they seemed to quickly access an ecstatic state, frenetically dancing to yoga singer Krishna Das's live devotional music, with their eyes closed. I felt more inhibited, but I tried not to criticize myself for it and made the decision that I needed to experiment with LKM. Soon after, I found myself uplifted and connected, then quickly and skeptically wondered if I was just being overly impressionable. After all, I was surrounded by people who seemed blissfully free. But I decided that I didn't need to analyze; my doubts were just my mind trying to spoil my freedom. In my personal quest for inspiration, I didn't want to obsess over why something moved me; I just wanted to go with it.

As a professional, however, I aim to link the approaches I teach to science. Were Rachel's reservations about self-compassion warranted? Barbara Fredrickson, the professor I mentioned earlier who studies the power of positive emotions, researched the very LKM I learned from Sharon, a practice that involves directing feelings of kindness to both yourself and others. In a randomized control trial, Fredrickson and her colleagues looked at whether thinking more loving thoughts would improve people's lives, offering employees at a Detroit technology company six hour-long meditation sessions, each including roughly twenty minutes of LKM. The sessions also included twenty minutes for questions, and twenty minutes of suggestions for daily practice. On average, participants also tried the LKM for eighty minutes over the course of the week on their own. In total, they practiced for roughly fifteen minutes a day. Here's what Fredrickson and her team found: Upon completing LKM training and using the approach on their own between meetings, participants experienced increased feelings of love, joy, gratitude, and contentment, as well as self-acceptance, mindfulness, and positive relations with others. *"The evidence reveals that one way to outpace the hedonic treadmill is to begin a practice of LKM,"* she wrote. While these improvements took time to appear, peaking at the end of the course, the employees did in fact report heightened life satisfaction.

Fredrickson once predicted that positive emotions expand our thinking and attention, which prevents us from getting stuck in a narrow place of threat and instead creates ample opportunities for connection. Her theory, called "broaden and build," explains that it's hard to create lasting joy when you're coming from a negative place. You have the choice to either solidify that pessimism or purposefully generate more positivity.

What worked for Fredrickson's study subjects can work for you too. You don't need to wait for a lover (or anything else) to improve your life. Each one of us, like Rachel, can find ourselves painfully alone or try to generate good vibes, which makes us magnets for even more closeness. Taking a bit of time to think loving thoughts toward others every day can heighten your happiness, particularly if you're caught in negative feelings around dating. After all, a problem inherent in dating is that there are no guarantees you'll meet someone whom you'll feel a loving connection to—which can understandably make you feel rather cynical. As an alternative to falling into frustration, LKM offers an immediate opportunity to build positive feelings. If you're prone to self-judgment, this practice will you help you exercise a competing skill set, one that works as an antidote to ruminating and helps buffer you from stressful events. In case you're concerned about the time involved, to be clear, I'm suggesting spending roughly five to fifteen minutes of being mindfully present (as we'll cover in later chapters) and doing five to fifteen minutes of loving-kindness meditation each day. Hopefully, you'll discover that these breaks will actually save you time from having to recover from negative experiences.

If you'd like to give loving-kindness a try, do a quick Web search (type "Sharon Salzberg loving-kindness meditation" into your search engine) and you'll find a YouTube video of Sharon guiding the practice. If you'd prefer to read instructions and guide yourself, the box below offers an overview. As with any meditation, if your mind moves off topic, come back to the moment, with compassion (what an appropriate time to treat yourself with kindness and remember that all minds wander).

How to Practice Loving-Kindness Meditation

Sit upright, with your eyes either closed or open and focused on a single point (wandering eyes can lead to wandering minds). For five minutes, go through the list of groups below, and pick someone in each category to offer the loving-kindness statements that follow: (For example, for my benefactor, I thought of my treasured grandfather, Emil. He's deceased but I can still really picture him, focused and joyful, and I'd consider each sentence slowly: *May he be safe. . . . May he be happy. . . .* In bringing his image to mind, I immediately feel warmth and gratitude, then I move on to myself.)

- ♥ A benefactor (someone who naturally inspires loving feelings, perhaps someone who has helped or inspired you)
- ♥ Yourself ("May I be safe. . . ." "May I be happy. . . .")
- ♥ Someone you know is having a hard time (e.g., Brooke)
- ♥ A familiar face (e.g., your mail carrier)
- ♥ A difficult person (e.g., a neighbor with an incessantly barking dog)
- ♥ All beings, everywhere

The statements of loving-kindness go as follows:

May _____ be safe. May _____ be happy.
May _____ be healthy. May _____ live with ease.

Spend about one to two minutes on a person from each of these categories, really picturing your chosen person as you repeat the phrases above. Also, consider what it would look like for your people to experience the well-wishes above.

When I first learned LKM, I found myself trying to come up with original people for each category every day, which felt more like an exercise in creativity and took me away from focusing on the good intentions themselves. Ultimately, it was more helpful for me to think of a set person for each of the categories above and then generate deeper feelings, rather than scratch the surface and move on to another person the next day. You may want to stick with your selected people for a week or a month, whatever seems like a good plan for you.

While I believe that LKM will improve your life, my hope is that you're not simply practicing for *you*, but more sincerely fostering compassion for both yourself and others. I like to do this practice when I see people who are homeless—I don't necessarily want to offer money yet it seems callous to disregard another's struggle. If you tend to worry about others in a way that won't actually help them, as I found myself doing when I heard about Brooke's betrayal, these practices may feel like a more productive way of harnessing your mental energy. Recently, I mentioned to a psychologist friend who lived right across the street from a newly opened top-rated coffee shop that I'd been going out of my way to pick up my morning espresso there, and was surprised when my words led to a concerned look on her face. "I don't go there," she told me. I looked puzzled so she continued, "The man who's had a coffee cart on the corner for years is my 'familiar face' in my LKM and I'm sure his business is hurting now, so I'm religious about staying loyal to him." I was moved by how her practice had led her to build a loving connection with a relative stranger.

Similarly, if you think that focusing a lot on breathing seems irrelevant, this approach might feel like a purposeful addition to your mindfulness practice. Strategically, you can even practice LKM while walking, driving, or waiting in line. You may discover that you end up in a more pleasant frame of mind than if you'd let your mind run wild.

How does LKM work? The practice is a powerful form of *mental rehearsal*. As I explained to Rachel, when you envision something, you activate the same part of the brain that is actually used to perform that behavior. In a study where participants were asked to imagine a "sunny sky," their pupils dilated as if they were actually in the sun, which suggests that imagining is actually preparing. Athletes and performers of all kinds use mental rehearsal to get ready for challenging realities; this strategy has even been considered for surgeons performing complicated neurosurgery, to improve accuracy.

Mental rehearsal isn't just about performance; it's also about managing emotions. In DBT there's a strategy known as *coping ahead* which involves realistically imagining challenges you'll face and mentally rehearsing how you'll navigate. Unlike avoiding or worrying, this tool prepares you for the future in a productive way. One way Rachel coped ahead was by practicing LKM before she went on dates, knowing she had a tendency to disapprove of herself and her prospective partner. Instead of allowing herself to fall into that tendency, she generated more uplifting, compassionate emotions and noticed that she ended up feeling more patient and connected with both herself and her dates.

Contributing Is a Win-Win Opportunity

So far, we've touched on increasing loving thoughts to heighten our positive feelings and actions. Now, we'll focus on why giving to others matters. One of the worst feelings is worthlessness. And one of the biggest sources of meaning is feeling like you're making an impact. When I ask my clients about what they yearn for when they think about how much they want a romantic relationship, a lot of them generously describe wanting to lovingly do sweet things for someone, like buying a new crush's favorite black licorice from a hidden specialty store. It's exciting to map out ways to make a person's day, especially if you get to witness that person erupt into a surprised grin. But to enhance your sense of well-being and reduce depending on a lover to act lovingly, I suggest that my clients think about other ways to give that are linked to their values.

Contributing can serve as a powerful reminder of your unique strengths and also as a perspective-enhancing vacation from fo-cusing on your struggles. Recently, I was feeling grumpy, mostly due to unhelpful thoughts like *I've had this flu for weeks and have so much to do that will never get done.* . . . Then, coincidentally, I saw someone I'd recognized from a GoFundMe campaign, a young man, Demonte, who was shot twenty-eight times outside his home in a rough neighborhood in a random act of violence. Before his trauma, Demonte had worked at a juice bar I fre-quented. Though I'd never seen him there, his story quickly spread and I wondered about him. Then, in the middle of my perceived stress, I noticed him standing at the juice store visiting his old coworkers. I recognized him from his photo and ap-proached him to tell him that I'd been thinking of him, asked how he was feeling, and complimented his strength. I was blown away when he answered, "Pretty good," and offered me a mas-sive smile and hug. My entire week shifted, and though I'd hardly given much, just hoping he was well and offering a few affirming words expanded my attention in remarkable ways (im-mediately, I felt fortunate to merely have the flu).

My chance encounter was lucky, but purposefully putting yourself in a place that enables you to see your life more flexibly is always possible—and can reliably improve your mood. Like LKM (which counts as contributing), doing things for others creates positive emotions that build a chain of experiences that enhance your well-being. In a multisite study on the effects of giving, spearheaded by psychologist S. Katherine Nelson and her colleagues at the University of California, Riverside, people were asked to do something either for themselves or for others. The researchers found that giving to others improved the partic-ipants' moods more powerfully than self-soothing. The authors concluded: "People who are striving to improve their happiness may be tempted to treat themselves to a spa day, a shopping trip, or a sumptuous dessert . . . however, when happiness seekers are tempted to treat themselves, they might be more successful if they opt to treat someone else instead."

This research reminded me of a friend of mine who tried a novel solution to a broken heart. Years ago, when walking away from a painful relationship, she bumped into a person who handed her a pamphlet describing an organization that financially supports children in impoverished countries. When she got home, she did a bit of research and was moved to discover that a nominal contribution would cover a child's school supplies and lunches for a year. She signed up and soon after, received periodic letters in Spanish written in thick crayons from a grateful little boy; she joked about losing a bad boyfriend and finding herself a good kid. When her parents complained that they had no grandchildren, she told them they had a grandson in Colombia. And when dates didn't go well and her job felt pointless, thinking about her role in this boy's life immediately lifted her up. My friend's experience has been replicated in research. Positive psychology expert Elizabeth Dunn and her team looked at differences in emotions after spending on either oneself or another person. They found that donating even $5 contributed to happiness more significantly than spending on oneself. With holidays like Valentine's Day and concepts like romantic gestures, it can be easy to forget the joyful fact that there are so many other ways to show your loving self.

Thinking Through the Details

When we first started meeting, Rachel told me that she felt like she was withering away, that trying to act upbeat at work and on dates felt like a "pointless waste of time and energy." Since her problem was feeling like she was giving and not getting much back, we worked on her trying to give in a way that felt more meaningful but also feasible. Some of the ideas we came up with included her spending a bit of time talking to her roommate (who was also having a hard time) and mailing a sick relative a care package. When she did these things, she reported back that they enhanced her sense of purpose more than listening to a guy on a date ramble on. These generous actions took a bit of energy, but ultimately left her more invigorated.

To help create time for giving back we targeted ways she could let go of activities that depleted her. As I mentioned, Rachel worked in the wedding industry, and received frantic e-mails from engaged couples at all hours. We decided that she would stop responding after work. (When she did, she stopped receiving constant messages that made her feel like her own needs came second to those of people marrying.) My wise friend and NYU chaplain Rabbi Yehuda Sarna suggests making space for contributing in your life by telling friends or an employer: "On Tuesdays, I tutor someone and I need to be there at 6 p.m. Would it be possible for me to routinely leave at that time, and I can work later on Wednesdays?" After all, just because you don't have a child doesn't mean people don't depend on you. You deserve to show up for these people. Remembering that truth will increase your self-respect and generate respect from others.

There will be times when you give, and you don't feel particularly moved. Once, when I was struggling and also volunteering, I visited an elderly woman with dementia and cancer. Sometimes, I felt like my life had meaning if I could offer this lovely woman something; other times, I found myself mired in less generous thoughts, like: *It's not fair, I try my best to do right and can't meet anyone who tries to do the same*, which, as you'd expect, made my mood plummet, and was a distraction. It helped to remind myself that right in the middle of contributing, we may not always feel as positively as we'll ultimately feel. Again, the intent is giving, not getting; volunteering isn't a loan of goodness that will be returned to you. There were many days when my older friend acted angrily, accusing me of not visiting for months (due to her illness), which didn't feel good in the moment. Eventually, though, I focused on why I had signed up to visit her in the first place: to offer love, not receive it. As with any activity, it makes sense to think about what may work well for us to maintain the habit. Would you rather volunteer with a group, like Habitat for Humanity, or one-on-one, as a Big Sister? Would it make more sense for you to give less formally but routinely, such as offering sincere compliments to people who may otherwise go unnoticed? Also, think about which populations pull at your heartstrings: Children? Seniors? Pets? Once you've generated a few ideas, do some research, then mark your calendar with plans to help others.

Rachel and I let go of the goal of her feeling better and instead aimed for her to give her best. In a study led by empathy expert Sara Konrath, researchers found that volunteering for selfless reasons increased longevity, but only when acts of kindness were performed generously, rather than for self-oriented reasons. There are opportunities like singles meet-ups at soup kitchens or charity committees that offer the chance to both give back and also meet new people. These seem like great ways to meet like-minded souls with good hearts, but to heighten the power of giving, if you find your attention divided between trying to find a partner and focusing on a cause, it might be smart to supplement these sorts of events with ones that feel more purely altruistic.

Skip the "It Could Be Worse" Speech

It can feel incredibly frustrating when someone tells you to "look at everything that's going for you" or to "think of the positives" in a distressing situation. After my breakup, someone congratulated me, saying, "At least you've spared yourself a divorce!" Not surprisingly, this didn't make me suddenly feel lucky. I think the approach of quickly trying to look for the good is bound to backfire, because it feels dismissive of pain. A crucial part of self-compassion is *noticing* pain and adding kindness.

So instead of trying to find good in the middle of an upsetting experience, which seems like trying to avoid accepting discomfort (in chapter 9, you'll learn more about acknowledging your emotions as they unfold), you might consider practicing a few minutes of gratitude at a more opportune time. Just as practicing compassion reduces your tendency to think critically or pessimistically, if you're prone to seeing the negative, purposefully scheduling windows to redirect your attention to appreciate what's going well can create good feelings and protect you from hopelessness. Many of my clients, especially ones who tend to be perfectionists, selectively remember how they "messed up" but overlook when they've done something right. So instead of lying awake circling over your mistakes and ongoing to-dos, a nice alternative may be practicing gratitude for a couple of minutes, then spending a moment purposefully noticing what you've done well, which also seems like a better way to prepare for a good night's sleep. Rachel could readily list what was going wrong, but it took more effort to think of what was going right for her (e.g., health, good friends). These brief practices helped Rachel build a more thankful mindset.

One of my favorite lessons in gratitude comes from sociologist and bestselling author Martha Beck in her book *Expecting Adam*. She recounts a special moment with her son, Adam, who has a diagnosis of Down syndrome. For Christmas, she wrapped a gift and also wrapped a set of batteries, separately. Adam saw the package of batteries first, ripped open the paper, and assumed the batteries were his gift. He jumped up and down, overjoyed and overwhelmed with appreciation for all of the uses of household batteries. Over the years, when I'm struggling, I try to think about Adam's appreciation. I don't want to minimize pain; there is so much of it to face at times. Yet researchers explain that spending a few minutes each day noticing what you feel grateful for truly does increase happiness.

Take a Quick Gratitude Break

♥ For just two minutes, I invite you to think of what you are grateful for. (Be sure not to judge what's on your list as being too small or worry that you don't deserve what you have.)

♥ Then take a minute to notice what you've accomplished today that you feel proud of.

♥ How do you feel after this exercise?

♥ Is there a time each day when you can schedule in gratitude?

Like LKM and contributing, creating a gratitude routine doesn't need to take too much time. Spending just a couple of minutes each day listing three things you feel grateful for (in an app, notebook, or with a friend) will feel better than zooming in on what didn't go well that day or scrolling over depressing news. According to psychologist Robert Emmons, gratefulness feels more replenishing than comparing yourself to others; the latter makes you feel less-than or regretful. In a study led by researcher Adam Geraghty and his colleagues, people prone to worry were told to list up to six things a day that they felt grateful for. This simple exercise boosted their hope as powerfully as more complicated strategies like challenging unhelpful thoughts.

One of the reasons gratitude matters, as I told Rachel, is that it not only improves our mood and our health (people who feel thankful are better able to relax and sleep, and even tend to exercise more), but it also increases the ability to connect with others. People like Demonte and Beck's son, Adam, with their grateful ways, are instantly endearing. In a study spearheaded by social psychologist Lisa Williams, high school students were paired with mentors. Later, mentors who received a handwritten thank-you note (and were told that it was written by the mentee) rated the mentee as warmer and expressed more interest in continuing a relationship with the student, even offering contact information to stay in touch. Once again, the words I've heard my clients repeat, that they need to "play it cool" on dates, don't hold up. People are attracted to those who are grateful, but gratitude is also a powerful way for *you* to remember that there is good in your life, no matter how bad dating can feel. As speaker and author Byron Katie asks, "Do you want to meet the love of your life? Look in the mirror." When you see your incredible self, you won't feel like your worth lies outside of you and you'll also be more likely to keep good company.

CHAPTER 8

Detox Your Mind

It is the mark of an educated mind to be able to entertain a thought without accepting it.　　—ARISTOTLE

I WAS A virgin when I graduated college," confessed Jessica, a graceful thirty-three-year-old teacher during one of our initial sessions together. "I didn't want a drunk encounter with someone I'd never see again." That seemed reasonable enough, except she then worried that she'd made "too big a deal of sex," and that her lack of experience would appear "awkward" to anyone she met now that she had graduated. So, at twenty-five, instead of focusing on finding the connection she craved, she decided to "just get it over with to seem normal," and slept with someone she met one night at a bar. "I was semi-drunk," she acknowledged. After that, since she'd given up on making sex "special," she slept with a bunch of other guys to, as she explained, "feel ready" for when she met someone who mattered.

As I looked at Jessica, I thought about the stories I've heard from other patients who've gone through similar patterns of hopeless thinking, which can hold us back from what we want in love—and life. I feel a sense of genuine empathy when people describe ways they bump into pain, like Jessica, who told me about not only feeling hurt, but also contracting an STD in her quest to feel "normal" with regard to relationships. She got me thinking about how quickly certain ideas can permeate our minds, then go on to affect our moods and actions, all of which makes it more difficult to let our values guide our behavior. In this chapter, you'll learn to watch your thoughts so that you can remain true to what matters most to you.

Jessica valued emotional closeness and wanted sex to feel meaningful. That is, until fear took over and thoughts like *I waited too long* and *Something must be wrong with me* eroded her feelings of self-worth. Then she felt she had no choice but to turn the experience of intimacy into a training camp rather than something to savor. To be clear, I'm not saying that all sex merits the sanctity of romance or even knowing your partner's last name; that decision is up to you and your inner wisdom. What I want to stress is how our thoughts influence our self-perception and behaviors, going on to shape our life experiences.

A powerful example of how thoughts can torture us comes from Memorial Sloan Kettering pain specialist Gavril Pasternak, who tells the story of a woman treated for breast cancer who comes in worried about pain in her back, convinced that the disease has returned. Once Pasternak examines her and gives her the relieving news that she is cancer-free, her discomfort drops to the point that she no longer needs pain medication. Mental events can create real physical feelings. Like the cancer patient, Jessica could have reduced her suffering if she hadn't jumped to such disheartened conclusions.

If your intention is to build a life that you love, right now, it's hard to imagine embracing that process with a negative playlist on repeat in your head. Linda, a fifty-five-year-old client, repeatedly explained to me: "Men my age want to date women in their forties. That means I can either force myself to date someone who is eighty or deal with loneliness." Her ex-husband, she told me, had found a new younger love, which was bad enough. But her habit of foreseeing lying next to an octogenarian was debilitating. I'm not a prophet so I couldn't make Linda any promises, but I felt certain that pessimistic thinking wasn't making her life better.

Seeing Your Mind

Do you ever notice yourself having thoughts that aren't improving your quality of life, like Jessica or Linda? Take a minute to list a few of these. In the pages to come, we'll experiment with ways to get unstuck from these unhelpful thoughts but before we get there, let's cover some practical information on managing feelings. If you can mindfully notice your thoughts and emotions, catching them before they intensify, you'll have an easier time coping. Research from James Gross, an expert in the science of regulating emotions, has found that the sooner you intervene and try to change a negative emotion, the better—though any time is better than never. In Linda's case, I explained that she'd have an easier time managing her hopeless feelings if she was able to notice the thought *My only dating option is an eighty-year-old*. Then she could consciously reconsider that thought, reminding herself that she isn't psychic, so how could she know? In contrast, by not noticing her thoughts and intervening by treating herself kindly earlier in the negativity cycle, Linda was at risk of descending into a pit that would be hard to get out of, running with a negative prediction that might not happen, then ruminating on it until she was in tears.

Notice how I said that Linda could pay attention to and shift her thoughts, not suppress them. In one of his most famous articles, Gross looked at what happened when people tried to push away thoughts versus change their thoughts. He discovered that the act of suppressing (as we covered in chapter 4) gets in the way of experiencing and expressing joy. Thinking differently, on the other hand, can increase feelings of well-being, reduce negative emotions, and increase connection with others (more on this in chapter 10). In Linda's case, that might mean changing the thought *Only eighty-year-olds will like me* to *I'd like to date someone who cherishes me and whom I'm attracted to.*

Like many of the single clients I meet, Linda felt pretty sure that the only cure for her situation was to secure a partner. She also warned me that in the past, the kind of stress she was experiencing had dragged her down into a serious depression. Linda's words were insightful. The more we think certain thoughts, the more they show up automatically. If your thoughts are negative, they can create unpleasant moods that make you susceptible to more sad thoughts, and on and on. Thoughts, moods, and sensations have a way of merging and building on each other; once they get going, they can seem endless.

A Dose of Mindfulness

There's a way, however, to help prevent depression in people at risk, like Linda. Cognitive psychologist Zindel Segal and his team discovered that teaching patients Mindfulness-Based Cognitive Therapy (MBCT), an approach that teaches people to become more aware of negative moods and thoughts, then to observe those moods and thoughts to prevent a depressive spiral and interrupt the negative cycle. Segal and his colleagues developed an eight-week program that teaches people how to focus on day-to-day experiences, like physical sensations and breathing, then apply a similar nonjudgmental approach to their thoughts and emotions. By practicing skills such as scanning our body, watching our breath, and noticing subtleties we often tend to overlook (like the taste of a single raisin), it's possible to attend to details like facial tension and random thoughts. Impressively, studies on MBCT confirm that the training is as effective as medication in reducing the risk of relapsing into depression.

I'm not suggesting that people struggling with depression shouldn't take medication. What I'm highlighting is that practicing mental strategies can help you avoid a prolonged mood dip, even if you feel vulnerable or slightly down. The techniques used in MBCT can help with a wider range of issues too. In a Brown University study on social stress and depression led by researcher Willoughby Britton, people were given five minutes to prepare for a speech, then told to present it, with no notes, using a microphone, while standing in front of bright lights, cameras, and a judge who (unbeknownst to the presenters) had been instructed to give no feedback. (Just writing about this makes me anxious!) The subjects who learned MBCT felt less anticipatory anxiety and recovered more quickly after their speeches, compared to those who hadn't learned the techniques. What this means is that increasing awareness of thoughts can facilitate recovery in tough situations. Not only does mindfulness reduce pain, practicing paying attention seems to enhance joy. In a study at the University of Oxford, led by experts Gaëtan Cousin and Catherine Crane, healthy adults who participated in

MBCT reported increased positive moods, possibly because they were less apt to engage in self-critical thinking, compared to those who hadn't done the program.

One of my mottoes is that talk (and thoughts) are cheap without actions to go along with them. So I'd like to have you try some ways to begin to practice mindfulness. The truth is, however clearly you grasp the concept of mindfulness, you won't get the benefits unless you try it, though I wish I could get the same benefit from understanding principles as I do from applying them to my life, since I love to read and don't really enjoy slowing down. The good news is that you don't have to put in a lot of time meditating to reap the benefits. When I was on Segal's mindfulness retreat for therapists, he told us that MBCT graduates who practiced what they'd learned for just *three minutes* a day (most people practiced the breathing space you'll learn in the next chapter) were able to maintain their mindful progress! So when clients ask me how long I recommend practicing meditation, I suggest three to twenty minutes a day, ideally at the same time every day (maybe right after your morning coffee), since making something a habit reduces effort. That said, you're the expert in your own life, so do what works best for you.

Know too that there are so many resources available to help you become comfortable with mindfulness. If you like learning in a group setting, there are mindfulness classes offered in many cities throughout the country. There are also books, including Sharon Salzberg's *Real Happiness*, that offer great how-to advice on getting started. Many of my clients enjoy mindfulness apps and talks on the topic, such as Tara Brach's podcasts and the guided practices on the Web site of Dan Harris, author of *10% Happier*.

Now, LET'S ACT MINDFUL:

Three Minutes Toward a Healthier Life

I'd love for you to take a few minutes to give mindful breathing a try. Mindfulness includes tracking your thoughts. To do that, you need to learn to pay attention. Begin by setting a timer for three to ten minutes. Sit in a relaxed position, with your spine tall. If you're sitting in a chair, place your feet firmly on the ground; if you're on the floor, fold your legs comfortably. Once your body is in a position that's comfortable and sustainable, it's easier for your mind to get on board. Next, bring your full attention to your breathing, just noticing each inhale and exhale. What's so important about focusing on breathing? Well, since the breath is always there, it's continuously available for you to use as a focal point. As mindfulness master Jon Kabat-Zinn says, "As long as you are breathing, there is more right with you than wrong, no matter how ill or hopeless you may feel." I love that sentiment and I hope that your breath reminds you of that fact. As you try to focus on your breathing, know that your mind will probably wander. That's totally normal. Instead of concluding that you've *failed*, then giving up and following your train of thought wherever it goes (*What's on my to-do list?*), aim to see distractions as a time to practice compassionately coming back to your breath.

Helpful or Not

Now that we've touched on one of the first steps toward mindfulness—specifically cultivating attention by focusing on your breath—I want to tell you how that habit will help you think differently. Observing the breath builds the skill of watching, which, in the same way, helps us learn to notice our thinking without getting stuck in thoughts. The point is to notice any unhelpful thoughts, then untangle from these thoughts to regain some perspective, using the techniques outlined below:

Option 1: Some of my clients worry about simply watching their distressing thoughts and letting them go in case some of those thoughts happen to actually be useful. If you notice yourself thinking thoughts that might be helpful, you can invest time trying to think in a healthier way, a technique known as *cognitive reappraisal*. Life is often ambiguous (particularly when it comes to dating), which means there are lots of ways we can interpret things. So why default to the worst possible conclusion? Instead, you can change the way you interpret a situation— or *reappraise* it—so that it's more constructive. Jessica, for instance, could notice her thought that sex would feel *awkward*, and reappraise that thought to something like: *I'll know someone is respectful if he honors my needs.*

Try thinking more usefully yourself. If you go on a date and the person never calls, instead of just deciding, *I'm unlikable*, reflect on whether there is something relevant to the situation that's worth considering, such as: *I was in a bad mood and distracted. Next time I'll* . . . By transforming an unhelpful conclusion into more accurate information, you can use your mind to solve problems rather than create undue distress.

Option 2: When your thoughts are clearly unhelpful (e.g.,

I'm going to be alone unless I want to date a man with dentures), and they feel so upsetting and overwhelming that reappraisal seems out of reach, you can try something called *mindfulness of thoughts*. This technique means looking at your thoughts in a different way—as mere mental events rather than realities. Simply put, mindfulness is thinking differently about thinking. Just because you have a thought doesn't mean you must believe that thought. This approach is a healthier alternative to ruminating, which is inviting thoughts in and focusing on them obsessively.

My hope is that you'll experiment with both of these techniques. Studies suggest that each of them can lift you out of a sad mood, though reappraising may take a bit more mental effort. What's nice is that these two strategies work synergistically. The more mindful you are, the more readily you'll be able to change your thoughts. And both techniques are easier than feeling hopeless!

Fact-check Your Own Thoughts

To reappraise your thoughts, you can check the factual content of what you're thinking or saying. Many of my clients find this technique extremely helpful. For example, Rachel, whom you met in the introduction to this book, once casually described herself as "picky."

"What do you mean when you say that?" I asked.

"I go on a date and it's like, *Ugh, this person's not for me*," she clarified. "One guy out of every seven seems okay," she approximated.

I didn't want Rachel to force herself to feel different than she did, but I also wondered how she knew right away that someone wasn't "for her." After all, it's depressing to feel like you're wasting time searching for someone who doesn't exist. To get more

information about whether these dates were actually a bad fit or
if her conclusions were judgments rather than facts, I wrote out
these prompts for us to work through (based on Linehan's
"checking the facts" exercise):

Fact-check Your Thoughts

1. Describe the event.
2. What are my interpretations? (Look out for judgments
   and worst-case-scenario thoughts.)
3. What is my emotion and how intense is it (1 to 10 scale)?
4. What are other possibilities? What's the likelihood of
   the worst happening? If the worst does happen, how
   will I cope?
5. Does my emotion fit the facts? How do I feel now?

When Rachel and I did the exercise, she came up with the
following:

1. Event: Went on a date last week, saw this guy and immediately felt disappointed that he wasn't my "type."
2. Interpretations: I DON'T like him. He's annoying. He
   talks nonstop. My friends will hate him. This is a total
   waste of time. I'll never meet someone.
3. Emotions and intensity: Irritation, 6; Hopelessness, 7.
4. Other possibilities: He's not attractive but he's not unat-
   tractive. Sometimes my sense of chemistry changes once I
   know someone. He talked a lot on our date, but some people talk more when they're nervous. . . . He isn't representative of every guy in the world. I can cut a date short if I'm
   sure he's not for me. . . . Worst case is I waste 1.5 hours.

5. Assessment and current feelings: Emotion didn't fit the facts. Irritation and hopelessness are now a 2.5, a tiny bit more curious, like was he really *that* bad?

Obviously, I wanted Rachel to feel thrilled with her dates; I didn't want her to question her desire for connection, like Jessica once had. But it also seemed risky for her to apply definitive evaluations to people she barely knew. When you have a strong sense of true clarity, you don't need to play devil's advocate with yourself or displace your real insights with doubts. But there *are* times when we jump to conclusions that are way off (like on my first date with Adam, whom I initially judged as a "frat boy" because he had been part of a fraternity more than a decade earlier). Coincidence or not, after Rachel and I worked on checking the facts, she estimated that one out of every four guys were probably worth a second date. More important, she didn't feel as pessimistic about her future.

It's no accident that one of the prompts in the fact-checking exercise includes considering *what's the worst that could happen?* At times, we get so swept up by an emotion or thought that we don't follow through and imagine that whatever the outcome, we'll most likely manage to cope. The worst is rarely as bad as we think.

All of this reminds me of a former client, Tracey, a partner at a respected law firm, who told me that she was terrified she was going to be fired because her team wasn't bringing in business and her salary was high. When I asked her what she'd do if she lost her job, she looked confused, as if she'd expected me to reassure her that it wouldn't happen. Truthfully, I *didn't* actually believe she'd be laid off; what I was aiming for was to get her to think flexibly and strategically.

Once she gave it a bit of thought, she admitted, "I've never really thought that scenario through. My kids are out of the house, so I could sell our place, downsize, travel, teach, and find a part-time job with better hours," she told me, looking semi-relieved. Prior to this conversation, her primary focus was on how not to get fired; she was preoccupied with envisioning the humiliation of ending her career as a "failure" instead of reflecting on the possible positives of not going to the office every day. Together, we also worked on helping her reappraise that initial bleak assessment by checking the facts, moving toward truer statements: Her performance reviews were always stellar and the firm was in a financial crisis that extended far beyond her team.

A few weeks later, Tracey told me that she felt less anxious and more confident in her ability to cope, whatever happened with her job, so much so that we stopped meeting regularly. Then, months later, she came to my office for a visit, in gym clothes. She was happy and wanted to share her news: "The firm made cuts and I was let go," she told me. She received a good severance package and discovered that she was finding joy in her new freedom. While not everyone is lucky enough to have that kind of financial flexibility, what seems universally true is that when we move from feeling blinded by thoughts to more realistic assessments, it's easier to harness our resources to consider, *how can I can cope?*

Levity Is the Soul of Wit

In our first meeting, Dave, a client and photographer in his forties, told me how much he loved his wife and son. Then he broke eye contact, and he looked ashamed as he confided that he'd come to see me because he couldn't stop thinking about suicide. "I'm not depressed," he clarified. Yet, at different times, his mind whispered intrusive thoughts like *You should die . . . maybe you should jump out of that window. . . .* These thoughts were so upsetting that if one entered his mind, he quickly rushed home and crawled into bed. He'd felt so haunted by these frightening messages and by his lack of ability to control them that he decided to take a leave from work. "Do I need to go to a psychiatric hospital?" he asked.

Dave was both surprised and relieved when I told him I didn't think so. Clearly, he wanted to live and was motivated to stay safe. In our subsequent sessions, I worked on helping Dave notice his thoughts as mental events that weren't always rational or possible to control. "Telling yourself not to think about windows means you'll end up thinking about windows," I explained. "Trying to make a thought go away guarantees that it will stick around."

To help Dave take a different approach to thinking, I invited him to go for a walk with me instead of our usual sit-down session. He looked confused but was a good sport, and when we got outside, I instructed him to go and do whatever he wanted, no matter what I said. Then, I lurked behind him saying things like, "raise your left arm," "freeze," "go home, no one wants you out," while he continued strolling (this is an ACT-inspired exercise). Our outing helped Dave realize that he could ignore my strange suggestions (which he did) as he could notice and distance himself from upsetting thoughts that entered his mind. Despite my commands, or his thoughts, he could choose to go about his life freely, even when his mind wasn't making it easy. More seriously, Dave needed to notice that if his mind said *You should die*, he could continue to enjoy his life.

While you may never experience thoughts as extreme as Dave's, all of us have unexpected, upsetting, self-critical thoughts at times, thoughts that don't move us in a positive direction. I know that there are times when I set out to exercise in the early morning, and my mind throws me ideas like: *you're tired, you have so much to do, tomorrow is a better day to work out.* My mindfulness of thoughts practice has helped me see these mental events as opportunities to get out of my head and into my values of health and action, independent of my motivation.

In our next session, Dave and I talked about another technique—singing your thoughts, which can help you remember that thoughts are sounds and syllables, not literal prescriptions. After we reviewed this concept, I asked Dave to pick an upbeat song to apply to the thought *I should die.* The following week, he arrived with typed sheets so we could both sing along, excitedly passing me a folded piece of paper. He'd chosen the Haddaway song "What Is Love?" and introduced me to a clip of the song from a *Saturday Night Live* episode, which made the exercise even more hilariously helpful. Here are the lyrics we belted out: "What are thoughts? Thoughts can't hurt me, they can't hurt me . . . no more." Gradually, in his life, when those destructive thoughts came up, instead of panicking he learned to associate them with our song and the *Saturday Night Live* skit, which felt freeing, he told me, especially since the "die" thoughts quickly got in the way of logical reasoning. We also did some fact-checking around why he wanted to live, using photos and notes on his iPhone that reminded him of events he was looking forward to and people he loved.

My patient Linda, who was worried that only elderly men would find her attractive, also tried combining more mindful thinking and fact-checking, and found the results cathartic. When we did the latter, she reflected that she'd seen wedding announcements in the newspaper featuring women her age who were marrying men the same age. She also remembered she'd attended a wedding of a friend who'd remarried someone younger. And while she wasn't excited by the idea of singing her thoughts, she liked the idea of just watching them, of seeing them as visitors. We also noticed certain situations elicited mental packages for her—a whole grouping of negative thoughts. When her son mentioned her ex-husband, for instance, she knew she was at risk of falling into the *he's thriving and I'm suffering* bundle. As New Year's Eve approached, she expected the *this will be another year I'll be alone* headline. Anticipating what she was in for, mood-wise, helped her move past opening this sort of mental spam.

On a personal note, as I've been writing, all sorts of negative thoughts have come up for me. (Yes, unfortunately, practicing mindfulness doesn't permanently prevent self-doubt from ever cropping up again, but it does help to contain it.) I've caught myself thinking, *Why spend time writing something no one will read?* At other moments, I've worried, *People will see this and think it's not helpful enough!* or *It's unprofessional and bad luck to share details about my personal life in a book.* My mind also sends me critical messages before and after public speaking engagements. When I notice those thoughts, I do the same things I teach my patients: I focus on what I value—spreading hope based on science—and adopt the attitude, *thank you, mind.* Almost always, these thoughts evaporate and even if they stick around, they don't direct my behavior. As uncomfortable as it feels, I know I win a round that my mind loses when, despite my fears, I continue to write and seek speaking engagements.

Dating can feel harder, and provoke especially desperate thoughts. Before I found mindfulness, I used to get stuck in a state of anticipated aloneness, thinking, over and over, *I'll never meet someone I actually like.* That inevitably led to thoughts like *Maybe I should just forget about chemistry* and prompted actions like scanning past dates I'd had that were only so-so and platonic friendships for romantic possibility. After hearing about a friend who started an unexpected relationship with a once platonic pal, I even awkwardly asked one guy friend what he thought about us as a couple (*at least I like his company*, I justified). The truth was, I wasn't actually interested in being with this guy romantically, and let me tell you, I seriously wished I'd done some fact-checking before *that* conversation.

Another time, I went on a date with someone I later discovered was a bachelor on a reality dating show. When I watched the show months after our one date, the series (accurately) depicted him as arrogant and unkind. Yet when he never called me after our meeting, I blamed my own inadequacies for his silence. Like Jessica, my negative thoughts prevented me from seeing what I knew to be true: that he wasn't someone I wanted to be close with. Thank goodness the tools I learned through my professional development helped me get unbrainwashed from my own mind.

Calling Out Thoughts That Won't Help

While we all have our own idiosyncratic assumptions, there are a few ideas I hear often enough that they're worth addressing one by one. These can be especially limiting when it comes to feeling good. Do you notice yourself having any of these thoughts?

1. But what if . . .

It is totally normal to want guarantees in areas of our lives that matter to us most. Uncertainty can feel grueling, especially when we're waiting for big news (or a text message). It can feel remarkably frustrating that there is no insurance policy available for our personal and romantic life. If there were, I'm betting that many of us would pay a larger premium than we pay on home, health, and car coverage combined. But sadly, it's impossible to know for sure whether we'll meet someone, and if we do, there is no warranty protecting our union for the long term.

Accepting uncertainty is a crucial part of happiness in life. Researchers who have studied what kind of thinking predicts psychological problems have found that *intolerance of uncertainty* is high up on the list. Fearing the unknown and finding the possibility of negative outcomes unacceptable is terribly stressful, which may be why it can lead to psychological problems.

Life can change at any moment, for better or worse. Doing some fact-checking to remind yourself that you can't predict your future may not be as satisfying as knowing something will work out fabulously. But it's also less anxiety-provoking than dreading that the worst is definitely going to happen (e.g., *I'll be alone forever*). Instead of searching for certainty, which is impossible, we can practice reappraisal—shifting our focus to think about what we *can* control, then taking actions that are consistent with our values. We can remember that we have the option of choosing to date only people who make us feel good. We can appreciate that our relationship status doesn't warrant shame or dictate how we spend our day.

What else can we do? We can notice our thoughts, as we've

talked about, and in doing so, normalize them, perhaps reassuring ourselves by saying, *Of course we care.* That's more productive than ruminating or begging others to promise us that everything will work out (technically known as *reassurance seeking*). As tempting as the latter feels, it won't successfully alleviate anxiety.

Focusing on the breath can also be a powerful call to gratitude and to the collective fact that all we know for sure is this very moment. Another nice antidote to fearing the worst is maintaining hope and optimism. In case you're thinking that *optimistic* is another word for naive, in a study at Santa Clara University in California led by psychologist David Feldman, 160 college students were asked to list seven goals they hoped to achieve by the end of the year. They also completed questionnaires that measured their levels of hope. Later, the students were invited to share their progress. The more hopeful (or optimistic) the students had been about their goals, the more progress they'd made. Hope preserves our inner resources so we can put our energy toward achieving what matters most, like building a life filled with love and meaning.

2. There's something wrong with me.

Like Dave, some of my clients are convinced that there's something truly wrong with them that requires they sit on the sidelines of life. Even if you describe having "baggage" from breakups or experiences in your childhood, it's possible to do some reappraising, to enter the moment and remember that growth is possible with the right approach. I promise you, that approach *isn't* believing that you're forever flawed.

If you do some fact-checking and confirm that you truly have psychological problems that affect your relationships, there are accessible solutions that work. Even my clients who have faced traumas or serious psychological problems now, for the most part, enjoy healthy, satisfying relationships. And you don't necessarily need a lifetime of therapy or expensive residential treatment centers to reclaim your life. Mindfulness helps people who struggle with impulsive urges, all from the comfort of home. Michael Twohig, a psychologist at Utah State University, taught people coping with sex addiction various skills, including tracking their behaviors, observing and accepting their urges and thoughts, focusing on values, and entering the present moment. After the eight-week course, participants reported an 80 percent reduction in problematic pornography viewing, and were able to maintain those improvements three months later.

I mention all this because even if you think you have hangups or serious psychological problems, there are science-based approaches that can liberate you. With the help of an expert, you can find freedom. And you will never win wellness by bringing a case against yourself.

3. I'm single (and I'm ashamed about it).

Guess what? You're actually not "single." Why? Because your relationship status is not who you are. Defining yourself as your relationship status (especially a relationship status you may not like) isn't helpful, nor is it accurate. The same goes for using words to describe yourself that you don't like or that don't actually describe who you are. Jessica, for example, was pretty stuck on the "virgin" description, rather than seeing herself as a fun, thoughtful, spiritual woman with many friends. Tracey, the attorney I mentioned, would have likely defined herself as a "partner at a firm," in large letters, instead of "helpful mom" and "lifelong learner." I use these examples to remind you that narrowing in on one aspect of who you are tends to be limiting. It makes more sense to more flexibly zoom out to see the full picture of yourself; once you do, others might too.

To broaden your thinking, it can help to make a list of at least a dozen words and phrases that describe who you are (*empathetic, a hard worker*). After you've finished, scan your list and notice whether you've made one attribute more central than others, like your appearance. Then remind yourself that when you overidentify with a particular label, you're diminishing all that you truly embody. None of us is a collection of physical attributes, or a career, or a relationship status. We're all so much more than that. Applying mindfulness techniques can help broaden your perspective of yourself.

The next time negative ideas are lurking in your mind, I hope you'll try checking the facts and also experiment with the mindfulness of thoughts concept you've learned. To recap, some of the unhealthy thoughts and behaviors I've touched on so far include:

- I'll be happy if I meet someone.
- It's cathartic to think this through, again and again. . . .
- I missed my chance to end up with my soul mate.
- I can't deal with my feelings; I should just settle.
- I'm a failure because I'm not getting what I've worked toward.
- I can only _____ when I have a partner.

At first, you may notice taking a new approach feels tougher than reverting to your habitual ways of thinking. To stay motivated, consider this quote from Lao Tsu, the Chinese philosopher and Taoist: "When I let go of what I am, I become what I might be."

CHAPTER 9

Watch Your Mood

Genius is the ability to renew one's emotions in daily experience.　　　　　—PAUL CÉZANNE

M Y FEELINGS ARE overwhelming," Nicole, a normally outgoing forty-year-old, told me. She was at an impasse with her boyfriend; after a year of dating, she wanted him to commit to their relationship and take steps toward getting engaged. "We're both in our forties. Shouldn't we know what we want by now?" she wondered. But despite the fact that they got along and laughed often, he said he wasn't ready. He also insisted on maintaining contact with an ex-girlfriend, which consistently left Nicole feeling upset and insecure. She was clear, she said, that she couldn't continue to stay with him under these circumstances, but she also dreaded the pain of a breakup. "I'll really miss him—and I hate the risk of not knowing if I'll find someone I love as much." Her affective forecasting (aka those predictions about what we think we'll feel in the future) promised an emotional storm ahead, and her day-to-day wasn't going so well either. She told me that she could hardly enjoy experiences she'd once cherished, like being with her friends or reading. Instead, she constantly felt like she was on the brink of a loss she could prevent if only she made the right move. Just as bad, it was hard for her to focus at her job in client relations. She found herself obsessing over her relationship at her desk and, occasionally, crying in the bathroom, all of which led to a pileup of work that created more stress. When she spent time with Mr. Not Ready, she struggled to enjoy the moment and admitted that she felt impatient and yelled at him "for no reason."

Nicole hoped I had an answer for her, or that I could assure her that an ultimatum would ultimately work. But after she explained her dilemma in our first session, I told her that although she seemed incredibly upset and I wanted to help, I wasn't omniscient and couldn't directly tell her what to do. Desperate for guidance, she laid out her options: "Either I break up with him, and maybe he'll come around; or I keep waiting until he's ready," she said.

All I knew for sure was that Nicole couldn't break up with her emotions. That's why I offered her a third choice: to learn ways to cope, no matter what she decided. In this chapter, you'll also explore ways to navigate the inevitable ups and downs you'll face whether on your own or in a partnership and strategies for how to manage when you feel your most vulnerable.

In one of our early meetings, I asked Nicole how she was feeling. "Bad," she said, then rolled her eyes when I pushed her to be more specific, to notice and name her feelings. I knew this seemed like a stereotypical "therapist move." Eventually, she said, "sad, anxious, and angry." I wasn't trying to be pedantic but rather, strategic: Brain studies, including one spearheaded by psychologist Matthew Lieberman, confirm that when people are shown emotionally evocative images, if they label the emotions the images provoke, like "angry," or "scared," they can dampen the response of the brain's emotional center, the amygdala. Conversely, in a study led by psychologist Todd Kashdan where subjects were rejected by others, researchers found that not being able to differentiate between various emotions they were experiencing actually exacerbated feelings of low self-esteem.

The ability to pinpoint emotions—your own and those of other people—is a cornerstone of emotional intelligence. I want to help you learn to label your feelings, which will give your reasonable mind (aka logical abilities) the chance to have a word with your emotion mind so you can determine whether your emotions are helpful or unhelpful in any given situation. Let's start by taking a look at how you typically experience your emotions. Do any of these descriptions resonate with you?

a. My emotions tend to linger.
b. I have little control over my feelings; situations dictate my experience.
c. My actions are based on my emotions.
d. All of the above.

Many of my clients circle "all of the above," especially when they are in the midst of feeling something intensely. Certain people seem to experience what Linehan describes as *emotional vulnerability*, and notice that their emotions last longer and reach greater depths than others. While some of us may find ourselves innately prone to feeling intensely, all of us are at risk of being dominated by our emotions if we don't learn the right approach to sitting with them.

But experiencing emotions more deeply isn't necessarily a bad thing. Many people who experience emotions powerfully also notice that they feel heightened joy too. When I pointed this out to Nicole, she acknowledged, "I'm the kind of person who laughs so hard that my stomach hurts." However, she was skeptical that she could adjust her feelings: "I can't imagine that I'll get over this or stop feeling so passionately about so much."

Growing up, she told me, she'd known people in her community who faced tragic losses. A few seemed to mourn and move on; others seemed to be in a permanent state of grieving, always looking pained. "Don't you think that has to do with a person's degree of loss, not the 'tools' someone uses?" she asked. "I mean, maybe the inconsolable person had a special relationship that couldn't be replaced. Maybe it's *not* about managing emotions."

Certainly, every situation is complex and I would never blame someone who is suffering, nor tell them that they should somehow be more resilient. Yet I encouraged Nicole to experiment with trying tactics to increase her *emotion regulation*, managing her feelings in ways that aligned with her goals, since this ability relates to both overall well-being and improved relationships.

Your Beliefs About Emotions Influence How You Cope

My first step was to help Nicole target her thoughts about her feelings. Just as in other areas of life, believing you can cope with your emotions actually predicts that you will be able to manage them well. Moreover, trusting that your actions will create the outcomes you crave can be a huge source of hope and meaning. As I've emphasized in the preceding chapters, your relationships, daily experiences, thoughts, and emotions can improve in ways you may not anticipate, especially when you're in the midst of a crisis. That's important to remember, because you're more likely to try new strategies if you have faith that they will be effective.

Let's take a look at how beliefs about emotions impact us. In a study at Stanford University, psychologist Maya Tamir and her colleagues asked more than four hundred incoming freshmen to reflect on their theories about emotions. As I aimed to do by asking the questions at the start of this chapter, the researchers were hoping to discover which students assumed their emotions were unchanging, which anticipated that they were malleable, and how these beliefs affected how easily they adjusted to the challenging transition to college.

Here's what they found: 40 percent of students described their emotions as fixed (just as Nicole believed). The remaining 60 percent felt they had some control over their emotional life, and this group reported experiencing fewer negative emotions, more positive feelings, and increased social support.

Maybe you wonder how it's possible to know if the mere belief that coping is possible makes people more resilient, or if this group just happened to face less stress. In a study designed by Yochanan Bigman, a professor at Hebrew University in Israel, subjects were given a placebo pill and told that it would improve their memory along with the side effect of making it easier to regulate their feelings. Afterward, they were shown a video meant to arouse a strong emotional response. Those who anticipated that they'd be better able to cope with their emotions did so more successfully than a control group. Trying new ways of managing definitely takes work, so my hope is that you adopt the attitude that it is possible to change your relationship with your emotions and then discover, firsthand, that emotions don't have to rule your life.

To start to chip away at negative beliefs about emotions, it's helpful to appreciate what emotions do for us. From an evolutionary and psychological perspective, we have emotions for good reason. Emotions *communicate to us, influence others,* and *drive our behavior,* as Linehan has detailed. Nicole's feelings, for instance, made it clear to her that she wanted security in the form of a relationship that was going to last. When she authentically showed her noncommittal boyfriend that she was feeling sad, as tears ran down her face, her emotions communicated more poignantly than words ever could that her needs weren't being met.

I've talked previously about how unhelpful "playing games" and suppressing emotions can be, both in your day-to-day life and in your relationships. In case you're wondering whether Nicole expressing her genuine feelings was off-putting, researchers studying attraction found that people tend to be more drawn to others when they are confident that they can read that person's emotions. It's neither good for you nor endearing to others to hide how you feel, since closeness depends on communication, as research led by neuroscientist Silke Anders proves. Just because Mr. Not Ready wasn't proposing didn't mean Nicole's open expressions of emotion weren't useful. When you judge your feelings as "too much" as Nicole did, you're likelier to try to suppress them. Yet, again, pushing feelings away rather than practicing acceptance can ultimately leave you feeling more stressed.

A great way to know if you're open to your emotions is to ask yourself: *Am I willing to be with what I feel?* Shifting your perspective so that you can appreciate how emotions can help guide you is a nice way to move past seeing them as burdensome. As much as most of us don't like feeling dissatisfied, sadness can move us to take steps toward achieving what we crave. Similarly, if you're bored and frustrated at work and constantly distract yourself with Google Chat and a buffet of media sites, you run the risk of missing the message that you may regret how you're spending your hours.

If it's hard to believe that sitting with unpleasant feelings can be more helpful than escaping them, consider whether avoiding your emotions has worked for you in the past. In my office, I keep a unique trinket used by many ACT therapists, a Chinese finger trap. In case you're not familiar with this toy, when you stick your index fingers simultaneously into each end of this flexible woven bamboo cylinder and reflexively pull your fingers away from each other, you won't be able to extricate your fingers; they'll be stuck in the cylinder. The only way to free your fingers from the trap is to relax and stop pulling. A parallel approach holds true when it comes to our emotions. To live expansively, you need to sit with your feelings, especially ones that feel tricky, rather than indulge in the urge to push unpleasant emotions away.

Untangling an Emotion to Change How You Feel

As helpful as emotions can be, there are also times when they don't fit the facts or their intensity is disproportional. An important step in managing emotions is learning to differentiate *justified* from *unjustified* emotions. Nicole sitting with sadness about Mr. Not Ready makes a lot of sense when she is trying to make a decision about their relationship. But if her sadness feels so intense that she is constantly distracted at work, or unable to muster the strength to move forward, that pain is no longer useful.

The strategies I describe on the next pages (based on Linehan's Emotion Regulation unit) will provide you with a range of techniques to help you to manage your emotions rather than the other way around. As you'll see, an emotion has different components, each attached to a potential liberating course of action. What's nice about this model is that it's possible to intervene at multiple stages of feeling; it's not an all or nothing process.

Remember to keep in mind, again, that the earlier you try to manage your emotions, the easier it will be. It's usually simpler to reduce vulnerability, problem solve, and watch your thoughts before an emotion escalates. Once you're especially vulnerable and deluged by painful thoughts, it takes a lot of work not to act on your emotions.

THE STEPS TO MANAGING AN EMOTION

Vulnerabilities ⇨ Add positives

Situation ⇨ Problem solve

Interpretation ⇨ Check the facts/mindfulness of thoughts

Changes in body/action urges ⇨ Notice and do the opposite

Emotion ⇨ Observe and describe

Aftereffects ⇨ Practice mindfulness

1. Assess Your Vulnerabilities ⇨ Add Positives to Increase Resilience

Before we experience an emotion, there are factors that influence how intensely we'll react. When we're feeling more vulnerable (e.g., we're hungry, tired, or lonely), we're likely to respond more intensely. Think about it: Have you noticed that on a morning after you've gotten a good night's sleep, gone to an invigorating cardio dance class, sipped a delicious matcha, and arrived at work early, without rushing, you feel less irritated by an event that would normally bother you? The good news about *vulnerabilities* is we can notice them so they don't seize us. We can also schedule positive actions to increase our resilience, as we've already covered. Besides her tendency to experience emotions intensely, Nicole told me that some of her vulnerabilities were her age and the fact that she'd had a boyfriend (for years) who couldn't commit to moving in together. These contributed to her feeling especially defeated by her boyfriend's indecisiveness.

Take a few minutes to reflect on and list some of your vulnerabilities. Once you're aware of what makes you more susceptible to reacting strongly to stressors you can work on increasing your wellness. Practicing mindfulness is one way to strengthen your ability to recover from challenges. Actually, psychologist Joanna Arch, at the University of Colorado, Boulder, and her colleagues discovered that college students who spent fifteen minutes trying guided focused breathing exercises before looking at negative images felt less affected by those images and more willing to tolerate them. Another way to reduce vulnerability is to think about what you value and what brings you joy (as we covered in chapters 5 and 6). These practices are like emotional deposits in your bank account that provide a safety net when inevitable withdrawals hit you.

Once you have a sense of your personal vulnerabilities and what replenishes you, you can be more proactive. If you know that you feel emotionally vulnerable when you spend too much time alone at home, making plans and getting out can prevent you from plunging into emotion mind. A yoga teacher friend once told me that she feels especially alone when she doesn't have physical connection in her life. Rather than jump into bed with strangers, which isn't her style and also increases her vulnerabilities (more on this later in the chapter), she tries to schedule ten-minute chair massages and goes to yoga classes where students partner up and physically assist one another. She also validates herself, acknowledging that it's natural for an affectionate person like her to crave physical contact.

2. Pay Attention to the Situation ⇨ Problem Solve

After assessing your vulnerabilities, next comes *situation*, the event, thought, or feeling that triggers an emotion. In Nicole's case, thinking about her boyfriend's unwillingness to commit prompted her sadness. Whenever she thought about it, she got upset, and she felt even worse when she and her boyfriend spoke about their future and he said he couldn't make any promises.

It's possible to change how you feel about a situation by doing some *problem solving*. In Nicole's case, she could either break up with Mr. Not Ready or change her mind to truly accept that she wouldn't be getting engaged in the near future (and possibly never) if she stayed with him. As I've said, everyone deserves to pursue what matters to them. However, if Nicole somehow decided that she didn't care about formalities like a marriage license and wedding ceremony, her acceptance would count as problem solving—she'd no longer be in a situation where she felt dismissed. In real life, many experiences, like Nicole's, can't be quickly resolved. That's when you need to recognize if you're wisely accepting whatever is or if you're passively remaining in situations you'd be better off changing. Earlier, I used the example of emotions being a clue that you're not fulfilled in your job. In that scenario, I wouldn't necessarily recommend packing the contents of your desk and running out of your office. In fact, problem solving might include taking on new responsibilities at work, finding a meaningful volunteer position one evening a week, seeking a stimulating class, or researching other opportunities. As you see, in generating solutions, it's useful to brainstorm lots of options. Starting therapy was one way Nicole tried to problem solve. Take a couple of minutes to see if there's a situation you notice yourself in that might be worth improving. Next, choose a good first step to try.

3. Catch Your Interpretations ⇨ Check the Facts/Mindfulness of Thoughts

Another aspect of an emotion cycle is noticing your *interpretations*. So much of how we feel has to do with how we think. Nicole could choose to interpret her partner as *loving and anxious*, based on his parents' difficult relationship. She could also interpret his behavior as *manipulative*. One interpretation will likely generate patience, while the other is likely to produce anger. Again, *fact-checking* and *mindfulness of thoughts* are powerful ways to get unstuck from interpretations. As we covered in chapter 8, Nicole might notice that her boyfriend had never been close to proposing to anyone, so his behavior was not a specific rejection of her. Nicole could also simply notice thoughts such as *I'll never find someone who likes me as much as I love him*, rather than believe them. Be careful, though, not to delude yourself in the process of checking your interpretations. I'd never want Nicole to dismiss her desire for a life partner under the guise of compassionately reappraising her boyfriend's ambivalence.

4. Notice Your Body's Changes and Urges to Act ⇨ Act the Opposite of Unjustified Emotions

The combination of vulnerabilities, the situation that's provoking you, and your interpretation of that situation can affect your body and motivate you to take action. Facing a threat gets the heart racing, the sweat glands pumping, and in general, impels us to run. But that doesn't mean you should always act on your urges, since acting on an emotion intensifies it. A big part of how we feel has to do with how we act, which is why acting on emotions isn't necessarily cathartic (especially when the emotion isn't justified).

When I first met Nicole, she worried that something was wrong with her for loving someone so ambivalent. I wondered if, just as Nicole's behaviors (acting in love) heightened her infatuation, Mr. Not Ready's actions (pulling away) diminished his loving feelings. When I shared these thoughts with Nicole, she felt a bit better for understanding that her emotions and experiences made sense.

IS "HOOKING UP" WISE?

One of the features of dating today, especially in an app-driven world, is getting physical with someone, fast (aka acting on love). Some of my clients complain that they're interested in people they barely know or feel lonely as someone lies next to them. It's a dilemma: On the one hand, you want connection, so should you take what you can get—physical contact without an emotional bond? Is it possible to start a good relationship in your bedroom? In considering the model of emotions and how actions impact emotions, it seems like enjoying sex with relative strangers could create "love" that might not be quite real but instead be based on your emotion mind, since you don't have enough information. A mix of social media stalking, fantasizing, and trying to win someone over, especially coupled with an interpretation like *I'll be so much happier with a partner*, would leave anyone entranced.

Can anyone keep it casual? One client of mine had lots of commitment-free passion without ruminating or lusting. After years in a monogamous relationship, she wasn't looking for more than fun and in her quest was more attuned to her own needs than to wooing others. I'm not prescribing that path if you're looking for a relationship, but the combination of her situation and her behavior created the boundaries she needed to separate her heart from her body.

But how do you manage if you want a real relationship yet don't want to feel too into it before you know if the other person is worth your headspace and bed space? Before acting, you might weigh the pros and cons of getting in bed quickly, based on your past experience. You might also watch the thought that you have to *relax* to prove likable. While instant chemistry feels nicer than nothing, some people notice that experiencing euphoria too soon can lead to a brutal withdrawal.

Acting Opposite, Step-by-Step

If all of us are at risk of creating feelings through our actions, how can we change the way we feel? There's a DBT skill known as *opposite action*, and many of my clients find it powerful. Have you ever pushed yourself to go out with friends despite feeling a bit sad and lethargic, then notice that you leave feeling energized? That's one example of acting opposite. At times, acting opposite won't immediately feel good—I say that the ultimate goal of acting opposite isn't to *feel* better, but to *live* better. Like I've mentioned, I don't enjoy public speaking; it leads to all sorts of imposter thoughts and anxious feelings. Yet I immediately accept invitations and quickly prepare, instead of procrastinating. After a speech, I don't always feel better, but it's empowering to know that it's okay to feel afraid and proceed with courage. I'm sure you have examples of situations where you chose a meaningful action over what you were in the mood to do and ended up feeling enriched by your decision.

Doing the opposite shouldn't feel artificial. It isn't about thinking hostile thoughts as you act pleasantly. Your mind and body need to be aligned so that you're mindfully taking a meaningful step. For instance, if your emotion is fear, the aim of acting opposite isn't *appearing* calm, but *doing* what you'd do if you weren't afraid, like my public speaking example. Try acting opposite yourself and notice if you feel freer.

Acting Opposite to Live Differently

1. First, identify the emotion you want to change, along with the intensity of the feeling.
2. Describe your urges to act.
3. Act the opposite of those urges all the way.
4. Notice your current emotion and its intensity.

♥♥If your emotion didn't change, notice if other emotions arise, like feelings of accomplishment.♥♥

After Nicole and I discussed acting opposite, she tried this technique in lots of different ways. She practiced speaking gently instead of indulging in her urge to yell, which she had learned only made her more angry. Next, she decided that begging Mr. Not Ready to "put a ring on it" or obsessing about his being her only option wasn't making her feel empowered. She promised him that she'd take a few weeks off from analyzing and discussing their relationship trajectory given that they were at a standstill and their discussions didn't feel productive. After a month-long hiatus from engagement talk, Mr. Not Ready still wasn't ready. In the meantime, Nicole and I had spent time talking about her values. She told me that she cared a lot about maintaining her self-worth and the related goal of finding commitment within a relationship.

Eventually, after adding tons of positives to her life including fully participating in activities with friends, and changing her interpretation that her boyfriend was her only romantic option, she decided to deal with the situation. Courageously, she acted opposite of her fear of being alone and broke up with Mr. Not Ready. "At this point in my life, I want to be with someone who wants to build a future together," she explained. Her newly ex-boyfriend was upset and also, finally, had a clearer understanding of how hurt Nicole had felt. Nicole broke up with Mr. Not Ready wholeheartedly, without compulsively checking her messages or fantasizing about his coming back. In those first few weeks it's likely Nicole would have felt better with Mr. Not Ready by her side than she did right after they parted ways, but that wouldn't be prioritizing her value of self-respect.

Nicole told me that she found practicing the three-minute breathing space (you'll find the exercise in the pages ahead) helpful in maintaining her perspective and preventing her from ruminating. She practiced this mindfulness exercise in the morning when she woke up and during stressful moments after the breakup, when her mind wandered to her ex. When her friend got engaged, she made a point of noticing her thoughts (*Maybe I should call him and see what he's up to.*) as well as her emotions (envy, sadness), and physical sensations (a lump in her throat). Then she brought her attention to her breath, noticing that it felt shallow, and she tried to breathe more deeply. Finally, she expanded her awareness beyond her breath, relaxing her face and body, which calmed down her feelings and her urges to act. Instead of calling her ex-boyfriend and telling him that she missed him, she decided to put her phone away.

After a couple of months during which she tried living in the moment, as well as acting opposite (e.g., getting up when she felt like sleeping), she noticed that her love for her ex was fading. She was moved by how helpful (and also difficult) her actions felt and excited to recognize that her emotions no longer ruled her life.

5. Appreciate Your Emotion ⇨ Observe and Describe Your Experience

The combination of a situation, thought, and action build an *emotion*. As Nicole discovered and we touched on earlier in this chapter, when you can be specific about how you feel you're apt to end up more confident that you can cope. The more precise you can be about what's going on (e.g., My sadness is a 7 on a scale of 1 to 10), the easier it is to find solutions. When Nicole attended to her emotions she got a clearer sense that staying with her boyfriend gave her flickering moments of joy under a dark haze of vulnerability. That realization helped her break up with him so she could pursue a clearer future. Studies led by neuroscientist Lisa Feldman Barrett and her team suggest that people who are more skilled in figuring out what they're feeling are likelier to use strategies to reduce negative emotions and increase positive ones than people less able to distinguish their emotions. When you can identify exactly what you're feeling and how intensely you're experiencing it, you can both appreciate the message of that emotion and also decide if you need to work on modifying your feelings.

6. Look for Aftereffects ⇨ Practice Mindfulness

Emotions come and go, like visitors passing, unless we invite them in to stay. Ruminating is one way we prolong emotions, according to emotion researchers Philippe Verduyn and Saskia Lavrijsen. Similarly, you can get stuck in a cascade of emotions by judging your feelings. If Nicole felt anxious about her relationship, then judged that anxiety as *pathetic*, she'd likely feel worse, not just fearful but also ashamed. When you judge your feelings, you suffer. Think about it—you can feel sad, or depressingly sad about feeling sad. Panic is another case—it's an example of fear of fear. That's why it's important to differentiate between your emotions and your reactions to them. Les Greenberg, a psychologist who developed Emotion-Focused Therapy, clarifies that the first feeling is the *primary emotion*. What we feel after we judge that emotional experience is known as a *secondary emotion*. Secondary emotions create misery and also divert you from the main event—the message your emotion is relaying to you.

After you feel an emotion, aim to observe and describe it,

rather than judge it, or get muddied in secondary feelings. Bringing your awareness to your emotions is a mindfulness practice that can free you. Like watching thoughts, you'll be more able to manage your emotions when you're consciously aware of them.

Another Three Minutes of Mindfulness

Mindfulness doesn't have to be difficult or take a long time. Zindel Segal, one of the developers of MBCT, recommends an exercise called the "three-minute breathing space," which can help you act in ways that align with your long-term goals. This practice nicely moves through some of the components we've covered that contribute to the experience of an emotion. One aspect of the exercise I especially love is how it invites you to be aware of your thoughts and feelings, then drop down into the breath, then expand your attention again, so that your attention shifts rather than gets stuck in a thought or feeling. To begin, set a timer for three minutes, then sit in a comfortable position with your eyes closed or gazing comfortably at a single point.

Three-Minute Breathing Space

1. For a minute, notice: *What thoughts are going through my mind? What am I feeling in this moment?* Notice thoughts as mental events, just words passing through, bringing a quality of openness to any sensations or emotions you observe for a minute.
2. Next, bring your attention to the physical sensation of breathing, attending to your belly expanding and contracting.

3. Finally, scan your body as a whole. Notice your posture, facial expression, sensations, and the breath.

    You can do this practice anywhere, whether at home or as you go about your day.

Managing Your Emotions When You're Single and Don't Want to Be

I'd love for you to take a few minutes and think about how you might use the model of emotions to holistically improve your feelings about being single. How can you: reduce your vulnerabilities, problem solve, notice your interpretations, and act opposite? How might you label your emotions and reduce their aftereffects? Personally, I used these techniques to manage my feelings (after breaking up with my fiancé, on many disappointing Saturday nights, after bad dates, and during long stretches of no dates . . .). To reduce vulnerability, I delved into mindfulness and scheduled exercise classes that led to a surge of endorphins and connected me to new people. At times, I had to problem solve: saying no to random setups urged on me by people who didn't know me well, like the time a friend's mother wanted me to meet a man visiting from Singapore for a few days or someone tried to persuade me to go on a date with someone decades older than me. I could have watched the interpretation that there was no one eligible in either my area or age group, but instead I reflected on how nice it was that people wanted to help. That didn't mean I needed to go out with anyone available. I also had to do a lot of opposite action around shame, including not carrying myself like I was less-than. Noticing and naming my emotions helped me see that none of them were permanent—I went from contentment, to fear, to sadness—and back again.

Getting Ready for Emotion Regulation

I understand that some of what I'm suggesting may seem difficult—particularly if acting opposite requires breaking up with someone. But one part of the emotional regulation process that I love is that you can tailor how you do it depending on your needs, your vulnerabilities, and the situation. You can flexibly move between strategies to find what works best for you.

Still, in the midst of facing problems, we may feel depleted and find ourselves especially at risk of not investing much effort into managing well. If you observe an emotion that seems over-whelmingly intense, you might need to first recharge before you begin the steps in the process described earlier. When emotions are high, self-soothing can feel more useful than something like fact-checking.

Before breaking up, for example, Nicole booked a haircut, made a week's worth of plans with people, picked out some up-lifting playlists and books, and had her values chart (chapter 5) handy. She needed to participate in experiences that helped her enter the moment. In times of crisis, some of the additional strategies Linehan recommends as ways to increase *distress toler-ance* include changing your body temperature, doing intense ex-ercise, and relaxing your muscles. Nicole found that going to a high-intensity interval training class, taking a cold shower, and breathing deeply as she scanned each muscle group from head to toe, releasing tension, invigorated her, preventing her from get-ting stuck in her mind and reminding her of her strength. It may sound extreme, but one DBT tool includes dipping your face in ice water when emotions feel overwhelming. Basically, by cooling your face down, you slow your heart rate and oxygen can be redirected to other organs. People are genuinely shocked by how this can induce calm during times you feel flooded with emotions. If you're thinking this would never work, as I tell my clients, "Don't believe (or discount) anything I say until you try it."

Speaking of trying, now would be a great time to create two lists, one for home, and one for when you're on the go, of items and suggested activities that replenish you. Recently, I loved reading about Tim Ferriss's tip of taking a mason jar, decorating it, and labeling it "The Jar of Awesome." Each day, you can put a little note inside the container describing what went well or what you feel grateful for. On a tough day, looking at a handful of these reminders, taking a bath, and reading a funny article would certainly help me feel more confident in my ability to cope. On the go, reaching for my favorite lip gloss, looking at photos on my iPhone, and listening to fun music can give me the boost I need to then manage my emotions in the ways described earlier in this chapter.

Unexpectedly, after a couple of months apart, Mr. Not Ready called Nicole. He'd been going to therapy, had disconnected from his ex-girlfriend, and had worked through his commitment concerns as well. "Are you nuts?" his therapist had asked, when he described wanting to stay friends with his ex. Nicole was happy to report this to me, feeling vindicated in her feelings and decision to stand up for herself and let him go rather than forcing herself to accept the status quo. Mr. Not Ready had spent the time after their breakup thinking about life with Nicole and realized that he cherished her and loved her and the stability she brought to his life much more than he wanted "freedom" to explore with others. "I know I love you and I'm sorry for making you doubt that," he told her.

After months spent noticing her pain and moving forward, Nicole needed time to gather information and observe her emotions before making a decision. After some space and thought, she realized that her feelings of love were still there. As long as he respected her values, she could make this decision with her heart and her mind, and she told him she was ready. Soon after, they got engaged. More important, Nicole felt as if she could manage on her own—and manage her emotions. That ability would stay with her—and it will stay with you, whether or not there's a diamond on your finger.

CHAPTER 10

Say Goodbye to Feeling Lonely

If I am not for myself, who will be for me? If I am only for myself, what am I? And if not now, when?

—RABBI HILLEL

MADISON, FORTY-THREE, RUSHED to meet me from her office at a major tech company, where she is a senior executive. As we settled into our chairs at Starbucks, I looked at my radiant friend in awe. The day before, she had run the New York City Marathon, despite her demanding job. "How did you do it?"

We started by discussing her weekend. "It was my sixth marathon but unfortunately, I had this awful nausea that tortured me from mile fifteen on," she complained, sighing.

"But you finished?" I asked, wondering how she'd mustered the grit to continue when others would have quit.

"I finished," she confirmed. "My best friend, Rob, another guy, Jacques, and I ran together and it was just one foot in front of the other."

I'd met Madison five years earlier through her boyfriend, Spencer, my charismatic fitness instructor. I was one of many who cherished his supportive yet kick-butt classes and movie-star looks. Madison was always parked front and center in the room and we got into the habit of chatting for a few minutes after class, sweating and exhausted, but happy.

Madison had met Spencer years earlier, when they were both living in a smaller city. First they were friends, and soon after, they began to date, and seriously. When Madison landed a better job at another company in New York, Spencer followed at her urging. In the beginning, she covered both their living expenses and helped network for him. Spencer exudes this laid-back surfer vibe, which, counterintuitively, worked well for him as a fitness coach, since someone casually telling you to continue holding a long plank position for minutes seems more tolerable than someone screaming frenetically. Madison is more of a go-getter; she's chic, rushing about energetically, always jumping on opportunities. As I thought about their personalities, I couldn't imagine Spencer developing his cultlike following without Madison's strategizing.

So I wasn't entirely surprised when, after five years together, Madison confided in me that they weren't clicking. "Honestly, I've thought about breaking up for a long time, but after all this time together, I don't want to be alone in my forties," she told me. They were both kind and likable, so I could imagine them respectfully coexisting without much drama. However, as she continued to advance in her career, Madison grew agitated that Spencer wasn't more of a self-driven powerhouse. Still, she waited before doing anything. "I went through an awful breakup in my twenties, and I just don't want to go through that agony again." I'm not sure which came first, her feelings or their distance, but Spencer moved from their bed to the couch, and eventually, he got his own place.

What happened next stunned me. Less than a year after he'd moved out, Madison stumbled upon Spencer's wedding photos on Facebook, then shots of him caressing his new wife's baby bump. But Madison's equanimity about the whole thing touched me even more. Unlike many people, she didn't fall apart over it. "I'm not gullible; he must have connected with her before he moved out," she acknowledged. That was hard—even worse was the fact that Spencer had often questioned the construct of marriage during his relationship with Madison, yet now he'd be starting one, wedding ceremony and all.

Many people, including me, would feel devastated by the end of a long relationship followed by an ex's near-instantaneous marriage to someone else. But Madison kept going without moping or venting, continuing to train for her race, and dealing with her emotions so gracefully that she was able to quickly connect with someone who mattered to her, someone loyal and kind, who was, she said, "a good choice," not a rebound. Only a few weeks after technology punched her with a glimpse inside Spencer's wedding and his new wife's burgeoning belly, Madison met Jacques—one of the men with whom she eventually ran the marathon—through a mutual friend.

How did she keep thriving? "Don't get me wrong, the whole thing sucked," she admitted. One of the attributes I love most about Madison is that she's real—she doesn't pretend to be some sort of psychological or spiritual warrior. She's more of a disciplined athlete, plotting her practice schedule. When she told me about her most recent marathon, I didn't picture her looking Olympian, I imagined her looking obviously uncomfortable but moving forward nevertheless. Now, sipping her cappuccino, she acknowledged that she'd suffered, but had chosen to accept the outcome, forcing herself to connect with others and stay in the moment rather than obsessing over Spencer's new life. As we went through the play-by-play of the moment when she saw

Spencer's wedding photos as she stood on a train platform returning home from a weekend away with her friend Rob and some other friends, Madison told me that good company had been her lifeline.

Closeness is essential for all of us, and in this chapter you'll learn about ways to reduce feelings of loneliness, no matter what. When Madison and Spencer broke up, she didn't just lose a boyfriend, she lost a community. Most of her friends, like me, were part of her ex's circle. And these people, many much closer than she and I were, had commented enthusiastically on those wedding photos on Spencer's Facebook wall, leaving Madison feeling shunned. "I lost my person and my people," she said.

Yet she'd found new people. Given the number of my clients who tell me how hard it feels to find close friends, especially if you're new to a city, or, like Madison, if your ex gets most of the friends, I wondered how she and her friend Rob had met. I hadn't heard his name before and didn't know him from the gym. She explained that they'd only gotten close after her breakup. "He's a manager at a clothing store I love," she told me. "We'd chat, then I opened up about what happened," she continued. "I'd barely mentioned the breakup since I didn't want the news spreading around. But after I told him, we started hanging out, had a blast, and now we're like family."

Madison says her relationships with her friend Rob and a few others were instrumental to her not falling apart after the split. A Chapman University study of twenty-five thousand people led by sociologist Brian Gillespie found that the two biggest predictors of life satisfaction are quality of friendships and job engagement. Madison told me that friends allowed her to continue to excel at work and even use her job as an opportunity to take a break from the pain in her personal life.

How to Feel Lonely

While Madison made it sound simple, she transcended a lot of the barriers that can thwart relationships. I'd love for you to take a few minutes to ask yourself if you notice anything that may be holding you back from feeling closer to others.

Based on what I see when I talk to my clients (and what I know about myself), I've come to believe that there are four main paths to loneliness:

a. Judging ourselves
b. Judging others
c. Judging our time: *I'm busy!*
d. Judging the importance: *Why bother?*

Many people assume that the trick to feeling less lonely is making plans, improving communication, and upping your likability. But there's actually a crucial, more subtle cause of loneliness, one that starts with you. Christopher Masi and a team of researchers at the University of Chicago analyzed more than seventy-seven research studies to pinpoint what created feelings of loneliness. They found that *maladaptive social cognitions*, or negative thoughts related to interpersonal situations, were strong predictors of loneliness, and that thinking differently turned out to be the most powerful way to feel more connected.

After her painful breakup, Madison could have easily thought: *Why make new friends given that my old ones dumped me?* But if she had, she'd have missed the joy her new friendships offered. Because even if you push yourself to go out, if you're stuck in your head, or automatically dismiss the people around you, you'll likely end up alone no matter how many people are in the room.

It's sometimes easy to forget that you don't have to be single to feel lonely. Many of my clients assume that their married friends don't experience loneliness; I've made that mistake too. Years ago, a married friend confided that she felt lonely and I wondered about the strength of her relationship. Now, I understand what she meant. As wonderful as my partner, Adam, is, there are times when his eyes start slowly closing just as I'm ready to talk about my day. As Madison knew intuitively, to feel connected, we need a core *group*, not a single person. Specifically, Robin Dunbar, an anthropologist and psychologist at the University of Oxford, famously suggested that to be happy, most people need a group of roughly five people with whom they can deeply bond.

You might worry, as many of my patients do, that likability is an innate skill that people either have or don't. But everyone is capable of finding closeness, married or not. And we can all increase our capacity to foster and sustain relationships.

Making and Keeping Friends

Building relationships doesn't have to be complicated, though many of us make it that way. In particular, we get stuck focusing on seeming exciting or "cool," which is just another example of ways to feel painfully apart with people. We don't need to combine the trendiest outfit with the most hilarious, captivating story to draw others in, whether a potential new friend or a date. I'm convinced that connecting with people can be easier than we assume.

I like to teach people who worry about their social skills a DBT acronym—GIVE—that simplifies how to get close to others:

Gentle

Interested

Validating

Easy manner

Let's start with *gentle*. A couple of years ago, I spent time with Monty Roberts, a horse trainer celebrated for rounding up horses without whips, but with a nice, gentle tone and respectful stance. I'd visited his horse farm to learn more about how best to motivate clients to make powerful life changes, but I nearly panicked as I watched Monty, then in his late seventies, enter a small corral with a wild, bucking horse many times his size. Remarkably, within about fifteen minutes, by Monty's offering the spirited animal space and warm body language, the horse was following him, rather than running away or charging. Monty's technique, which embodied patience and compassion, showed me that even flighty animals, like wary humans, will quickly engage when someone comes across as respecting them.

Notice that gentleness isn't just about your words—it's also about your body language and facial expressions. Many of my clients have remarked that when they're feeling anxious or lonely, others don't perceive them as warm or approachable; instead, they may seem to have an implicit "do not disturb" sign. It makes a lot of sense: Our faces convey feelings. That's a wonderful thing, especially when we want to wordlessly let others know that we need support. But noticing and modifying your facial expressions can help you invite others in and also influence your mood. Again, DBT offers a brilliant solution to the dilemma of wanting closeness even when feeling distressed, called the *half-smile*.

The truth is, you can change how you feel by changing your face. By raising your lips slightly, like a quarter of an inch, you release forehead tension and end up looking more Buddha, less bitter, and feeling more serene too. (To be clear, this isn't a forced, fake smile, like when you're posing for a picture. You can make sure you feel relaxed and also appear comfortable and natural by practicing in front of the mirror.) If you're skeptical, research has shown that there is a facial feedback loop in which the brain communicates to the face and the face communicates with the brain. So relaxing your expression can affect your mood. Interestingly, studies have found Botox injections (that dampen the ability to frown) actually ease feelings of depression. Half-smiling is a natural remedy and a great example of acting opposite (the skill we talked about in chapter 9). Madison constantly wears a half-smile. I've been practicing the expression since studying DBT and I'm continuously surprised by how much calmer and kinder it makes me feel, especially if I'm impatiently waiting in line for my morning coffee or stuck in traffic.

Often, as I mentioned earlier, people worry that they need to up their ante to impress, like a reality TV or Instagram story star. You can draw others in by being *interested* (Susan Cain explores this beautifully in her bestseller, *Quiet*). Instead of worrying about performing, attentively listening is a gift. Ultimately, we all want to feel seen and heard. While any one of us can satisfy an urge for entertainment with thousands of channels replete with gifted performers and comedians, your wholehearted attention is something only *you* can offer.

When I volunteered at a suicide prevention hotline, initially, I wondered how I'd manage to quickly connect with struggling strangers. A huge focus of our training was *validation*, which means communicating your understanding and acceptance of another person's emotions, thoughts, pain, and desires. Just as invalidating someone's feelings or words creates distance, it's pretty remarkable how validation increases closeness and intimacy. Validation isn't sounding fake, like an insincere therapist uttering, "It sounds like you're feeling . . ." It's also the opposite of being defensive or saying something like "I totally get it," which no one ever does. It's taking a genuine interest and expressing how someone's experience makes sense.

GIVE isn't crucial just for starting relationships; the technique also maintains them. For example, if you worry that stating your preferences will alienate others, adopting a sympathetic, *easy manner* sets a nice tone to express yourself. The same way beautiful music at peak volume is migraine-inducing, most people react adversely to feeling pressured. Yet so many people think they need to powerfully project. A client of mine spent tons of money working with a dating coach who insisted he "take charge." This person already had a pretty authoritative delivery, and when he noticed this wasn't working, at work or with women, he reluctantly tried a more mellow manner, which put him at ease, as well as those around him.

GIVE might sound simple, and in some ways, it can be. But the technique requires gestures, like making eye contact and paying attention, which are impossible to do if you're transfixed by technology. If you meet up with someone who is preoccupied with texting someone else, you probably won't feel seen or heard. Instead of feeling resentful or writing the person off as "rude," this is a great opportunity to combine GIVE and a skill you'll learn in the pages to come, known as DEAR MAN. It drives me crazy when I'm with someone who is absorbed with his or her smartphone while I wait, restlessly. It makes me feel invalidated—like I don't matter. I try not to take this personally and have practiced smiling and saying, "You know me and my mindfulness, I think we'll have more fun if we're together. Do you have an urgent message you're waiting for?" If whoever I'm with says "no," I warmly ask them if we can both agree to stow our gadgets since I think this will prove more relaxing. (I can tell you, with a nice delivery, you won't put someone off.) Making this request can feel difficult, but it's better than feeling alone, with others, and feeling resentful.

Thinking in a Less Lonely Way

Another exercise I love is called TIC TOC, a tool used in CBT that helps people think more adaptively. Given that unhelpful thoughts can fuel loneliness, thinking more constructively is one way of reducing experiences of loneliness. First attributed to the founder of CBT, Aaron Beck, and later described by psychiatrist David Burns, TIC stands for **T**ask **I**nterfering **C**ognitions, and TOC stands for **T**ask **O**rienting **C**ognitions. This sounds complicated, but basically, it involves watching your mind so you can more flexibly replace ideas that get in your way with ones that motivate you.

TIC TOC is often used to help people address thoughts that fuel procrastination, but I like to use the strategy more generally to target mental barriers that affect us in areas of our lives that matter. If your goal is getting close to others, TIC TOC can help you observe appraisals that keep you alone so you can swap them with ones that connect you with other people. Again, many people worry about how they come across or assume that they're unlikable or unworthy, or, just as unhelpful, that they're uniquely complex, like an edgy jigsaw puzzle piece. Both TICs can leave you feeling like you'll never connect. My friend Cory Newman, who directs Beck's research and treatment center, encourages clients who worry in social situations to replace those TICs with a TOC: "You only fail if you bail," which motivates people to show up and is more practical than assuming that any of us can magically intuit other people's possibly negative opinions.

The ability to swap automatic unhelpful thoughts with more encouraging ones takes awareness, willingness, and effort. I know how hard doing that can feel. Months after my wedding, I faced some TICs like *close friends don't care about me.* These thoughts were leaving me lonely. As I've mentioned, the majority of my close friends married roughly seven years before I did. I vividly remember scraping together money to purchase thoughtful wedding gifts for my friends. Even six months after my wedding, some friends I'd considered close hadn't reciprocated with a present. I appreciated that friends were generous in attending, but the fact that close friends who lived ten minutes from the wedding venue didn't so much as use a Bed Bath and Beyond coupon to get something small hurt my feelings.

Instead of more mindfully thinking that these missing gifts were an oversight, I ruminated a bit on the memories of traveling for their weddings and going alone, while most of them lived close by and arrived as part of a couple. I think the most painful rut was thinking that our dearth of presents meant my friends didn't like me.

Adam suggested I call one of my best friends in the still gift-less group to try to get some answers, but I already felt vulnerable and the last thing I wanted to do was reenact a Larry David–esque plot full of uncomfortable faux pas.

Later, when I looked at our wedding album, it struck me that my friends looked sincerely elated. I also noticed that I wasn't getting anywhere with my TICs, like *I need to meet better friends.* Ultimately, I decided to practice some CBT on myself. I reconsidered: *I can buy my own plates* and *my friends paid their babysitters for hours to dance with us.* My TOCs were linked to my values, like giving people the benefit of the doubt and being close to others, and immediately freed me from feeling like a needy pariah. I felt like I had my old friends back again.

Just as I got stuck in harmful TICs after my meaningful big day, I often hear clients talk about how others disappoint them. Many complain that they're always the ones to remember birthdays or initiate plans; they feel bummed that their gestures aren't reciprocated.

Once we work on not personalizing others' oversights with thoughts such as *some people just aren't as detail-oriented*, my clients almost always notice that they feel more connected than when they're keeping score, even if the other person's behavior doesn't change.

Interestingly, research has found that reframing our relationships can make us feel less alone. Psychologists differentiate between *perceived support* and *received support*, and highlight that when it comes to reducing the risk of depression, *perceived support* is more important than actually receiving support. Believing you're cared for, which may have a lot to do with thoughts that allow for feeling connected, matters more than actual support. I love the TOC *People are doing the best they can.* In contrast, the TIC *They should do better* gets in the way of bonding and feeling close.

Consciously adopting thoughts that promote relationships expands our community. In the days immediately following the tragedy of September 11th, Sharon Salzberg helped volunteers who'd spent days digging for bodies cope with what they were experiencing. One evening, a student approached her and confessed, "I feel weird saying this with everything that has happened, but I'm really upset because after the attacks, no one called me to find out if I was okay. Nobody." Each day, this woman faced dozens of dire missing person posters on street corners and overheard phones buzzing as people desperately tried to reach their loved ones. To be at the center of a calamity and to feel as if no one cares if you're alive would be totally depressing.

Instead of getting paralyzed by TICs like *No one will ever care about me*, with her mindfulness practice and Sharon's help the student worked on transforming her thoughts to the more motivational *I have to change my life*. And she did. Years later, Sharon met her again and the woman recounted that after noticing her own pain, she courageously tried to implement shifts in her life. Instead of escaping or acting helpless, she joined a synagogue and engaged with a community.

Remarkably, even for people with an *anxious attachment style* who seriously fear that people will disappoint them, it's possible to enjoy closeness. (For more on this topic, *Attached,* by Amir Levine and Rachel Heller, is a fantastic book.) Understandably, an anxious style takes a toll on one's well-being and can make it hard to stay close to others. In contrast, being mindful, like that 9/11 volunteer, can allow you to enter into relationships with less baggage and judgments that can destroy happiness. As a study led by psychologist David Creswell reports, when older adults participated in an eight-week mindfulness class, they not only reported feeling less isolated, but also had reduced inflammatory genes associated with stressors like loneliness.

When You're "Busy," or Not in the Mood

In addition to staving off loneliness by noticing judgments about others (and yourself), to feel more connected, pay attention to your thoughts about your schedule. Do you often feel like you're too busy to socialize or that you'd rather lie low than socialize (not that the latter can't be valid)? Admittedly, I've convinced myself that I *just don't have time* to make plans. Then I stumbled on a refreshing dose of rebuke in the form of an opinion piece by Tim Kreider in *The New York Times*. Kreider writes, "If you live in America in the twenty-first century you've probably had a lot of people tell you how busy they are." He then acknowledges that people who work in ICUs or spend their days shuffling between multiple minimum-wage jobs probably *are* justifiably exhausted. However, most of us fill our schedules with unnecessary tasks or misjudge how limited our time actually is. Kreider concludes, "I suppose it's possible I'll lie on my deathbed regretting that I didn't work harder . . . but I think what I'll really wish is that I could have one more beer with Chris, another long talk with Megan, one last good hard laugh with Boyd. Life is too short to be busy."

I don't doubt that your time is a precious commodity (which is why I'm so moved that you're reading this book). But illogical as it sounds, the less time you devote to work, the more productive you may end up being. In a 2006 study, the accounting firm Ernst & Young found that employees' year-end reviews improved roughly 8 percent for each additional ten hours of vacation they took. And those who took the most time off were less likely to leave their jobs.

Still, being with others might not always feel like your first choice of things to do, especially after a long week of work. It can feel challenging to rally after work and organize weekend plans. It *is* easier to go out if you have a partner who fills your free moments with opportunities to bond with a good group. While I do want to validate the challenges in making time to connect, the research on the risks that come along with loneliness suggests that connecting is worth the exertion. Creating closeness with others can keep you resilient, while feeling lonely seems to intensify pain. Loneliness isn't just a painful feeling; it increases your risk of sickness and death. Psychologist Julianne Holt-Lunstad and her colleagues at Brigham Young University reviewed studies on relationships and mortality (examining more than three hundred thousand people) and concluded that those who were integrated in their communities were *half* as likely to die early as their more socially isolated peers. Shockingly, loneliness is twice as dangerous as obesity in terms of its effect on your health; it also increases the risk of mortality to the same extent as smoking cigarettes.

Let me be clear—when I talk about being lonely, I am *not* talking about being single. As I've mentioned before, neither your relationship nor your marital status matters in terms of loneliness. What does matter is your involvement in community and activities. A multisite study led by Candyce Kroenke followed nearly three thousand nurses with cancer and found that those with a large network of friends were *four times* more likely to survive than those who had fewer relationships.

And despite stereotypes of seniors being isolated, a study by experts Maike Luhmann and Louise Hawkley that surveyed more than sixteen thousand German adults found that loneliness seems to peak at ages thirty and sixty, and dips around ages forty and seventy-five. Interestingly, the authors found that people who lived alone were less lonely, so we can't assume that these age differences relate to marrying and divorcing. Given the fact that loneliness isn't ageist or resolved by moving in with someone (and as an aside, if you know you don't want to live alone, there are intentional communities that connect like-minded people), again, it's worth increasing the support you feel, *now*.

Loneliness can also compromise your ability to think clearly. In the introduction, remember, I talked about anticipated aloneness reducing intelligent thought, and research suggests that it may also reduce your ability to process social cues. In animal studies, social isolation *actually* diminishes brain size, and in humans, brain studies show that people who describe themselves as lonely show reduced density in a brain region linked to social cognition (the left posterior superior temporal sulcus, to be exact). This finding is so interesting—and so depressing. When we crave companionship most, we may be most at risk of misreading social cues in ways that leave us feeling disconnected, for instance misjudging another person's forgetfulness as maliciousness. Slowing down and deciding to judge others less and remembering that a lonely mind may be clouding your perspective can help you think more clearly—and get you more connected.

Bad Company

I've often suggested that my clients join groups to connect with others who have similar values, such as Single Mothers by Choice, volunteer groups, or CrossFit classes. Will getting out there actually alleviate your loneliness? It depends. . . .

I feel a bit guilty to admit this since I care about abstaining from gossiping, but for years I spent time with close friends having conversations about how *guys were the worst* and how coupled friends *should do better* about staying in touch. At the time, these conversations seemed like an informal support group. But eventually I realized that getting together to talk about loneliness isn't a cure for loneliness. As one of my clients told me while reflecting on her time in a talk therapy group, sharing misery wasn't as helpful as she imagined. Rather, hearing others describe how they practiced tools like mindfulness to change their outlook felt more encouraging.

She was on to something. A remarkable project known as the Framingham Heart Study has followed three generations of Massachusetts residents since 1948, people who have generously invited scientists to uncover themes that unfold across their lifespans. When looking at Framingham participants, loneliness researcher John Cacioppo and his colleagues at the University of Chicago noticed a powerful effect of loneliness: It seems to be contagious, like the flu. When one person in a group started to share their lonely feelings, those close to them were also affected, and were 50 percent likelier to feel lonely as well.

To enjoy the benefits of connecting, your best bet is to enter the moment with others. Madison, for instance, doesn't spend her time with Rob discussing Spencer and his new life. Instead, when I asked her what she and Rob like to talk about or do, she mentioned their shared passion for running and watching reality TV shows. Like Madison, we all have stressors we can vent about, since dating is full of them, but to really feel happiest, we do best by appreciating good company.

Feeling Less Lonely While You're Flying Solo

Just because you're by yourself doesn't mean you have to be bad company. Recently, I was on my way to a lecture, and I had time to spare and felt hungry, in a neighborhood where I happened to know a lot of people, including many clients. While I often sit at restaurants by myself in neighborhoods where I feel more anonymous, I'll admit that I worried that getting caught eating alone would feel uncomfortable. I imagined myself telling the host, "Just one," and feeling pathetic. Then I took a moment to step back, mindfully. That's when I realized that in announcing "Just one," and looking down, I was setting the table for feeling less-than. I put my iPhone away and confidently said, "One, please!" Then I ate with my eyes up and found myself enjoying comforting Indian food on my dinner date.

Technology can be another version of bad company. I totally understand that it's easier to see what people are up to without having to make the effort get together in person. You no longer need to sit across from someone to see a new haircut or hear about an epic Halloween party. Yet in the same way that a sex toy (hopefully) isn't a substitute for a partner, social media seems like a poor substitute for plans with people you care about. Given the choice of receiving lots of posts on your Facebook wall or having a celebratory dinner out with friends, I'd bet that seeing friends in real time, in real life, will always feel nicer.

So many people complain about long-distance romantic relationships, of wanting an in-person partner, instead of a mix of FaceTime and WhatsApp, it seems strange that any of us would settle for those tech replacements in our other relationships. Now, I don't want to sound like the parent of a teenager bossily trying to curb your screen time. But in my own life and in the lives of my clients, I've repeatedly seen that swapping people for tech gadgets hijacks joy. One piece of evidence: As social media use climbs, rates of loneliness are also increasing. Plus, there's no doubt in my mind that social networking can lead to TICs (e.g., *They got together and didn't invite me*), stealing time and energy better used for seeing people in real life. Time online consumes us, enhancing the busy trap. The more you devote to others, in person, the closer you'll feel.

Overcoming Paralysis by Analysis

You can also curb loneliness by doing some problem solving, especially if you're caught in a situation that's not working for you. Some people worry that asserting themselves might seem too aggressive. Others get trapped in the TIC *people should know better.* My sense, influenced by principles in DBT, is that it's inevitable that you'll face dissatisfaction in relationships. Given this fact, the ability to repair relationships is more important than preventing a rift in the first place. Instead of ruminating on how best to bring up an issue that bothers you or worrying that saying something about a touchy topic will ruin a relationship, try the following DBT strategy, a great acronym known as DEAR MAN, that sets the stage to strategically ask for what you need instead of obsessing and feeling paralyzed.

Here's how it works:

> **D**escribe the facts
> **E**xpress how you feel
> **A**ssert or ask for what you want
> **R**einforce/reward
> **M**indful
> **A**ct confident
> **N**egotiate, if needed

I love this formula because you can use it to simplify tough topics. For example, a friend, Kate, told me that she'd recently ended a few friendships. "Why?" I asked. Kate, now thirty-eight, is a remarkable single mother who married young and tragically, as her husband was diagnosed with cancer and died soon after the birth of their daughter. Extroverted and yearning for company, she tries to schedule plans with friends in advance and looks forward to having activities on her calendar. She is also able to enter the moment, and I always have a blast when we're together. Yet despite the fact that she doesn't tend to ruminate or spread loneliness, Kate noticed that some of her friends took their plans so casually that they'd ask to reschedule just hours beforehand. "If they know what I've been through and they're flaking out on me anyway, I'm not going to waste my time anymore," she told me, explaining her recent decision to end a relationship with a friend who'd canceled once again. I felt for her and told her about the DEAR MAN technique. If her friend understood that Kate needed reliability, she might think twice before canceling again.

I didn't think it was enough for Kate to just embrace TOCs like *they mean well*, or *things pop up last minute*, but I felt she could benefit by actually doing something to increase her friends' empathy and reliability. Together, we worked on how she might talk to her friend who was prone to canceling at the last minute. The premise of DEAR MAN is that you need to set the stage and lay out what happened (Describe the facts) and allow others to get a sense of your experience (Express how you feel). Next, we tell them what we hope for (Assert) and link that to something that matters to them (Reinforce). Your delivery is Mindful, so you don't get distracted with a whole list of grievances or lose sight of what you're asking for, nor do you dilute your request with unnecessary apologies (Act confident). Finally, you might need to Negotiate (e.g., if Kate's friend were to ask to reschedule, she could give her more notice). This approach works well in asking for what matters to you in all your relationships—from your co-workers to the person you're dating. It's about being clear on what happened, your emotions, and your request, and thoughtfully thinking about why this would work well for you both.

Kate and I worked on her approaching her friend with something like this: "I know you have a lot on your plate now. And I love how, when I asked you last week about going to that new sushi place, you said, 'Let's do it!' So I booked a table and a babysitter. I looked forward to seeing you, especially because this month is rough with Father's Day. So it would mean a lot if you pick a time for plans that you're confident will work, or, if something comes up, you give me enough notice to invite someone else. I'll keep on the lookout for the best new hot spots and we always have so much fun together." (That's the reinforce, which clarifies why your request would also work well for another person. We're all driven by incentives.)

Kate sent a quick, transparent e-mail. Her friend was apologetic, and Kate discovered that once she stated her needs mindfully, she wouldn't have to give up a relationship or obsess on how this person previously disappointed her or might hurt her again in the future. Instead, she was optimistic that she had a friend she could count on.

I could have practiced a DEAR MAN with friends who didn't get me wedding gifts, but ultimately I chose not to because my objective was feeling closeness, not getting nice stuff. I decided that if my friends acted like they cared about me, I could embrace the theory that they were forgetful and this TOC turned out to be enough to allow me to drop my sense of disconnection. But I've resorted to the technique many times in other situations, including once requesting that my friends resist focusing on my dating life when we got together, as if that were the only thing that defined me, or telling my parents that I didn't want their well-intentioned but ultimately unhelpful advice when it came to my romantic relationships, though I valued their emotional support. Madison could have employed a DEAR MAN to talk to friends who hadn't reached out to her about how she was doing post-breakup but had posted lots of exclamation points on her ex-boyfriend Spencer's wall about his wedding. But since her ultimate goal was to try to separate from him, she decided to skip reclaiming the relationships they once shared and put her energy into building new friendships instead.

Thought Is Cheap

Now I want to validate and deliver a DEAR MAN to *you*. It's incredibly painful to want a partner and to not have one now and/ or to feel as if your relationships aren't as fulfilling as you'd hoped. We all deserve closeness, and just thinking more forgiving thoughts isn't a cure for that desire. I want you to *feel* more satisfied with relationships, and touched by the people in your life. That requires really taking a look at how busy you truly are, making space for connection, and getting vulnerable. Could you select a couple of people who seem interesting whom you might want to GIVE to? Are there people in your life to whom you want to deliver a DEAR MAN, in the service of increasing the depth of our friendships? Can you plan a date with a friend and strategize how to circumvent spending another night lamenting loneliness? Mindfully letting go of unhelpful judgments, combined with taking on productive behaviors, will help you build the ultimately supportive squad. I hope you can pick a few of these ideas to experiment with because you deserve the company you crave.

CONCLUSION

Single, and Serene About It

We never know how high we are
Till we are called to rise;
And then, if we are true to plan
Our statures touch the skies—
—EMILY DICKINSON

EVEN IF FACEBOOK gives you the option to describe your relationship status as "It's complicated," we don't need things to be complicated with others or within ourselves. Interestingly, the word *single* is related to the word *simple*, from the Latin *simplex*. We can live simply and happily at any point in our lives by letting go of worries and judgments, and remembering that we're complete, whether we're single and satisfied, actively dating, or in a relationship. I also find it telling that the origin of the word *happy* is the Old English word *hap*, meaning by chance or good fortune. Finding love *may* make you happy. We can all generate examples of people who found love and seemed elated. But we can also dig deeper, to purposefully create joy.

For more than a decade, I looked like the picture of contentment, smiling, running to yoga, and pursuing a career in psychology. Yet inside, I felt like I wasn't *good enough* because I was single, and I struggled to find peace of mind. Once I decided to focus on measuring my worth by focusing on my values and living mindfully, I felt empowered and at ease.

I also have clients who are going through all the motions of happiness, yet don't feel free. Beyond appearing like we have it together, we deserve to achieve a more accepting and compassionate state of mind. That can feel hard to do during times of loneliness, especially in a society that continues to shout that there's something wrong with independent women. It drives me crazy to hear how often women are asked, "Why are you still single?" as if our relationship status is not just chance, but something to justify.

In writing this book, I've shared more about my personal life than I generally do (with colleagues and clients alike). So when I started showing the manuscript around to a few people, I felt especially vulnerable, wondering if my stories were professional and wanting to make sure my prescriptions felt worthwhile. When I sent a draft of the book to my friend Cory Newman, who teaches therapists around the world to do their best work, I found myself empathizing with clients waiting to hear from someone after a date, especially when he sent me a brief e-mail one week later asking to set up a time to talk. Cory's curt reply and absence of a reassurance like "this is great!" left me apprehensive, though anticipating our phone meeting felt like a tiny fraction of how unsettling awaiting romantic validation once felt to me.

"You didn't really write a book on being single . . ." Cory said in our call, and I felt my face warming and my heart rate accelerating as I noticed feeling ashamed and anxious. "You wrote about advances in living well," he (thankfully) continued. Cory was right. The recommendations in this book aren't only for those searching for intimacy. Focusing on your values, learning to enter the moment, and taking steps toward living a fulfilling life, independent of circumstances (like whether or not you have a partner), applies to all of us (including anyone who puts you in a position of having to defend your relationship status).

I hope to give you a dose of respectful support for all those times the pangs of loneliness dull your bright light. It can truly feel hard to be single or unhappily coupled —I don't want to minimize that for a second or to have you think that wanting a loving relationship is all in your head. The suggestions in this book aren't meant to imply that you somehow need fixing. Rather, I want to honor that it can be painful to not have something you want. It is certainly distressing to be invalidated by others. The tools I've offered here come from a place of tremendous admiration, and they aim to promote well-being, particularly if you notice yourself falling into any of the habits I described in part 1. These strategies aren't meant to add more work to your life—they are meant to enhance your freedom. They are the same tools I practice to get unstuck, personally, and continue to use every day. I also prescribe these to anyone who asks me about how to live optimally.

In the Hebrew language, there are numerical values associated with words that are said to offer meaningful insights. The word "love," *ahava*, shares the identical value as the word "one," *echad*, highlighting that the function of love is to unify. Whether you are either by yourself or in the company of others, it's important to strive for becoming united within, so you don't get torn apart by negative thoughts, feelings, or actions. You are whole and worthy of love no matter what you think in moments of anticipated aloneness. I hope the reminders in this book help you remember that.

REFERENCES

Introduction

Baumeister, R. F., J. M. Twenge, and C. K. Nuss. "Effects of Social Exclusion on Cognitive Processes: Anticipated Aloneness Reduces Intelligent Thought." *Journal of Personality and Social Psychology* 83(4) (2002): 817–27.

Harker, L., and D. Keltner. "Expressions of Positive Emotions in Women's College Yearbook Pictures and Their Relationship to Personality and Life Outcomes Across Adulthood." *Journal of Personality and Social Psychology* 80(1) (2001): 112–24.

Kabat-Zinn, J. *Full Catastrophe Living: Using the Wisdom of Your Body and Mind to Face Stress, Pain, and Illness.* Revised ed. New York: Bantam Books, 2013.

Killingsworth, M. A., and D. T. Gilbert. "A Wandering Mind Is an Unhappy Mind." *Science* 330 (Nov. 12, 2010): 932.

Linehan, M. M. *DBT Skills Training Handouts and Worksheets.* 2nd ed. New York: Guilford Press, 2015.

Lyubomirsky, S., L. King, and E. Diener. "The Benefits of Frequent Positive Affect: Does Happiness Lead to Success?" *Psychological Bulletin* 131(6) (2005): 803–55.

Stillman, T. F., R. F. Baumeister, N. M. Lambert, A. W. Crescioni, N. DeWall, and F. D. Fincham. "Alone and Without Purpose: Life Loses Meaning Following Social Exclusion." *Journal of Experimental and Social Psychology* 45(4) (2009): 686–94.

Chapter 1

Allen, J. "Partners Main Source of Happiness Around the Globe: Poll." 2012. www.reuters.com/article/us-valentine-poll-idUSTRE81D10U20120214.

Barnhofer, T., J. M. Huntenburg, M. Lifshitz, J. Wild, E. Antonova, and D. S. Margulies. "How Mindfulness Training May Help to Reduce Vulnerability for Recurrent Depression: A Neuroscientific Perspective." *Clinical Psychology Science* 4(2) (2016): 328–43.

Baumeister, R. F., K. D. Vohs, J. Aaker, and E. N. Garbinsky. "Some Key Differences Between a Happy Life and a Meaningful Life." *Journal of Positive Psychology* 8(6) (2013): 505–16.

Blackwell, L. S., K. H. Trzesniewski, and C. S. Dweck. "Implicit Theories of Intelligence Predict Achievement Across an Adolescent Transition: A Longitudinal Study and an Intervention." *Child Development* 78(1) (2007): 246–63.

Brickman, C. "Hedonic Relativism and Planning the Good Society." In *Adaptation-Level Theory: A Symposium*. Edited by M. H. Apley. New York: Academic Press, 1971.

Crum, A. J., and E. J. Langer. "Mind-Set Matters: Exercise and the Placebo Effect." *Psychological Science* 18(2) (2007): 165–71.

Crum, A. J., P. Salovey, and S. Anchor. "Rethinking Stress: The Role of Mindsets in Determining the Stress Response." *Journal of Personality and Social Psychology* 104(4) (2013): 716–33.

Danner, D. D., D. A. Snowdon, and W. V. Friesen. "Positive Emotions in Early Life and Longevity: Findings from the Nun Study." *Journal of Personality and Social Psychology* 80(5) (2001): 804–13.

DePaulo, B. M., and W. L. Morris. "The Unrecognized Stereotyping and Discrimination Against People Who Are Single." *Current Directions in Psychological Science* 15(5) (2006): 251–54.

Dweck, C. S. *Mindset: The New Psychology of Success*. New York: Ballantine Books, 2007.

———. "Can Personality Be Changed? The Role of Beliefs in Personality and Change." *Current Directions in Psychological Science* 17(6) (2008): 391–94.

Fredrickson, B. L. *Love 2.0: Creating Happiness and Health in Moments of Connection*. New York: Plume, 2014.

Gilbert, D. T., E. C. Pinel, T. D. Wilson, S. J. Blumberg, and T. P. Wheatley. "Immune Neglect: A Source of Durability Bias in Affective Forecasting." *Journal of Personality and Social Psychology* 75(3) (1998): 617–38.

Greitemeyer, T. "Stereotypes of Singles: Are Singles What We Think?" *European Journal of Social Psychology* 39(3) (2009): 368–83.

Hölzel, B. K., J. Carmody, M. Vangel, C. Congleton, S. M. Yerramsetti, T. Gard, and S. W. Lazar. "Mindfulness Practice Leads to Increases in Regional Brain Gray Matter Density." *Psychiatry Research* 19(1) (2011): 36–43.

Hölzel, B. K., U. Ott, H. Hempel, A. Hackl, K. Wolf, R. Stark, and D. Vaitl. "Differential Engagement of Anterior Cingulate and Adjacent Medial Frontal Cortex in Adept Meditators and Non-Meditators." *Neuroscience Letters* 421(1) (2007): 16–21.

Irwin, M. R., R. Olmstead, E. C. Breen, T. Witarama, C. Carrillo, N. Sadeghi, J. M. Arevalo, P. Nicassio, R. Bootzin, and S. Cole. "Cognitive Behavioral Therapy and Tai Chi Reverse Cellular and Genomic Markers of Inflammation in Late Life Insomnia: A Randomized Controlled Trial," *Biological Psychiatry* 78(10) (2015): 721–29.

Johnson, D. R., and J. Wu. "An Empirical Test of Crisis, Social Selection, and Role Explanations of the Relationship Between Marital Disruption and Psychological Distress: A Pooled Time-series Analysis of Four-wave Panel Data." *Journal of Marriage and the Family* 64(1) (2002): 211–24.

Kaplan, R. M., and R. G. Kronick. "Marital Status and Longevity in the United States Population." *Journal of Epidemiology and Community Health* 60(9) (2006): 760–65.

Lucas, R. E., Y. Georgellis, A. E. Clark, and E. Diener. "Reexamining Adaptation and the Set Point Model of Happiness: Reactions to Changes in Marital Status." *Journal of Personality and Social Psychology* 84(3) (2003): 527–39.

Lutz, A., L. L. Greischar, N. B. Rawlings, M. Ricard, and R. J. Davidson. "Long-Term Meditators Self-Induce High-Amplitude Gamma Synchrony During Mental Practice." *Proceedings of the National Academy of Sciences of the USA* 101(46) (2004): 16369–73.

Lyubomirsky, S., K. M. Sheldon, and D. Schkade. "Pursuing Happiness: The Architecture of Sustainable Change." *Review of General Psychology* 9(2) (2005): 111–31.

Morris, N. "Through Meditation, She Makes Happiness an Inside Job." *Los Angeles Times* (2011). http://articles.latimes.com/2011/feb/19/local/la-me-beliefs-meditate-20110219.

Pikhartova, J., A. Bowling, and C. Victor. "Is Loneliness in Later Life a Self-Fulfilling Prophecy?" *Aging & Mental Health* 20(5) (2016): 543–49.

Salzberg, S. *A Heart as Wide as the World*. Boston: Shambhala, 1999.

Segal, Z. V., P. Bieling, T. Young, G. MacQueen, R. Cooke, L. Martin, and R. D. Levitan. "Antidepressant Mono-Therapy vs. Sequential Pharmacotherapy and Mindfulness-Based Cognitive Therapy, or Placebo, for Relapse Prophylaxis in Recurrent Depression." *Archives of General Psychiatry* 67(12) (2010): 1256–64.

Wilson, T. D., and D. T. Gilbert. "Affective Forecasting: Knowing What to Want." *Current Directions in Psychological Science* 14(3) (2005): 131–34.

Wilson, T. D., T. P. Wheatley, J. M. Meyers, D. T. Gilbert, and D. Axsom. "Focalism: A Source of Durability Bias in Affective Forecasting." *Journal of Personality and Social Psychology* 78(5) (2000): 821–36.

CHAPTER 2

Baer, R. A. "Self-Focused Attention and Mechanisms of Change in Mindfulness-Based Treatment." *Cognitive Behavioral Therapy* 38(Suppl. 1) (2009): 15–20.

Chung, M. "Pathways Between Attachment and Marital Satisfaction: The Mediating Roles of Rumination, Empathy, and Forgiveness." *Personality and Individual Differences* 70 (November 2014): 246–51.

Davis, R. N., and S. Nolen-Hoeksema. "Cognitive Inflexibility Among Ruminators and Nonruminators." *Cognitive Therapy & Research* 24(6) (2000): 699–711.

Downey, G., and S. I. Feldman, "Implications of Rejection and Sensitivity for Intimate Relationships." *Journal of Personality and Social Psychology* 70(6) (1996): 1327–43.

Genet, J. J., and M. Siemer. "Rumination Moderates the Effects of Daily Events on Negative Mood: Results from a Diary Study." *Emotion* 12(6) (2012): 1329–39.

Joinson, A. N. "'Looking At,' 'Looking Up' or 'Keeping Up With' People? Motives and Uses of Facebook." *Proceedings of the SIGCHI Conference on Human Factors in Computing Systems* (2008): 1027–36.

Jostmann, N. B., J. Karremans, and C. Finkenauer. "When Love Is Not Blind: Rumination Impairs Implicit Affect Regulation in Response to Romantic Relationship Threat." *Cognition and Emotion* 25(3) (2011): 506–18.

Kaiser, R. H., J. R. Andrews-Hanna, C. A. Metcalf, and S. Dimidjian. "Dwell or Decenter? Rumination and Decentering Predict Working Memory Updating After Interpersonal Criticism." *Cognitive Therapy Research* 39(6) (2015): 744–53.

Keune, P. M., V. Bostanov, B. Kotchoubey, and M. Hautzinger. "Mindfulness versus Rumination and Behavioral Inhibition: A Perspective from Research on Frontal Brain Asymmetry." *Personality and Individual Differences* 53(3) (2012): 323–28.

Killingsworth, M. A., and D. T. Gilbert. "A Wandering Mind Is an Unhappy Mind." *Science* 330 (Nov. 12, 2010): 932.

Martin, L. L., A. Tesser, and W. D. McIntosh. "Wanting but Not Having: The Effects of Unattained Goals on Thoughts and Feelings." In *Handbook of Mental Control*. Edited by D. M. Wegner and J. W. Pennebaker. Englewood Cliffs, NJ: Prentice Hall, 1993.

McLaughlin, K. A., and S. Nolen-Hoeksema. "Rumination as a Transdiagnostic Factor in Depression and Anxiety." *Behavior Research and Therapy* 49(3) (2011): 186–93.

Mischel, W. *The Marshmallow Test: Why Self-Control Is the Engine of Success.* New York: Little, Brown and Company, 2014.

Mischel, W., Y. Shoda, and P. K. Peake. "The Nature of Adolescent Competencies Predicted by Pre-School Delay of Gratification." *Journal of Personality and Social Psychology* 54(4) (1988): 687–96.

Nolen-Hoeksema, S. *Women Who Think Too Much*. New York: St. Martin's Press, 2003.

Nolen-Hoeksema, S., and C. G. Davis. "'Thanks for Sharing That': Ruminators and Their Social Support Networks." *Journal of Personality and Social Psychology* 77(4) (1999): 801–14.

Nolen-Hoeksema, S., J. Larson, and C. Grayson. "Explaining the Gender Difference in Depressive Symptoms." *Journal of Personality and Social Psychology* 77(5) (1999): 1061–72.

Nolen-Hoeksema, S., and J. Morrow. "A Prospective Study of Depression and Post-Traumatic Stress Symptoms Following a Natural Disaster: The 1989 Loma Prieta Earthquake." *Journal of Personality and Social Psychology* 61(1) (1991): 115–21.

Nolen-Hoeksema, S., E. Stice, E. Wade, and C. Bohn. "Reciprocal Relations Between Rumination and Bulimic, Substance Abuse and Depressive Symptoms in Female Adolescents." *Journal of Abnormal Psychology* 116(1) (2007): 198–207.

Papageorgiou, C., and A. Wells. "Metacognitive Beliefs About Rumination in Recurrent Major Depression." *Cognitive and Behavioral Practice* 8(2) (2001): 160–64.

Rawn, C. D., and K. D. Vohns. "The Importance of Self-Regulation in Interpersonal Functioning." In *Self and Relationships: Connecting Intrapersonal and Interpersonal Processes*. Edited by K. D. Vohns and E. J. Finkel. New York: Guilford Press, 2006.

Roberts, H., E. R. Watkins, and A. J. Wills. "Cueing an Unresolved Personal Goal Causes Persistent Ruminative Self-Focus: An Experimental Evaluation of Control Theories." *Journal of Behavior Therapy and Experimental Psychiatry* 44(4) (2013): 449–55.

Rose, A. J. "Co-Rumination in the Friendships of Girls and Boys." *Child Development* 73(6) (2002): 1830–43.

Senkans, S., T. E. McEwan, J. Skues, and J. R. P. Ogloff. "Development of a Relational Rumination Questionnaire." *Personality and Individual Differences* 90 (Feb. 2016): 27–35.

Starr, L. R. "When Support Seeking Backfires: Co-Rumination, Excessive Reassurance Seeking, and Depressed Mood in the Daily Lives of Young Adults." *Journal of Social and Clinical Psychology* 34(5) (2015): 436–57.

Tran, T. B., and J. Joormann. "The Role of Facebook Use in Mediating the Relation Between Rumination and Adjustment After a Relationship Breakup." *Computers in Human Behavior* 49 (2015): 56–61.

Tronick, E., H. Als, L. Adamson, S. Wise, and B. Brazelton. "The Infant's Response to Entrapment Between Contradictory Messages in Face-to-Face Interaction." *Journal of American Academy of Child Psychiatry* 17(1) (1978): 1–13.

Watkins, E. "Constructive and Unconstructive Repetitive Thought." *Psychological Bulletin* 134(2) (2008): 163–206.

———. "Depression Rumination: Investigating Mechanisms to Improve Cognitive Behavioural Treatments." *Cognitive Behaviour Therapy* 38(Suppl. 1) (2009): 8–14.

Wilson, T. D., D. A. Reinhard, E. C. Westgate, D. T. Gilbert, N. Ellerback, C. Hahn, C. L. Brown, and A. Shaked. "Just Think: The Challenges of the Disengaged Mind." *Science* 345 (July 4, 2014): 75–77.

Zawadzki, M. J., J. E. Graham, and W. Gerin. "Rumination and Anxiety Mediate the Effect of Loneliness on Depressed Mood and Sleep Quality in College Students." *Health Psychology* 32(2) (2013): 212–22.

CHAPTER 3

Carey, B. "Expert on Mental Illness Reveals Her Own Fight." *The New York Times* (2011). http://www.nytimes.com/2011/06/23/health/23lives.html?pagewanted=all.

Epstude, K., and N. J. Roese. "The Functional Theory of Counterfactual Thinking." *Personality and Social Psychology Review* 12(2) (2008): 168–92.

Gao, H., Y. Zhang, F. Wang, Y. Zu, H. Ying-Yi, and J. Jiang. "Regret Causes Ego-Depletion and Finding Benefits in the Regrettable Events Alleviates Ego-Depletion." *The Journal of General Psychology* 141(3) (2014): 169–206.

Gilbert, D. T., C. K. Morewedge, J. L. Risen, and T. D. Wilson. "Looking Forward to Looking Backward: The Misprediction of Regret." *Psychological Science* 15(5) (2004): 346–50.

Gilovich, T., V. H. Medvec, and D. Kahneman. "Varieties of Regret: A Debate and Partial Resolution." *Psychological Review* 105(3) (1998): 602–5.

King, L. A., and J. A. Hicks. "Whatever Happened to 'What Might Have Been'? Regrets, Happiness, and Maturity." *American Psychologist* 62(7) (2007): 625–36.

Leary, M. R., E. B. Tate, C. E. Adams, A. Batts Allen, and J. Hancock. "Self-Compassion and Reactions to Unpleasant Self-Relevant Events: The Implications of Treating Oneself Kindly." *Journal of Personality and Social Psychology* 92(5) (2007): 887–904.

Lee, S. W. S., and N. Schwartz. "Framing Love: When It Hurts to Think We're Made for Each Other." *Journal of Experimental Social Psychology* 54 (2014): 61–67.

Linehan, M. M. *DBT Skills Training Handouts and Worksheets*. 2nd ed. New York: Guilford Press, 2015.

Morrison, M., K. Epstude, and N. J. Roese. "Life Regrets and the Need to Belong." *Social Psychological and Personality Science* 3(6) (2012): 675–81.

Morrison, M., and N. J. Roese. "Regrets of the Typical American: Finding from a Nationally Representative Survey." *Social Psychological and Personality Science* 2(6) (2011): 576–83.

Saffrey, C., and M. Ehrenberg. "When Thinking Hurts: Attachment, Rumination, and Postrelationship Adjustment." *Personal Relationships* 14(3) (2007): 351–68.

Saffrey, C., A. Summerville, and N. J. Roese. "Praise for Regret: People Value Regret Above Other Negative Emotions." *Motivation and Emotion* 32(1) (2008): 46–54.

Shimanoff, S. B. "Commonly Named Emotions in Everyday Conversations." *Perceptual and Motor Skills* 58(2) (1984): 514.

Sparks, E. A., J. Ehrlinger, and R. P. Eibach. "Failing to Commit: Maximizers Avoid Commitment in a Way That Contributes to Reduced Satisfaction." *Personality and Individual Differences* 52(1) (2012): 72–77.

Stewart, A. J., and E. A. Vandewater. "'If I Had It to Do Over Again . . . ': Midlife Review, Midcourse Corrections, and Women's Well-Being in Midlife." *Journal of Personality and Social Psychology* 76(2) (1999): 270–83.

Wrosch, C., I. Bauer, G. E. Miller, and S. Lupien. "Regret Intensity, Diurnal Cortisol Secretion, and Physical Health in Older Individuals: Evidence for Directional Effects and Protective Factors." *Psychology and Aging* 22(2) (2007): 319–30.

Zeelenberg, M., and R. Pieters. "A Theory of Regret Regulation 1.0." *Journal of Consumer Psychology* 17(1) (2007): 3–18.

Zeelenberg, M., W. W. van Dijk, and A. S. R. Manstead. "Reconsidering the Relation Between Regret and Responsibility." *Organizational Behavior and Human Decision Processes* 74(3) (1998): 254–72.

Zhang, J. W., and S. Chen. "Self-Compassion Promotes Personal Improvement from Regret Experiences via Acceptance." *Personality and Social Psychology Bulletin* 42(2) (2016): 244–58.

CHAPTER 4

Ansari, A., and E. Klinenberg. *Modern Romance*. New York: Penguin, 2015.

Bond, F. W., S. C. Hayes, R. A. Baer, K. M. Carpenter, N. Guenole, H. K. Orcutt, T. Waltz, and R. D. Zettle. "Preliminary Psychometric Properties of the Acceptance and Action Questionnaire—II: A Revised Measure of Psychological Flexibility and Experiential Avoidance." *Behavior Therapy* 42(4) (2011): 676–88.

Fergus, T. A., J. R. Bardeen, and H. K. Orcutt. "Experiential Avoidance and Negative Emotional Experiences: The Moderating Role of Expectancies About Emotion Regulation Strategies." *Cognitive Therapy Research* 37(2) (2013): 352–62.

Gerhart, J. L., C. N. Baker, M. Hoerger, and G. F. Ronan. "Experiential Avoidance and Interpersonal Problems: A Moderated Mediation Model." *Journal of Contextual Behavioral Science* 3(4) (2014): 291–98.

Gross, J. J., and R. W. Levenson. "Hiding Feelings: The Acute Effects of Inhibiting Negative and Positive Emotion." *Journal of Abnormal Psychology* 106(1) (1997): 95–103.

Hayes, S. C., J. B. Luoma, F. W. Bond, A. Masuda, and J. Lillis. "Acceptance and Commitment Therapy: Model, Processes, and Outcomes." *Behavior Research and Therapy* 44(1) (2006): 1–25.

Hayes, S. C., K. D. Strosahl, and K. G. Wilson. *Acceptance and Commitment Therapy: An Experiential Approach to Behavior Change.* New York: Guilford Press, 1999.

Hayes, S. C., K. G. Wilson, E. V. Gifford, V. M. Follette, and K. Strosahl. "Experiential Avoidance and Behavioral Disorders: A Functional Dimensional Approach to Diagnosis and Treatment." *Journal of Consulting and Clinical Psychology* 64(6) (1996): 1152–68.

Impett, E. A., A. Kogan, T. English, O. John, C. Oveis, A. M. Gordon, and D. Keltner. "Suppression Sours Sacrifice: Emotional and Relational Costs of Suppressing Emotions in Romantic Relationships." *Personality and Social Psychology Bulletin* 38(6) (2012): 707–20.

Kashdan, T. B., V. Barrios, J. P. Forsyth, and M. F. Steger. "Experiential Avoidance as a Generalized Psychological Vulnerability: Comparisons with Coping and Emotion Regulation Strategies." *Behavior Research and Therapy* 44(9) (2006): 1301–20.

Kashdan, T. B., and J. Rottenberg. "Psychological Flexibility as a Fundamental Aspect of Health." *Clinical Psychology Review* 30(7) (2010): 865–78.

Leahy, R. L. "Sunk Costs and Resistance to Change." *Journal of Cognitive Psychotherapy* 14(4) (2000): 355–57.

Machell, K. A., R. G. Fallon, and T. B. Kashdan. "Experiential Avoidance and Well-Being: A Daily Diary Analysis." *Cognition and Emotion* 29(2) (2015): 351–59.

Moroz, M., and D. M. Dunkley. "Self-Critical Perfectionism and Depressive Symptoms: Low Self-Esteem and Experiential Avoidance as Mediators." *Personality and Individual Differences* 87 (Dec. 2015): 174–79.

Spielmann, S. S., G. MacDonald, J. A. Maxwell, D. Peragine, A. Muise, and E. A. Impett. "Settling for Less Out of Fear of Being Single." *Journal of Personality and Social Psychology* 105(6) (2013): 1049–73.

Srivastava, S., M. Tami, K. M. McGonigal, O. P. John, and J. J. Gross. "The Social Costs of Emotional Suppression: A Prospective Study of the Transition to College." *Journal of Personality and Social Psychology* 96(4) (2009): 883–97.

Tackman, A. M., and S. Srivastava. "Social Responses to Expressive Suppression: The Role of Personality Judgments." *Journal of Personality and Social Psychology* 110(4) (2016): 574–91.

Taitz, J. L. *End Emotional Eating: Using Dialectical Behavior Therapy Skills to Cope with Difficult Emotions and Develop a Healthy Relationship to Food.* Oakland, CA: New Harbinger, 2012.

CHAPTER 5

Baumeister, R. F. "Self-Control: The Secret to Life's Successes." *Scientific American* 312 (Apr. 2015): 60–65.

Boyle, P. A., L. L. Barnes, A. S. Buchman, and D. A. Bennett. "Purpose in Life Is Associated with Mortality Among Community-Dwelling Older Persons." *Psychosomatic Medicine* 71(5) (2009): 574–79.

Boyle, P. A., A. S. Buchman, R. S. Wilson, L. Yu, J. A. Schneider, and D. A. Bennett. "Effect of Purpose in Life on the Relation Between Alzheimer Disease Pathologic Changes on Cognitive Function in Advanced Age." *Archives of General Psychiatry* 69(5) (2012): 499–505.

Brooks, D. "The Moral Bucket List." *The New York Times* (2015). www.nytimes .com/2015/04/12/opinion/sunday/david-brooks-the-moral-bucket-list.html.

Fromm, E. *The Art of Loving*. New York: Harper Perennial Modern Classics, 2006.

Gottman, J., and N. Silver. *The Seven Principles for Making Marriage Work: A Practical Guide from the Country's Foremost Relationship Expert*. New York: Harmony Books, 2015.

Grant, A. *Originals: How Non-Conformists Move the World*. New York: Viking, 2016.

Kalanithi, P. *When Breath Becomes Air*. New York: Random House, 2016.

Kleiman, E. M., and J. K. Beaver. "A Meaningful Life Is Worth Living: Meaning in Life as a Suicide Resiliency Factor." *Psychiatry Research* 210(3) (2013): 934–39.

Langer, E. J., and J. Rodin. "The Effects of Choice and Enhanced Personal Responsibility for the Aged: A Field Experiment in an Institutional Setting." *Journal of Personality and Social Psychology* 34(2) (1976): 191–98.

McKeown, G. *Essentialism: The Disciplined Pursuit of Less*. New York: Crown Business, 2014.

Polk, K., B. Schoendorff, and F. O. Olaz. *The Matrix: A Step-by-Step Approach to Using the ACT Matrix Model in Clinical Practice*. Oakland, CA: Context Press, 2016.

Schaefer, S. M., J. M. Boylan, C. M. van Reekum, R. C. Lapate, C. J. Norris, C. D. Ryff, and R. J. Davidson. "Purpose in Life Predicts Better Emotional Recovery from Negative Stimuli." *PLOS ONE* 8 (2013): e80329.

Stillman, T. F., N. M. Lambert, F. D. Fincham, and R. F. Baumeister. "Meaning as Magnetic Force: Evidence That Meaning in Life Promotes Interpersonal Appeal." *Social Psychological and Personality Science* 2(1) (2011): 13–20.

Tashiro, T. *Happily Ever After: What Really Matters in the Quest for Enduring Love*. Ontario, Canada: Harlequin, 2014.

van Dijk, W., and M. Zeelenberg. "What Do We Talk About When We Talk About Disappointment? Distinguishing Outcome-Related Disappointment from Person-Related Disappointment." *Cognition and Emotion* 16(6) (2002): 787–807.

CHAPTER 6

Beck, A. T. *Cognitive Therapy of Depression*. New York: Guilford Press, 1979.

Boone, S. Personal interview. May 22, 2017.

Brach, T. "Accepting Absolutely Everything." Blog post. 2012. http://blog
.tarabrach.com/2012/05/accepting-absolutely-everything.html.

Brach, T. *Radical Acceptance: Embracing Your Life with the Heart of a Buddha*. New
York: Bantam, 2004.

Burzynska, A. Z., C. N. Wong, L. Chaddock-Heyman, E. A. Olson, N. P. Gothe,
A. Knecht, M. W. Voss, E. McAuley, and A. F. Kramer. "White Matter Integ-
rity, Hippocampal Volume, and Cognitive Performance of a World-Famous
Nonagenarian Track-and-Field Athlete." *Neurocase* 22(2) (2016): 135–44.

Cattrall, K. "How to Be a Parent . . . Without Being a Parent." September 15,
2015. http://www.bbc.co.uk/programmes/p0327zz8.

Centers for Disease Control and Prevention. "Adult Participation in Aerobic and
Muscle-Strengthening Activities." 2013. https://www.cdc.gov/mmwr/preview
/mmwrhtml/mm6217a2.htm?s_cid=mm6217a2_w.

Dimidjian, S., S. D. Hollon, K. S. Dobson, K. B. Schmaling, R. J. Kohlenberg,
M. E. Addis, R. Gallop, J. B. McGlinchey, D. K. Markley, J. K. Gollan,
D. C. Atkins, D. L. Dunner, and N. S. Jacobson. "Randomized Trial of Behav-
ioral Activation, Cognitive Therapy, and Antidepressant Medication in the
Acute Treatment of Adults with Major Depression." *Journal of Consulting and
Clinical Psychology* 74(4) (2006): 658–70.

Dobson, K. S., S. D. Hollon, S. Dimidijan, K. B. Schmaling, R. J. Kohlenberg,
R. J. Gallop, S. L. Rizvi, J. K. Gollan, D. L. Dunner, and N. S. Jacobson.
"Randomized Trial of Behavioral Activation, Cognitive Therapy, and Antide-
pressant Medication in the Prevention of Relapse and Recurrence in Major
Depression." *Journal of Consulting and Clinical Psychology* 76(3) (2008): 468–77.

Hausmann, L. M., A. Parks, A. O. Youk, and C. K. Kwoh. "Reduction of Bodily
Pain in Response to an Online Positive Activities Intervention." *Journal of
Pain* 15(5) (2014): 560–67.

Layous, K., J. Chancellor, and S. Lyubomirsky. "Protective Factors Against Mental Health Conditions." *Journal of Abnormal Psychology* 123(1) (2014): 3–12.

Linehan, M. M. *DBT Skills Training Handouts and Worksheets*. 2nd ed. New
York: Guilford Press, 2015.

Lyubomirsky, S., and K. Layous. "How Do Simple Positive Activities Increase
Well-Being?" *Current Directions in Psychological Science* 22(1) (2013): 57–62.

Marrs, R. Personal interview. January 25, 2017.

Martell, C. R., S. Dimidjian, and R. Herman-Dunn. *Behavioral Activation for
Depression: A Clinician's Guide*. New York: Guilford Press, 2010.

Medina, J., L. Hopkins, M. Powers, S. O. Baird, and J. Smits. "The Effects of a
Hatha Yoga Intervention on Facets of Distress Tolerance." *Cognitive Behaviour Therapy* 44(4) (2015): 288–300.

Otto, M. W., and J. A. J. Smits. *Exercise for Mood and Anxiety: Proven Strategies for Overcoming Depression and Enhancing Well-Being.* New York: Oxford University Press, 2011.

Wetherell, J. L., N. Afari, T. Rutledge, J. T. Sorrell, J. A. Stoddard, A. J. Petkus, B. C. Solomon, D. H. Lehman, L. Liu, A. J. Lang, and J. H. Atkinson. "A Randomized Control of Acceptance and Commitment Therapy and Cognitive Behavioral Therapy for Chronic Pain." *Pain* 152(9) (2011): 2098–107.

Chapter 7

Baumeister, R. F., E. Bratslavsky, C. Finkenauer, and K. D. Vohs. "Bad Is Stronger than Good." *Review of General Psychology* 5(4) (2001): 323–70.

Beck, M. *Expecting Adam: A True Story of Birth, Rebirth, and Everyday Magic.* 2nd ed. New York: Three Rivers Press, 2011.

Breines, J. G., and S. Chen. "Self-Compassion Increases Self-Improvement Motivation." *Personality and Social Psychology Bulletin* 38(9) (2012): 1133–43.

Dunn, E. W., L. B. Aknin, and M. I. Norton. "Spending Money on Others Promotes Happiness." *Science* 319 (Mar. 2008): 1687–88.

Emmons, R. A., and M. E. McCullough. "Counting Blessings versus Burdens: Experimental Studies of Gratitude and Subjective Well-Being in Daily Life." *Journal of Personality and Social Psychology* 84(2) (2003): 377–89.

Emmons, R. A., and A. Mishra. "Why Gratitude Enhances Well-Being: What We Know, What We Need to Know." In *Designing the Future of Positive Psychology: Taking Stock and Moving Forward.* Edited by K. Sheldon, T. Kashdan, and M. F. Steger. New York: Oxford University Press, 2012.

Fredrickson, B. L. "What Good Are Positive Emotions?" *Review of General Psychology* 2(3) (1998): 300–319.

Fredrickson, B. L., M. A. Cohn, K. A. Coffey, J. Pek, and S. M. Finkel. "Open Hearts Build Lives: Positive Emotions, Induced Through Loving-Kindness Meditation, Build Consequential Personal Resources." *Journal of Personality and Social Psychology* 95(5) (2008): 1045–62.

Geraghty, A. W. A., A. M. Wood, and M. E. Hyland. "Dissociating the Facets of Hope: Agency and Pathways Predict Dropout from Unguided Self-Help Therapy in Opposite Directions." *Journal of Research in Personality* 44(1) (2010): 155–58.

Gilbert, P., K. McEwan, M. Matos, and A. Rivis. "Fears of Compassion: Development of Three Self-Report Measures." *Psychology and Psychotherapy* 84(3) (2011): 239–55.

Hani, M., V. Vakharia, M. A. Kirkman, M. Murphy, and D. Nandi. "Practice Makes Perfect? The Role of Simulation-Based Deliberate Practice and Script-Based Mental Rehearsal in the Acquisition and Maintenance of Operative Neurosurgical Skills." *Neurosurgery* 72(Suppl. 1) (2013): 124–30.

Kannan, D., and H. M. Levitt. "A Review of Client Self-Criticism in Psychotherapy." *Journal of Psychotherapy Integration* 23(2) (2013): 166–78.

Kleiman, E. M., L. M. Adams, T. B. Kashdan, and J. H. Riskind. "Grateful Individuals Are Not Suicidal: Buffering Risks Associated with Hopelessness and Depressive Symptoms." *Personality and Individual Differences* 55(5) (2013): 595–99.

Konrath, S., A. Fuhrel-Forbis, A. Lou, and S. Brown. "Motives for Volunteering Are Associated with Mortality Risk in Older Adults." *Health Psychology* 31(1) (2012): 87–96.

Laeng, B., and U. Sulutvedt. "The Eye Pupil Adjusts to Imaginary Light." *Psychological Science* 25(1) (2014): 188–97.

Leary, M. R., E. B. Tate, C. E. Adams, A. Batts Allen, and J. Hancock. "Self-Compassion and Reactions to Unpleasant Self-Relevant Events: The Implications of Treating Oneself Kindly." *Journal of Personality and Social Psychology* 92(5) (2007): 887–904.

Linehan, M. M. *DBT Skills Training Handouts and Worksheets.* 2nd ed. New York: Guilford Press, 2015.

Lyubomirsky, S., K. M. Sheldon, and D. Schkade. "Pursuing Happiness: The Architecture of Sustainable Change." *Review of General Psychology* 9(2) (2005): 111–31.

Mongrain, M., R. Lubbers, and W. Struthers. "The Power of Love: Mediation of Rejection in Roommate Relationships of Dependents and Self-Critics." *Personality and Social Psychology Bulletin* 30(1) (2004): 94–105.

Neff, K. D. "Self-Compassion: An Alternative Conceptualization of a Healthy Attitude Toward Oneself." *Self and Identity* 2(2) (2003): 85–101.

Neff, K. D., and S. N. Beretvas. "The Role of Self-Compassion in Romantic Relationships." *Self and Identity* 12(1) (2012): 78–98.

Nelson, K. S., K. Layous, S. W. Cole, and S. Lyubomirsky. "Do Unto Others or Treat Yourself? The Effects of Prosocial and Self-Focused Behavior on Psychological Flourishing." *Emotion* 16(6) (2016): 850–61.

Salzberg, S. *Real Happiness: The Power of Meditation: A 28-Day Program.* New York: Workman, 2011.

Sarna, Y. Personal interview. November 7, 2016.

Warren, R., E. Smeets, and K. Neff. "Self-Criticism and Self-Compassion: Risk and Resilience: Being Compassionate to Oneself Is Associated with Emotional Resilience and Psychological Well-Being." *Current Psychiatry* 15(12) (2016): 19–32.

Whiffen, V. E., and J. A. Aube. "Personality, Interpersonal Context and Depression in Couples." *Journal of Social and Personal Relationships* 16(3) (1999): 369–83.

Williams, L. A., and M. Y. Bartlett. "Warm Thanks: Gratitude Expression Facilitates Social Affiliation in New Relationships via Perceived Warmth." *Emotion* 15(1) (2015): 1–5.

Wood, A. M., J. J. Froh, and A. W. A. Geraghty. "Gratitude and Well-Being: A Review and Theoretical Integration." *Clinical Psychology Review* 30(7) (2010): 890–905.

CHAPTER 8

Britton, W. B., B. Shahar, O. Szepsenwol, and W. J. Jacobs. "Mindfulness-Based Cognitive Therapy Improves Emotional Reactivity to Social Stress: Results from a Randomized Controlled Trial." *Behavior Therapy* 43(2) (2012): 365–80.

Carleton, R. N. "The Intolerance of Uncertainty Construct in the Context of Anxiety Disorders: Theoretical and Practical Perspectives." *Expert Review of Neurotherapeutics* 12(8) (2012): 937–47.

Cousin, G., and C. Crane. "Changes in Disengagement Coping Mediate Changes in Affect Following Mindfulness-Based Cognitive Therapy in a Non-Clinical Sample." *British Journal of Psychology* 107(3) (2016): 434–47.

Doron, G., D. Derby, O. Szepsenwol, E. Nahaloni, and R. Moulding. "Relationship Obsessive-Compulsive Disorder: Interference, Symptoms, and Maladaptive Beliefs." *Frontiers in Psychiatry* (2016). http://journal.frontiersin .org/article/10.3389/fpsyt.2016.00058/full.

Feldman, D. B., K. L. Rand, and K. Kahle-Wrobleski. "Hope and Goal Attainment: Testing a Basic Prediction of Hope Theory." *Journal of Social and Clinical Psychology* 28(4) (2009): 479–97.

Gross, J. J. "Antecedent- and Response-Focused Emotion Regulation: Divergent Consequences for Experience, Expression, and Physiology." *Journal of Personality and Social Psychology* 74(1) (1998): 224–37.

Gross, J. J., and O. P. John. "Individual Differences in Two Emotion Regulation Processes: Implications for Affect, Relationships, and Well-Being." *Journal of Personality and Social Psychology* 85(2) (2003): 348–62.

Hanley, A., E. L. Garland, and D. S. Black. "Use of Mindful Reappraisal Coping Among Meditation Practitioners." *Journal of Clinical Psychology* 70(3) (2014): 294–301.

Harris, D. *10% Happier: How I Tamed the Voice in My Head, Reduced Stress Without Losing My Edge, and Found Self-Help That Actually Works—A True Story.* New York: It Books, 2014.

Hayes, S. C., K. D. Strosahl, and K. G. Wilson. *Acceptance and Commitment Therapy: The Process and Practice of Mindful Change.* 2nd ed. New York: Guilford Press, 2016.

Kabat-Zinn, J. *Full Catastrophe Living: Using the Wisdom of Your Body and Mind to Face Stress, Pain, and Illness.* Revised ed. New York: Bantam Books, 2013.

Keng, S., C. J. Robins, M. J. Smoski, J. Dagenbach, and M. R. Leary. "Reappraisal and Mindfulness: A Comparison of Subjective Effects and Cognitive Costs." *Behavior Research and Therapy* 51(12) (2013): 899–904.

Kuyken, W., S. Byford, R. S. Taylor, E. Watkins, E. Holden, K. White, B. Barrett, R. Byng, A. Evans, E. Mullan, J. D. Teasdale. "Mindfulness-Based Cognitive Therapy to Prevent Relapse in Recurrent Depression." *Journal of Consulting and Clinical Psychology* 76(6) (2008): 966–78.

McEvoy, P. M., and D. M. Erceg-Hurn. "The Search for Universal Transdiagnostic and Trans-Therapy Processes: Evidence for Intolerance of Uncertainty." *Journal of Anxiety Disorders* 41 (Jun. 2016): 96–107.

Reid, R. C., J. E. Bramen, A. Anderson, and M. S. Cohen. "Mindfulness, Emotional Dysregulation, Impulsivity, and Stress Proneness Among Hypersexual Patients." *Journal of Clinical Psychology* 70(4) (2014): 313–21.

Salzberg, S. *Real Happiness: The Power of Meditation: A 28-Day Program*. New York: Workman, 2011.

Segal, Z., M. Williams, and J. Teasdale. *Mindfulness-Based Cognitive Therapy for Depression*. New York: Guilford Press, 2002.

Szalavitz, M. "The Pleasant Truths About Pain." *Psychology Today* (2005). https://www.psychologytoday.com/articles/200509/the-pleasant-truths-about-pain.

Teasdale, J., M. Williams, and Z. Segal. *The Mindful Way Workbook: An 8-Week Program to Free Yourself from Depression and Emotional Distress*. New York: Guilford Press, 2014.

Twohig, M. P., and J. M. Crosby. "Acceptance and Commitment Therapy as a Treatment for Problematic Internet Pornography Viewing." *Behavior Therapy* 41(3) (2010): 285–95.

Twohig, M. P., J. C. Plumb Vilardaga, M. E. Levin, and S. C. Hayes. "Changes in Psychological Flexibility During Acceptance and Commitment Therapy for Obsessive Compulsive Disorder." *Journal of Contextual Behavioral Science* 4(3) (2015): 196–202.

CHAPTER 9

Anders, S., R. de Jong, C. Beck, J. D. Haynes, and T. Ethofer. "A Neural Link Between Affective Understanding and Interpersonal Attraction." *Proceedings of the National Academy of Sciences of the USA* 113(16) (2016): E2248–57.

Arch, J. J., and M. G. Craske. "Mechanisms of Mindfulness: Emotion Regulation Following a Focused Breathing Induction." *Behaviour Research and Therapy* 44(12) (2006): 1849–58.

Bandura, A. "Self-Efficacy: Toward a Unifying Theory of Behavioral Change." *Psychological Review* 84(2) (1977): 191–215.

Barrett, L. F., J. Gross, T. C. Christensen, and M. Benvenuto. "Knowing What You're Feeling and Knowing What to Do About It: Mapping the Relation Between Emotion Differentiation and Emotion Regulation." *Cognition and Emotion* 15(6) (2001): 713–24.

Bigman, Y. E., I. B. Mauss, J. J. Gross, and M. Tamir. "Yes I Can: Expected Success Promotes Actual Success in Emotion Regulation." *Cognition and Emotion* 30(7) (2016): 1380–87.

Birk, J. L., and G. A. Bonanno. "When to Throw the Switch: The Adaptiveness of Modifying Emotion Regulation Strategies Based on Affective and Physiological Feedback." *Emotion* 16(5) (2016): 657–70.

Campbell-Sills, L., D. H. Barlow, T. A. Brown, and S. G. Hoffman. "Effects of Suppression and Acceptance on Emotional Responses of Individuals with Anxiety and Mood Disorders." *Behaviour Research and Therapy* 44(9) (2006): 1251–63.

Ferriss, T. *Tools of the Titans: The Tactics, Routines, and Habits of Billionaires, Icons, and World-Class Performers.* New York: Houghton Mifflin Harcourt, 2016.

Greenberg, L. S. "Emotion-Focused Therapy." *Clinical Psychology and Psychotherapy* 11(1) (2004): 3–16.

Gross, J. J. "Emotion Regulation." In *Handbook of Emotions.* 3rd ed. Edited by M. Lewis, J. M. Haviland-Jones, and L. F. Barrett. New York: Guilford Press, 2008.

Gross, J. J., and O. P. John. "Individual Differences in Two Emotion Regulation Processes: Implications for Affect, Relationships, and Well-Being." *Journal of Personality and Social Psychology* 85(2) (2003): 348–62.

Kashdan, T. B., C. N. DeWall, C. L. Masten, R. S. Pond, C. Powell, D. Combs, D. R. Schurtz, and A. S. Farmer. "Who Is Most Vulnerable to Social Rejection? The Combination of Low Self-Esteem and Lack of Emotion Differentiation on Neural Responses to Rejection." *PLOS ONE* 9 (2014). http://journals.plos.org/plosone/article?id=10.1371/journal.pone.0090651.

Kashdan, T. B., L. Felman Barrett, and P. E. McKnight. "Unpacking Emotion Differentiation: Transforming Unpleasant Experience by Perceiving Distinctions in Negativity." *Current Directions in Psychological Science* 24(1) (2015): 10–16.

Kneeland, E. T., J. F. Dovidio, J. Joorman, and M. S. Clark. "Emotion Malleability Beliefs, Emotion Regulation, and Psychopathology: Integrating Affective and Clinical Science." *Clinical Psychology Review* 45 (Apr. 2016): 81–88.

Kring, A. M., and D. M. Sloan. *Emotion Regulation and Psychopathology: A Transdiagnostic Approach to Etiology and Treatment.* New York: Guilford Press, 2009.

Lieberman, M. D., N. I. Eisenberger, M. J. Crockett, S. M. Tom, J. H. Pfeifer, and B. M. Way. "Putting Feelings into Words: Affect Labeling Disrupts Amygdala Activity in Response to Reactive Stimuli." *Psychological Science* 18(5) (2007): 421–28.

Linehan, M. M. *DBT Skills Training Handouts and Worksheets.* 2nd ed. New York: Guilford Press, 2015.

Roemer, L., S. K. Williston, and L. G. Rollins. "Mindfulness and Emotion Regulation." *Current Opinion in Psychology* 3 (Jun. 2015): 52–57.

Tamir, M., O. P. John, S. Srivastava, and J. J. Gross. "Implicit Theories of Emotion: Affective and Social Outcomes Across a Major Life Transition." *Journal of Personality and Social Psychology* 92(4) (2007): 731–44.

Verduyn, P., and S. Lavrijsen. "Which Emotions Last Longest and Why: The Role of Event Importance and Rumination." *Motivation and Emotion* 39(1) (2015): 119–27.

Williams, M., J. Teasdale, Z. Segal, and J. Kabat-Zinn. *The Mindful Way Through Depression*. New York: Guilford Press, 2007.

CHAPTER 10

Burns, D. D. *The Feeling Good Handbook*. New York: Plume, 1999.

Cacioppo, J. T., J. H. Fowler, and N. A. Christakis. "Alone in the Crowd: The Structure and Spread of Loneliness in a Large Social Network." *Journal of Personality and Social Psychology* 97(6) (2009): 977–91.

Cacioppo, J. T., and W. Patrick. *Loneliness: Human Nature and the Need for Social Connection*. New York: Norton, 2008.

Cacioppo, J. T., H. T. Reiss, and A. J. Zautra. "Social Resilience: The Value of Social Fitness with an Application to the Military." *American Psychologist* 66(1) (2011): 43–51.

Cacioppo, S., A. J. Grippo, S. London, L. Goossens, and J. T. Cacioppo. "Loneliness: Clinical Import and Interventions." *Perspectives on Psychological Science* 10(2) (2015): 238–49.

Cain, S. *Quiet: The Power of Introverts in a World That Can't Stop Talking*. New York: Broadway Books, 2013.

Creswell, J. D., M. R. Irwin, L. J. Burklund, M. D. Lieberman, J. M. Arevalo, J. Ma, E. C. Breen, and S. W. Cole. "Mindfulness-Based Stress Reduction Training Reduces Loneliness and Pro-Inflammatory Gene Expression in Older Adults: A Small Randomized Control Trial." *Brain, Behavior, and Immunity* 26(7) (2012): 1095–101.

Davis, T. J., M. Morris, and M. M. Drake. "The Moderation Effect of Mindfulness on the Relationship Between Adult Attachment and Wellbeing." *Personality and Individual Differences* 96 (Jul. 2016): 115–21.

Dunbar, R. *How Many Friends Does One Person Need? Dunbar's Number and Other Evolutionary Quirks*. Cambridge, MA: Harvard University Press, 2010.

Finzi, E., and N. E. Rosenthal. "Emotional Proprioception: Treatment of Depression with Afferent Facial Feedback." *Journal of Psychiatric Research* 80 (Sept. 2016): 93–96.

Gillespie, B. J., D. Frederick, L. Harari, and C. Grov. "Homophily, Close Friendship, and Life Satisfaction Among Gay, Lesbian, Heterosexual, and Bisexual Men and Women." *PLOS ONE* (2015). http://journals.plos.org/plosone/article?id=10.1371/journal.pone.0128900.

Hawkley, L. C., M. W. Browne, and J. T. Cacioppo. "How Can I Connect with Thee? Let Me Count the Ways." *Psychological Science* 16(10) (2005): 798–804.

Hennenlotter, A., C. Dresel, F. Castrop, A. O. Ceballos Baumann, A. M. Wohlschlager, and B. Haslinger. "The Link Between Facial Feedback and Neural Activity Within Central Circuitries of Emotion—New Insights from Botulinum Toxin–Induced Denervation of Frown Muscles." *Cerebral Cortex* 19(3) (2008): 537–42.

Holt-Lunstad, J., T. B. Smith, and J. B. Layton. "Social Relationships and Mortality Risk: A Meta-Analytic Review." *PLOS ONE* (2010). http://journals.plos.org/plosmedicine/article?id=10.1371/journal.pmed.1000316.

Kanai, R., B. Bahrami, B. Duchaine, A. Janik, M. J. Banissy, and G. Rees. "Brain Structure Links Loneliness to Social Perception." *Current Biology* 22(2) (2012): 1975–79.

Kreider, T. "The 'Busy' Trap." *The New York Times*, June 30, 2012. http://opinionator.blogs.nytimes.com/2012/06/30/the-busy-trap/?_r=0.

Kroenke, C. H., L. D. Kubzansky, E. S. Schernhammer, M. D. Holmes, and I. Kawachi. "Social Networks, Social Support, and Survival After Cancer Diagnosis." *Journal of Clinical Oncology* (2006). http://ascopubs.org/doi/full/10.1200/jco.2005.04.2846.

Levine, A., and R. S. F. Heller. *Attached: The New Science of Adult Attachment and How It Can Help You Find—and Keep—Love.* New York: TarcherPerigee, 2012.

Lewis, M. B. "Exploring the Positive and Negative Implications of Facial Feedback." *Emotion* 12(4) (2012): 852–59.

Linehan, M. M. *DBT Skills Training Handouts and Worksheets.* 2nd ed. New York: Guilford Press, 2015.

Luhmann, M., and L. C. Hawkley. "Age Differences in Loneliness from Late Adolescence to Oldest Old Age." *Developmental Psychology* 52(6) (2016): 943–59.

Masi, C. M., H. Y. Chen, L. C. Hawkley, and J. T. Cacioppo. "A Meta-Analysis of Interventions to Reduce Loneliness." *Personality and Social Psychology Review* 15(3) (2011): 219–66.

Olds, J., and R. S. Schwartz. *The Lonely American: Drifting Apart in the Twenty-first Century.* Boston: Beacon Press, 2009.

Ott, S. R., H. Verlinden, S. M. Rogers, C. H. Brighton, P. S. Quah, R. K. Vleugels, and J. Vanden Broeck. "Critical Role for Protein Kinase A in the Acquisition of Gregarious Behavior in the Desert Locust." *Proceedings of the National Academy of Sciences of the USA* 109(7) (2012): E381–87.

Santini, Z. I., A. Koyanagi, S. Tyrovolas, C. Mason, and J. M. Haro. "The Association Between Social Relationships and Depression: A Systematic Review." *Journal of Affective Disorders* 175 (Apr. 1, 2015): 53–65.

ACKNOWLEDGMENTS

First and foremost, I want to thank *you* for taking a look at this, since I imagine you have a lot going on in your life! It means so much to think of the possibility of your investing in this book.

Thank you to the experts—I am grateful to each social scientist I referenced who devoted many years of tireless work to teach us meaningful lessons. Ideas presented by Drs. Roy Baumeister, Tyler Stillman, Carol Dweck, Daniel Gilbert, Matthew Killingsworth, Sonja Lyubomirsky, James Gross, Susan Nolen-Hoeksema, Barbara Fredrickson, Richard Lucas, and Bella DePaulo were particularly influential to me. I'd also like to acknowledge all of the people who participated as volunteers in the studies described.

To my clients, professional mentors, and colleagues, I feel privileged to know you. My patients and their courageous explanations of their experiences moved me to write this book, and I am profoundly grateful for the opportunity to work with inspirational people. Relatedly, there are certain psychologists whose pioneering work has entirely changed my clients' lives, personally affected my life, and given me confidence that I can actually help people. When my patients thank me, I know it is mostly because I've been lucky to learn from the teachings of Drs. Marsha Linehan, Steven Hayes, Aaron Beck, Zindel Segal, and William Miller, all of whom have dedicated their careers to empathetically empowering people. I first trained in implementing evidence-based therapies at the American Institute for Cognitive Therapy and I'm grateful for the support of Dr. Robert Leahy and all of my former cherished associates in the practice. I've had many supportive mentors over the years whom I feel lucky to now consider friends—thank you especially to Drs. Simon Rego, Dan Goodman (aka Dr. Dan in the introduction), Lata McGinn, Debra Safer, Cory Newman, Dennis Greenberger, Josh Pretsky, and Emanuel Maidenberg.

Lots of people helped make my dream of writing a liberating and scientific dating book happen. People often ask me about how I found my thoughtful and responsive literary agent, Lindsay Edgecombe. I found her in another author's acknowledgments section and couldn't be happier to thank her now in mine. A huge thank you to my wonderful editors at TarcherPerigee, Stephanie Bowen and Amanda Shih, who got this message, cheered this book on, and provided wise guidance. Many thanks to the entire team at Penguin who made this concept into a beautiful book, and to Danielle Caravella, Brianna Yamashita, Ashley D'Achille, and Suzanne Williams for spreading the word. I learned so much about how to write from my brilliantly detailed editor, Paula Derrow. Early in my writing, I met Adam Grant, a bestselling author and stellar human, and his support of this project was instrumental. Many people I respect took time to meet and share stories and ideas and I am grateful to each of you.

In particular, I want to thank Sharon Salzberg, whose teachings guide me and my therapy practice. I am grateful that Richard Marrs patiently taught me about fertility treatments and that Sarah Boone helped me understand the foster adoption process.

And for my friends and family, I am lucky to have you in my life. Adam, I think I'm the first person to use the word "feminist" to describe you but you truly are. You support my career to the point that I feel like you're not only my partner, but also my professional publicist, and I love that we share a growth mindset. Sylvie, lovingly thinking of you growing up and dating shaped my message, and Eli, my excitement over your impending arrival a couple of weeks after my book deadline kept me going. To my mother, you've taught me from your example that I can chase my career. Despite your work as a surgeon, you've been an incredibly devoted bubbie. To my father, you always told me I could write books and I thank you for your faith and Roxbury Park trips with Sylvie. To Michelle and Rebecca, my sisters, you were always there to listen to my endless dating stories and offer advice, and Moshe, you're a great addition to our family. Thank you to my in-laws, Karen and Bill, for being supportive. Sonia, you're a gifted writer and you read over so many drafts of so many of my projects, I feel fortunate to be your niece, and Jimmy, you're the most generous uncle. My father's parents, Simon and Gita, were Holocaust survivors who taught me perspective and gratitude and I honor their memory. Sylvia "Ceiba" and Dr. Emil Seletz, my maternal grandparents—you mean the world to me, now and since day one. My biggest gift and greatest loss was your presence in my life. My message in this book is the one you gave me—that being "#1," or good enough just for being you, is your birthright. And I thank g-d for everything.

ABOUT THE AUTHOR

Photo © Sultan Khan

Jennifer L. Taitz, Psy.D., A.B.P.P., is a licensed clinical psychologist who specializes in evidence-based therapies. Dedicated to providing the highest level of expertise, she is board-certified in both Cognitive Behavioral and Dialectical Behavior Therapies (CBT and DBT). Dr. Taitz's mission is to compassionately offer proven tools to help people get unstuck and enhance their quality of life. Dr. Taitz is passionate about spreading research findings to solve common problems. She is the author of *End Emotional Eating*, which earned a seal of merit from the Association for Behavioral and Cognitive Therapies. After years of helping clients learn to be more mindful with themselves and others, Dr. Taitz increasingly noticed that popular dating books lacked psychological truths, which inspired her to write *How to Be Single and Happy*.

Dr. Taitz graduated magna cum laude from New York University and earned her doctorate at Ferkauf Graduate School of Psychology. She completed fellowships at Yale University School of Medicine and at the American Institute of Cognitive Therapy, where she directed the DBT program for many years. Dr. Taitz is a diplomate of the Academy of Cognitive Therapy and served as a founding board member of the New York City Association for Contextual Behavior Science. In addition to presenting at national and international conferences, Dr. Taitz often participates in interviews for major media outlets. Currently, she serves as a clinical instructor in the department of psychiatry at the University of California, Los Angeles, and maintains a clinical practice, LA CBT DBT. For more information, please visit drjennytaitz.com.

The author will donate a portion of her proceeds from *How to Be Single and Happy* to the charitable organization Distributing Dignity and Girls Not Brides member organizations.